Gib Hedstrom

Navigating Sustainable Growth

T0406273

Gib Hedstrom

Navigating Sustainable Growth

A Roadmap for Boards and Corporate Leaders

DE GRUYTER

ISBN 978-3-11-154858-6
e-ISBN (PDF) 978-3-11-154885-2
e-ISBN (EPUB) 978-3-11-154909-5

Library of Congress Control Number: 2025933608

Bibliographic information published by the Deutsche Nationalbibliothek
The Deutsche Nationalbibliothek lists this publication in the Deutsche Nationalbibliografie;
detailed bibliographic data are available on the internet at http://dnb.dnb.de.

© 2025 Walter de Gruyter GmbH, Berlin/Boston, Genthiner Straße 13, 10785 Berlin
Cover image: Jennifer Davey; Cover design: Britta Zwarg, Berlin
Typesetting: Integra Software Services Pvt. Ltd.

www.degruyter.com
Questions about General Product Safety Regulation:
productsafety@degruyterbrill.com

There is nothing more difficult to take in hand, more perilous to conduct, or more uncertain in its success, than to take the lead in the introduction of a new order of things.

Niccolo Machiavelli
The Prince (1532)

A leader takes people where they want to go. A great leader takes people where they don't necessarily want to go, but ought to be.

Attributed to Rosalynn Carter

Advance Praise

In a world that urgently needs business to lead with purpose and long-term vision, *Navigating Sustainable Growth* offers timely and practical guidance for boards and executives. Gib Hedstrom makes a compelling case that sustainable growth isn't just about doing less harm – it's about creating more value for society than we take. For leaders serious about building future-fit companies, this book is a vital resource.

Paul Polman, Former CEO
Unilever

The importance of sustainability in business is widely acknowledged, yet few grasp how to effectively integrate it into corporate strategy to drive growth. With a focus on best practices and actionable guidance, *Navigating Sustainable Growth* bridges this gap by providing a clear roadmap for leaders. Gib Hedstrom offers valuable insights and practical steps for driving sustainable growth. This book is an indispensable resource for any executive or board member committed to creating long-term value while addressing climate challenges.

Dave Regnery, Chair & CEO
Trane Technologies

The risk of climate change is widely recognized, but few understand how good governance can mitigate it. The famed "triangle" of governance – connecting directors, managers, and investors – must become a fulcrum for balanced approaches. That is the major lesson from *Navigating Sustainable Growth*. Gib Hedstrom is a true pioneer in climate governance, qualified by decades of board-level consulting work and influential publications. His newest book is packed with practical insights and steps for prospering on our planet while at the same time respecting it.

Alexandra Lajoux, Chief Knowledge Officer Emeritus
National Association of Corporate Directors

This book belongs on every CEO's desk. As climate risks to assets and society intensify and geopolitics become more complex, CEOs need an action-oriented guide that cuts through the noise. Companies committed to leading and growing sustainably must future-proof their businesses by embracing – not resisting – emerging regulations from the EU and beyond. Gib's book delivers that blueprint, just when it's needed most.

Mike Mabry, CEO
Global Resources International

https://doi.org/10.1515/9783111548852-202

In *Navigating Sustainable Growth*, Gib Hedstrom provides a roadmap for boards to enhance fluency, drawing on decades of helping boards and corporate leaders address the most challenging issues of the day.

Wendy Kei, Chair, Board of Directors
Ontario Power Generation

This isn't another book about why sustainability matters; this is the 'how.' Gib bridges the strategy gap between today's short-termism and the climate-aligned economy taking shape. Essential reading for boards, CEOs, and the next generation of business leaders in every MBA classroom.

Dave Stangis, Chief Sustainability Officer
Apollo Global Management

Boards can no longer treat climate as a side issue – it's as critical to long-term value as AI and digital transformation. Despite the pressure to deliver short-term results, management must assess how the company's strategy will deliver sustainable growth over the next five years and beyond. Gib Hedstrom offers the game plan to align corporate strategy with sustainability and secure resilience and profitable growth.

Jo Mark Zurel, Chair, Board of Directors
Fortis Inc.

The thing about *climate* is that it doesn't care what you think about it, like whether it's caused by humans or not. One way or another, a shifting climate will affect all corporations, everywhere. Companies that embrace the challenge are poised to reap the rewards and increase shareholder value. With *Navigating Sustainable Growth*, Gib Hedstrom lays out a practical, non-partisan action plan for corporate leaders and boards to achieve sustainable growth and profitability. This is a must read!

Bill Davis, CEO
Stance Capital

Gib Hedstrom's work here, much like that of his distinguished career in governance and sustainability, is an exemplar of high-quality research, logic, and practicality. Organizations that follow his advice will be well served in both the immediate and longer term.

Robert Galford, Board of Directors *[retired]*
Forrester Research

Navigating Sustainable Growth: A Roadmap for Boards and Corporate Leaders is essential for directors looking to learn more about the impacts of climate change, gain alignment between the board and management, and make boardroom discussions more productive and impactful. In Gib Hedstrom's feature "Climate and Sustainability for Boards" for *Directors & Boards*, he expertly explained why climate change is a pressing issue for directors and why the time is now for them to enhance their fluency and knowledge on the topic. If he can do that in six pages, imagine what he does with a whole book.

Bill Hayes, Editor in Chief
Directors & Boards

This is more than a guide – it's a wakeup call about the urgent challenges we face. Solving them will require public, private, and nonprofit leaders to work together in new and exciting ways. Only the private sector has the resources to move fast and deliver outcomes at scale. Gib Hedstrom has provided the framework for how corporate leaders, especially board members, can engage in ways that generate strong economic outcomes and durable solutions to the climate crisis.

Larry Selzer, President and CEO
The Conservation Fund

This is the guide C-suites have been waiting for. *Navigating Sustainable Growth* is a much-needed resource for executives committed to turning sustainability into a competitive advantage. This approach builds on Gib Hedstrom's decades with ESG Navigator helping hundreds of major companies. That platform has been incredibly helpful for conducting an honest assessment, gaining executive alignment, and preparing for board dialog. Now, having a practical 'how-to' guide to create alignment and stimulate the right type of board discussion is invaluable. The book speaks to each corporate function, blending boardroom insights with global best practices.

Jennifer Aspen Mason, CSO & EVP
J.M. Huber Corp

Timely, insightful, and action oriented. Over the next five years, customers will increasingly demand innovative solutions to climate and other material sustainability challenges. This book identifies how to capture emerging value creation opportunities – while avoiding the costs of inaction or delay.

Alexa A. Dembek, PhD, SVP, Chief Technology and Sustainability Officer
DuPont

In these critical decades of transition, successful companies will phase out the destructive business models of the past and grow those decarbonizing and dematerializing the value chain. Boards of directors have the vantage point and power to guide that strategic shift, and every corporate functional leader – and MBA professor – must weave climate and sustainability into their daily activities. *Navigating Sustainable Growth* helps boards, corporate leaders, and business schools to navigate a course toward sustainable business. Gib's book provides a timely, "how to" toolkit.

Jason Jay, Director, Sustainability Initiative,
MIT Sloan School of Management

In this terrific, highly readable book, Gib Hedstrom makes a clear and compelling case that you can't have a healthy business on an unhealthy planet. More importantly, he lays out a climate strategy every executive and board of directors should follow – one grounded in the volatile dynamics of this moment. It is a practical and insightful guide, worthy of study by every business leader – and anyone who strives to become one.

Joel Makower, Chairman and Co-founder
Trellis Group

Acknowledgments

In writing this book, I followed my grandmother's words of wisdom: *"too soon old, and too late smart."* I vowed to garner help along the way, especially sensing that the time to act on climate change is slipping away. We all need to get smart, quick.

Thirty years of work with executives of over 100 companies who challenged my assumptions and influenced my thinking, and the 150 global companies using ESG Navigator, shaped the early drafts. When I thought my content was good, I reached out to experts who could make it even better.

Jane Schindewolf's contributions are too many to count. Special thanks to Lucy Carmody, whose global expertise in finance and climate and excellent writing helped the text reach a new level. A group of global leaders sharpened certain arguments: Alexandra Lajoux on board oversight, Alex Gold on EU developments, Bill Davis on sustainable investing, Dean Slocum on social responsibility. Sophia Deery, Jen Davey, and Larry Krupp provided excellent support. Then, when all the content was close to final, Elsa Wenzel did her magic, cutting words, polishing messages, and offering new ideas.

I am most grateful to the longstanding clients who entrusted me to work on their behalf and meet with their CEOs and present to their boards. While far too many to name, special thanks to Scott Tew who challenged me to define world class climate and sustainability governance. Longtime colleague Bob Willard connected me with Sarah Keyes, who provided outstanding input and unselfishly introduced me to board members Wendy Kei, Jo Mark Zurel, and Gale Rubenstein.

None of this would have been possible without the initiative and constant support from Jaya Dalal and the De Gruyter team. You made the past 18 months enjoyable.

Finally, I have had the privilege of learning from an amazing group of mentors. Each guided me gently, clearing away the clouds to see my North Star. Professors Donald B. Potter (geology) and Burton V. Barnes (forest ecology) sparked an inner flame. Sigurd F. Olson said, *"Have faith in yourself and in what you want to do. Nothing is impossible."* He urged me to pursue a career in sustainability when the word meant something else, and no such career seemed possible. Patrick F. Noonan coached me over many years in board meetings. More recently, Jeremy Grantham planted the inspiration that the best working years may be after most friends retire.

May every reader be as fortunate to enjoy such incredible mentors.

https://doi.org/10.1515/9783111548852-203

About the Author

Gilbert (Gib) Hedstrom is widely recognized as a trusted advisor to business leaders on climate and sustainability issues that increasingly dominate the global agenda. He has reported directly to full boards and board committees of major corporations on over 70 occasions, often meeting with outside directors in executive sessions.

Gib's extensive experience with Fortune 500 boards led to his creation of ESG Navigator™ – developed at the request of board members. Endorsed and licensed by The Conference Board in 2020, ESG Navigator is the leading global sustainability benchmarking and strategic planning platform. Over 175 major global companies take advantage of the powerful analytics for CEO and board reporting.

After training in finance at General Electric, Gib spent 20 years at Arthur D. Little. He spearheaded environmental auditing in the US, which later expanded globally, and wrote the original environmental auditing standards as well as several books. Gib's team led several thousand audits across the globe. Later, as Vice President and Managing Director, he led the company's European environmental practice, including several years from Brussels. After returning to the US, he co-led the company's global sustainability practice.

Gib founded Hedstrom Associates in 2004, providing business consulting and executive counsel at the intersection of corporate governance and sustainability. For ten years, he ran The Conference Board's various executive sustainability councils. His clients have included dozens of leading global companies and high-profile assignments.

Gib has authored several books and written dozens of articles related to governance and sustainability. The National Association of Corporate Directors (NACD) featured the cover story article authored by Gib (with a client) titled "Transforming Board ESG Oversight" in the Fall 2022 issue of *Directorship*. In January 2025, *Directors & Boards* published his article "Climate and Sustainability for Boards." And, in May 2025, Gib and colleague Lucy Carmody launched The Climate Story (https://the-climate-story.com/), a free-to-access, 30-slide PDF summarizing the climate situation today and what to expect over the next five years.

Gib currently works with corporate leaders and boards keen to drive 'truly' sustainable growth over the next decade. He also instructs NACD's Virtual Briefing Desk course for sitting directors titled "Sustainability Oversight: Cutting Through the Noise."

Gib earned his MBA and MS (sustainability) from the University of Michigan, and a BA in economics and geology from Hamilton College. He has served on the board of the Erb Institute for Global Sustainable Enterprise, the University of Michigan, and several local non-profit boards.

He welcomes further discussion about governance and sustainable growth. Visit https://gibhedstrom.com/ and reach him at gib@esgnavigator.com.

https://doi.org/10.1515/9783111548852-204

To the generation raised under the shadow of climate change, burdened by the inaction of the past . . .

. . . and to the business leaders shaking off the temptation to pursue business as usual, creating the truly sustainable growth companies of the future.

Contents

Preface

Sustainability* has never been a question of *if*. It has always been a question of *when*. The when is now.

The developed world mostly has had a great run since the dawn of the Industrial Revolution and the US oil industry in the 1850s. But the underlying trends spell the end of that era and the dawn of a new one. Those trends are hardwired. To deliver sustainable growth, CEOs and **boards** must grasp sustainability in the right context, do an honest company assessment, fix board oversight, and deeply integrate sustainability into the core of the business.

This is a big ask – nothing less than *transforming* each company from the "old economy" fossil-fuel-based model of the past 150 years to a "new clean energy economy." Tomorrow's winning companies will capture value from helping customers and consumers decarbonize and dematerialize.

The Trump administration's actions may signal otherwise, but don't be fooled. The direction is clear. The challenge for every CEO and board member today is this:

 For Boardroom Discussion

As we work across the value chain, how can we build a profitable, growing company that approaches zero (negative) and even **net-positive** environmental and social impacts, and help our suppliers and customers do the same?

Wrong Timing

I was a few decades too early. After living in Europe in the mid-1990s, running Arthur D. Little's global environmental business, I returned to the US inspired by European companies taking action to create sustainable profits while focusing on people and planet.

So, in 1997, I was asked by independent directors in back-to-back Fortune 150 board meetings to develop a scorecard to help them measure progress. That was the first such scorecard. Twenty years later, there were over 100.

From 1998 to 2000, I learned that US companies were not ready to transform.

***Note:** Appendix B contains a list of Acronyms and Appendix C provides definitions for key terms. Both are highlighted in bold font the first time they appear.

https://doi.org/10.1515/9783111548852-206

I was a few decades too early

I was almost tossed out of Oklahoma when I asked the CEO of Kerr McGee, then a major oil and chemical company, about his climate policy. He told me, the outside expert on his environmental governance redesign team, never to mention the "C" word in his company or, for that matter, the state.

General Motors' top executives did not appreciate my suggestion that the company rebrand itself as "Global Mobility" after BP had rebranded as Beyond Petroleum. Instead of ushering me upstairs to the CEO's floor, they took me on a tour of the Hummer showroom.

Arch Coal's president figuratively raked me over the coals during my presentation on **climate change** that his boss (the CEO of Ashland) asked me to give his top team. At the end, the Arch Coal president asked me for my slides.

Sustainable Growth Revisited

Every CEO aims to deliver sustainable growth and profitability. As a financial trainee at General Electric (GE) in Pittsfield, MA, I learned about sustainable growth from Jack Welch, who ran GE's plastics business. He later set the standard every CEO aims to meet – demonstrating steadily rising growth and profitability over two decades.

Starting now, achieving sustainable growth will differ dramatically from in the past. The need to manage for the long term, however, remains the same.

 Pause for Reflection

Companies that manage for the long term, about five-to-seven years ahead, substantially outperform others, with **47 percent higher revenue growth over a 15-year period**, according to McKinsey & Company.

Looking ahead, the term "sustainable" will incorporate metrics for **climate risk**, decarbonization pathways, and **biodiversity** net gain – building intangible asset value from sustainability.

A Call to Action Now

The global signals shout out for a rapid unfolding of the old economy and launching of the new clean energy economy.

Why now?

The stark conclusion of **COP**28 (the 2023 United Nations Climate Conference) … was that we've missed the boat. It's already too late to gradually reduce carbon emissions to reach the Paris Agreement target of 1.5 degrees Celsius (1.5°C) of warming by 2050. That was confirmed in 2024, the first year the world recorded temperatures exceeding the 1.5°C threshold.

Three decades before COP28, the global sustainability conversation kicked off at the 1992 Rio Earth Summit. I was there, speaking to business leaders, listening, and learning. In Rio, climate scientists talked about sea level rise in fractions of an inch. From 2010 to 2024, the sea level near Savannah, Georgia, rose more than 7 inches.

The 2025 southern California wildfires signal that climate change impacts will become much more visible, even dire, over the next few years. It's impossible for any CEO to miss the more frequent and destructive storms, longer heat waves, heavier precipitation and rising seas.

The impacts on business are **material** and manifold. The insurance industry and capital markets are responding. This will increasingly impact key boardroom decisions, such as which new businesses to buy, old businesses to reshape or shed, new offerings to create, and new business partners to engage with.

Reflections from the Boardroom

Boards must own the climate and broader sustainability agenda – in collaboration with the CEO.

For more than 25 years, I have enjoyed a unique window into how they operate. As an advisor on environment, governance, and strategy for large multinationals, I have spent nearly 300 hours in more than 80 board meetings.

For seven years, a board committee chair called me before each meeting, requesting input to share with the CEO. In other meetings, a CEO asked me if he needed to fire a company president, a former CEO stepped down as the new one took charge, and a mining company board member dozed off during the discussion of a fatality.

Committee chairs have met with me in executive sessions, sans CEO or management present, on over 20 occasions, asking: "Is there anything else we need to know?" Specifically, they wondered:
- How should we be thinking about sustainability as a board?
- How do we stack up versus competitors, peers, and best practices?
- What actions should we take to capture value from sustainability?

During executive sessions at Fortune 500 company board meetings in 1997, independent directors asked if I could develop a scorecard to help them answer those questions.

My response was to create a platform in collaboration with the dozens of leading companies I had the privilege of working closely with. For ten years (2008 to 2018), I ran three executive sustainability councils for The Conference Board with 100 sustainability leaders from 75 major companies. Since 2018, I have hosted monthly webinars for corporate leaders discussing how to navigate sustainability. Working together, we created ESG Navigator, *by industry – for industry*.

The platform, later endorsed by The Conference Board, has provided over 200 large, global companies (mostly Fortune 500 or equivalent) with a peer network, insights, and benchmarks. Many share their assessment and analytics with the C-suite and board to guide long-term strategy.

A "How-to" Update of Prior Books

Armed with the experience I have gathered over the past several years discussing these issues with CEOs and boards, this book will not focus on *why* sustainability is important or *what* constitutes the current status of sustainability funds, regulations, reporting frameworks, and ratings.

Instead, the book focuses on *how boards, CEOs and their teams should think about, and act on, sustainability*, specifically:

- **Board members and CEOs** will find an easy-to-read summary aimed squarely at the boardroom, with proven key performance indicators (KPIs) to assess board structure, fluency, and meeting design.
- **C-suite executives** will see clearly how sustainability touches each business function and how to fully integrate sustainability into existing business practices.
- **Corporate secretaries** will find simple tools for use with the CEO and board.
- **Sustainability professionals** will understand how to think about sustainability as the C-suite and board does.
- **Educators** will learn how to discuss sustainability in highly practical ways.

I knew we were near the tipping point when I published *Sustainability: A Guide for Boards and C-suites* in 2017. I went out on a limb when I declared that climate change is *the defining issue of the early twenty-first century*. But I was pleased to learn that the book hit the mark.

- In 2018, leading company sustainability executives immediately ordered 50 copies each for senior executives and board. The same year, De Gruyter published my sequel, *Sustainability: What It Is and How to Measure It*.

- In 2020, The Conference Board endorsed ESG Navigator, the corporate planning tool underlying that book, making the platform available to some 1,200 corporate members worldwide.
- In 2022, the NACD published our article "Transforming Board ESG Oversight" as the cover story in its quarterly journal *Directorship*.

Today, the tipping point for sustainability stares us in the face. (I crystallized this in a feature article for the First Quarter 2025 *Directors & Boards* magazine, "Climate and Sustainability for Boards."[1])

The climate crisis is calling. Business leaders can likely count down the remaining years during which the old economy model of the Industrial Revolution and its reliance on international trade in oil plays out:

- **Insurance companies** and banks will increasingly limit exposure to high risk, potentially stranded assets.
- **Investors** will prioritize companies that deliver sustainable growth in terms of not only revenue and profits but also decarbonization, dematerialization, contribution to net-positive biodiversity impact, and societal value.
- **Competitors** will quietly and aggressively change their business models and offerings to deliver new economy offerings.

Rethinking sustainable growth can be uncomfortable. It requires smashing many norms we have taken for granted for generations. It is inherently long term – in a business world constantly pulled to the short term. It is complex. It is highly impactful.

And it is happening now.

Notes

1 Hedstrom, Gib, "Climate and Sustainability for Boards," *Directors & Boards*, January 2025.

Part One: **Calibrate**

Introduction

(The) rapid crystallization of climate change-related risks (has) highlighted the need for rapid decarbonization and scaling up of adaptation finance, bringing longer-term environmental risks into sharper relief.[1]
Rebecca Karnovitz, VP – Senior Credit Officer, Moody's Investor Service

A company is not sustainable unless it can create long-term, profitable growth – while earning its license to operate, innovate, and grow. That's what 'sustainable' has meant to CEOs in the past. But what will sustainable growth mean going forward?

Society is on a collision course: a rising global middle class continues to burn more fossil fuels, accelerating CO_2 concentrations, causing higher land and ocean temperatures and sea level rise. The result – growing economic impact of major weather events, causing insurance companies to react and financial markets to price-in risk and volatility.

How should companies respond?

 Pause for Reflection

It's hard to make a good argument for being less smart than your competitors about the major trends impacting your business.

It's almost impossible to miss the growing financial impacts of the rapidly warming planet and adverse weather events.
- **Companies** have faced **supply chain** disruptions and realize that **net-zero** greenhouse gas (**GHG**) emission goals are merely table stakes. *Fewer than one in five businesses with these goals, however, are on track to meet them.* Every large and mid-size company will soon need robust net-zero goals and a climate transition plan.
- **Customers**, especially from Europe, are demanding detailed, auditable information aligned with the overarching ambition of the European Green Deal. Approved in 2020, it aims to make the European Union climate-neutral by 2050. Current efforts may streamline the EU standards a bit, but will not change the overarching goal and direction.
- **Investors** see the risk of climate impacts and stranded assets growing as populations age, putting retirement plans at risk. They are using sustainability information to spur capital flows. Long-term investors such as pension funds and endowments expect companies to demonstrate that they have climate-competent boards.

https://doi.org/10.1515/9783111548852-001

- **Insurance companies** are addressing climate risk in profound ways, cutting insurance altogether in high-risk areas and increasing premiums elsewhere by a factor of two or three. This is happening globally, not just in Florida and California. Insurers are also creating new revenue streams with climate **transition risk** analytics businesses.
- **Banks** have begun restricting financing of carbon-intensive projects while disclosing their financing ratios of low-carbon to fossil fuel energy supply.

Meanwhile, deeply entrenched, often fossil fuel-dependent interests perpetuate the status quo and resist change.

Governments have failed to establish appropriate guardrails to manage the **externalities**.

 For Boardroom Discussion

CEOs and boards, as stewards of their enterprises, face this question: *How fast and how dramatically do we need to pivot to approach net zero and capture competitive value from the emerging economy that prioritizes decarbonization and resource efficiency?*

The first step for every executive and investor is to think about sustainability and its sister acronym **ESG**, referring to environment, social, and governance factors, the right way.

Sustainability: Magnitude and Urgency

Sustainability represents a 'once in a multi-generation' set of business opportunities – and risks.

Magnitude and Scale

The magnitude and scale of the opportunities are on par with the transition from the Agricultural Revolution to the Industrial Revolution.

This interface between major eras of history is where the magic of innovation happens. It is not unlike the ecological term *ecotone*, representing a transitional area of vegetation, such as between forest and field. These are the richest, most biodiverse places on earth.

Today's transformation is likely to unfurl as a condensed version of what happened 150 years ago. That was when, in a 30-year span, some of the world's most groundbreaking technologies emerged: the telephone (1876); the phonograph (1878); the incandescent light bulb (1879); the automobile (1886); Kodak camera (1888); electric street cars (1888); and the airplane (1903).

Business leaders now face the first major period of breakthrough innovation since the early 1900s. It is happening now. (See Figure 1.)

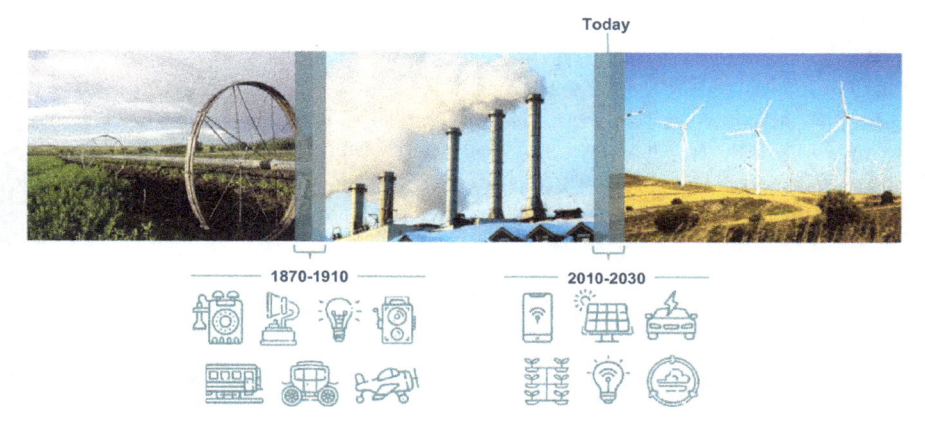

Figure 1: Transformative Innovation Periods

You might ask: are we not already well along with the energy transition implied in this figure? Coal plants have been closing as renewable energy and other green technologies have rapidly ticked upward. Leading companies have voluntarily set goals, reported progress, and engaged **stakeholders**.

Prolonging the Status Quo

Despite notable accomplishments, especially in Europe, in many ways, little has changed since the dawn of the Industrial Revolution. Think about it.
- Much of society continues to drive oil-fuelled vehicles and burn black rocks to keep warm. **In the US, fossil fuels represented approximately 80 percent of total energy in 2024.**[2] While almost 500,000 MW of coal power has been decommissioned since 2000, 1.27 million MW went online in China and India.[3]
- Only one in six (16 percent) of the world's largest 2,000 publicly listed companies are on track to achieve net zero in their operations by 2050.[4]

The more urgent the need for innovation and action to rapidly decarbonize, the greater the rift becomes between those prolonging the old economy and others accelerating the new one.

Even if lawmakers prolong the backlash against ESG in the US, disclosure requirements elsewhere will offset it.

 Pause for Reflection

Given the rapidly escalating scale of financial impacts, the question is: How fast will the transition take from the old 'take, make, waste' fossil-fuel economy to the new clean energy, **circular economy**? Could future events trigger a dramatic and swift change?

To paraphrase Rudiger Dornbusch's Law:

"The crisis takes longer to come than you expect, then it happens much faster than you would think possible."

The premise of this book is that the required, large pivot demands a step-change in mindset and leadership. The window for competitive differentiation and early mover advantage is closing fast. Innovators are already readying for take-off.

The tide will soon turn, and the race will be on globally to reap huge rewards from helping customers and society decarbonize.

It's Not About Compliance

One recent board committee meeting illustrated the challenge of seeing the future yet being stuck in the past.

In early 2023, I was invited to discuss sustainability at the board committee of a US manufacturer of water drainage products for commercial infrastructure projects. The US company served US markets and was facing limited pressure from Europe.

The board committee viewed climate risks cautiously focused more on pending US regulations than on pressure from Europe. They saw sustainability as compliance and were not yet ready to embark on a major transformation. Perhaps the conversation was too early, given the extreme weather events and climate impacts to come later that year throughout 2024, and into 2025.

The message: Many US companies focus far too much on sustainability through the regulatory compliance lens. This may be especially true of larger, global, US-based businesses. They are reluctant to rethink their current business model and portfolio.

This is a big mistake.

Pause for Reflection

The most important "aha" moment for any board member, CEO, or C-suite executive is to recognize that **sustainability is not about compliance or disclosure**.

Instead, sustainability requires courage and foresight to reimagine value creation.

It is about getting your heads and minds around the scale of the challenges and imagining how your business thrives in a rapidly decarbonizing future.

Urgency

A seismic shift is underway to build the new clean-energy economy. Yet almost all companies are stuck in the recent past. They are taking false comfort by making incremental improvements.

Meanwhile, China charges ahead, dominating the new clean-energy economy. They can only hope President Donald Trump continues with his "drill, baby, drill" focus. Yet the US today is already the world's largest oil producer and gas exporter.[5]

China produces 80 percent of the world's solar panel components, 60 percent of wind turbine capacity, and almost two-thirds of all electric vehicles (EVs). China also processes most of the minerals used in clean-energy technologies. Indeed, green technology is core to China's economy, and Chinese companies have found workarounds to trade barriers in the West.

Beijing's investments accounted for nearly half of global spending on clean energy and low-carbon manufacturing technologies in 2022, over half a trillion dollars. The US spent just $141 Bn in the same year.[6]

Climate: The Issue of Our Time

As we sit at the cusp of a transformative innovation period (Figure 1), climate change stands far and above all other issues.

If sustainability is an arrow that is piercing business as usual, then climate is the tip of the arrow. Appendix A contains a summary of **The Climate Story**, a logical, eight-step, data-rich summary for busy executives.

We are up against the clock to deal with carbon pollution and the many impacts a changing climate brings to businesses.

That represents business opportunity.

The hurricanes, fires, floods and droughts of 2023, the warmest year on record, represented a postcard from the future. Then came 2024, which was even warmer. The prolonged streak of abnormal heat continued into 2025 despite the arrival of La Niña ocean conditions, which typically bring cooler temperatures. And the early 2025 California wildfires brought the climate discussion to the kitchen table for many Americans.

In late 2023, the main headline out of the annual United Nations Climate Change Conference called COP28 was that, for the first time ever, more than 190 governments called for the world to "transition away from fossil fuels in energy systems in a just, orderly, and equitable manner." But that was not the biggest news.

 Pause for Reflection

The real news from COP28: **The world will *not* meet the widely understood Paris Agreement target** of holding global temperature rise to 1.5°C above pre-industrial levels by 2050.

Yikes. Normally, hitting a deadline early is good. But globally reaching the Paris pact's warming target 26 years ahead of schedule is not.

Global temperatures reached an increase of 1.6°C in 2024. The harsh realities of climate change are knocking at the front door of many in the developed world. Developing countries, by contrast, have grappled with coastal inundation and increased cyclonic activity in the tropics for decades.

Climate is also a threat multiplier.

- **Water:** As the old saying goes, we know the price of water when the well runs dry. In 2017, Cape Town prepared for "Day Zero," when municipal water supplies would switch off. With desalination technology proven, freshwater availability is essentially an energy challenge.
- **Biodiversity:** The rise in extreme weather events illustrates the negative impacts of a warming climate on biodiversity. Recent major wildfires (California, Chile, Canada, Athens, Maui) and floods (North Carolina, Brazil, Malawi, Italy, India, Vermont, Libya) have endangered habitats and plant and animal species.
- **Plastics:** Ninety-nine percent of plastics are sourced from fossil fuels. Their production will roughly double by 2050. This means more GHG emissions from production, transportation, use, and disposal. Compounding the issue, the volume of plastic waste continues to grow dramatically. Researchers are finding plastic pollution in human brains, lungs, arteries, and breast milk, not just in soil, oceans, and waterways.

This decade, **from 2025 to 2035, is the moment when all of this comes to a head**.

Every company should assume that climate is a material risk. Even those in relatively lower carbon industries should measure and report the full **value chain** impacts with the same rigor as they do their financial results.

To ground corporate leaders in sustainability, Chapter 1 provides an overview: definitions, the ESG backlash, sustainable investing, laws and regulations, reporting frameworks, and ratings.

Investors are Redefining Sustainable Growth

The financial markets are awakening to the impacts of climate change. The accelerating action by investors, exchanges, and regulators directly responds to the growing financial impact of a warming climate. Investors see the interaction between financial and systemic risks and use the phrase 'double materiality' to describe the risks posed *by* the company and *on* the company:

- The company's impacts on the environment and society contribute to issues like climate change.
- That, in turn, creates financial risks for almost every company.

A Changing of the Guard

For the past several decades, environmental groups such as Ceres and Environmental Defense Fund have been signaling warning signs. Today, major investors and asset owners have joined in. The investor-led initiative Climate Action 100+, for instance, engages some 600 global asset owners totaling $68 Tn in assets.

Moody's Investor Service best summarized the situation in its 2024 Outlook,[7] listing the following major drivers:

- **Green technologies and disruptive innovation** will buttress capital spending and accelerate the pace of the carbon transition.
- Increasing **climate and sustainability** disclosure requirements, especially mandatory disclosures about climate risk up and down the supply chain, pose a major challenge for companies and financial institutions.
- The increased frequency and severity of **extreme weather events** are causing mounting financial and economic losses.
- Investors now appreciate the **interplay between climate and natural capital** as environmental degradation accelerates.
- Decarbonization, demographics, and artificial intelligence (AI) are **reshaping the future of work**.

This provides an opening for companies to rethink sustainable growth.

Rethinking Sustainable Growth

Sustainable growth going forward means **more good, less bad**: more revenue and profits; less carbon and harm to nature.

Moody's Outlook paints a lucid picture of the future: the threat of climate and natural capital destruction, the need for rapid innovation in clean technologies, the risk of perpetuating the status quo, and the future of the workplace.

 Pause for Reflection

The message is clear. It reminds me of one of my favorite sayings:
Uber yourself before you get Kodak'ed

Moody's, and most investors, know that Millennials and Gen Zers will comprise over 70 percent of the workforce by 2030. These employees and customers will ask tough questions about how your company is addressing the climate crisis.

Chapter 2 provides the context for how investors will view sustainable growth in the near term. It also spells out exactly how CEOs and boards can get ahead of competitors by measuring and disclosing data supporting tomorrow's sustainable growth metrics.

The CEO/Board Misalignment

The board must own climate and sustainability, in collaboration with the CEO. It cannot be delegated.

Climate disclosure and regulatory requirements now clearly position climate risk as a material financial risk, placing oversight of a company's climate action within a board member's fiduciary duty.

Facts to Consider

- The median CEO tenure today in the S&P 500 public companies decreased 20 percent between 2013 to 2022, from 6 years in 2013 to 4.8 years in 2022.[8]
- Traditional strategic planning among Western companies focuses on a short-term, tactical horizon of one to three years ahead. Successful Chinese companies plan ten years ahead.

– A pivot to long term doesn't pay off for individual CEOs during their tenure, according to McKinsey & Company. Track companies beyond that, however, and it does pay off for shareholders.

The pressure on CEOs to deliver short-term results is, if anything, growing. A record 27 CEOs resigned in 2024 from companies engaged by activist investors, a nearly threefold increase from 2020.[9]

Transitioning a company to a low-carbon business model is complicated. It requires action spanning more than three years. It is the board's job to ensure metrics guide this planning and execution. If they wait too long, enterprise value could crash.

Figure 2 illustrates the critical role boards face in planning and executing over the five-to-seven-year horizon, given these facts:

– The CEO's focus in public companies is one to three years ahead.
– The board must focus on both the short and the long term.
– Climate impacts are intensifying rapidly.
– The opportunities offered by new solutions to climate change exist now.

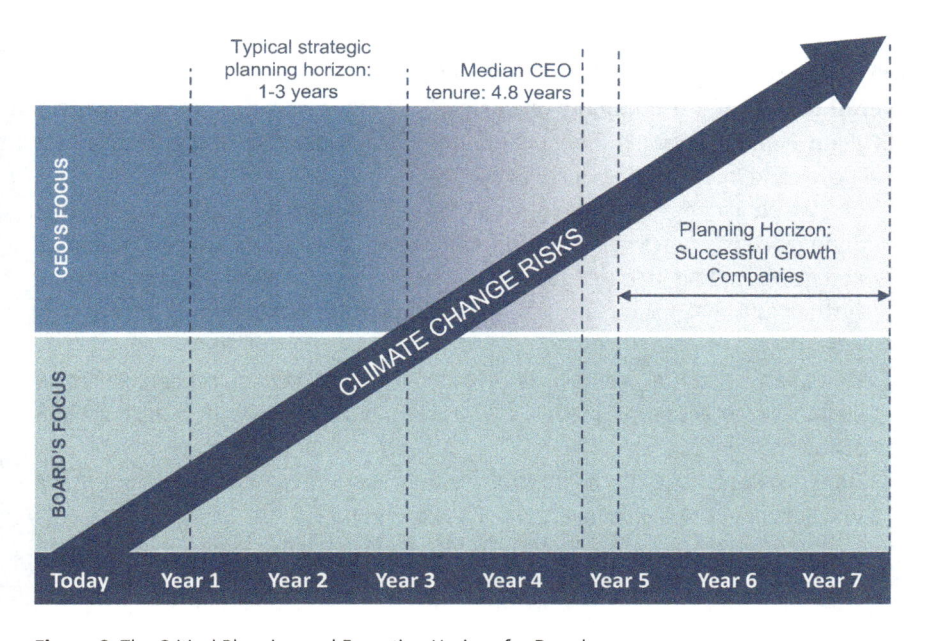

Figure 2: The Critical Planning and Execution Horizon for Boards

Short-term incentives motivate short-term behavior, such as cutting R&D expenses to increase profits. The board's role is especially critical since directors have a fiduciary responsibility to oversee long-term performance and since typical CEO compensation packages payout based on one-to-three-year performance. Consider the following:

- The average duration of executive compensation plans for CEOs of constituents of the MSCI All Country World Index was 1.7 years.[10]
- Eighty-nine percent of performance-based awards for the 250 largest US S&P 500 companies continue to be measured over a three-year period.[11]
- Equity award targets for large-cap companies in the MSCI USA Index were granted on an annual basis, even when the intent was to incentivize long-term performance.[12]

The common standard of three-year vesting falls short of long term. Instead, companies should incentivize long-term value creation in their leadership. Focusing on short-term returns as the primary metric in remuneration keeps companies stuck in short-term behaviors.[13]

Defining Questions for Boards and CEOs

The fundamental question boards and CEOs should ask today is, "**What is the overall impact of our company on society?**" In other words, as former Unilever CEO Paul Polman says: "Is the world better off because our company is in it?" Drill down and have business leaders ask:

- Can we plod along, making sure we comply and disclose the right information?
- Should we run toward the regulations from Europe, Singapore, California, and other leading jurisdictions? Do we assume similar regulations will spread further and that a company can gain competitive advantage by moving beyond them?
- How many years do we have to pivot from an old economy model to a new clean energy economy model – to transform and thrive in a zero-carbon economy?
- Do we risk missing the boat? Will we later say, "Whoops, we missed that!" like Borders Books, once overcome by Amazon?

For Boardroom Discussion

It's hard for boards, CEOs, and their teams to recognize the **urgency and magnitude** of action. Also hard is assessing the **time required** to review and refine the company's purpose and adjust the business model, portfolio of businesses, and offerings accordingly to attract tomorrow's employees.

Board oversight today means helping the CEO:

- **Articulate the company's full potential**, answering the question: How does our company make society better in the era of climate change?
- **Build a clear path** for creating long-term value for shareholders and value to society.
- **Communicate a compelling story** to current and future investors, employees, and customers.

Data suggests that *considerable misalignment lingers between C-suite executives and board directors on critical issues that relate to but are not limited to sustainability*. To close that gap, the first step is to conduct an objective, brutally honest assessment of your company through a sustainability lens. Chapter 3 elaborates areas of board-management misalignment and Chapter 5 provides guidance on how to conduct such an objective assessment.

Boards Must Own Climate and Sustainability

Boards are the most important decision-makers in the global economy. Directors face two options:

- Should our company charge ahead with one-to-three-year strategic plans, maximizing growth and profitability from our current business model?
- Or should we "open the aperture" and start by defining what our company should look like in five to seven years?

Most US companies have opted for the first option.

Let's Sit This Out

With the shifting politics, geopolitics, and regulatory messaging, it is tempting for many company executives to sit this out for a bit.

In principle, addressing the impacts of climate change and other substantial externalities belongs to governments. They define the guardrails. Companies, on the other hand, operate within those guardrails to create value by delivering solutions to customers.

Here's why most US companies essentially watch from the sidelines:
- Governments have placed extensive laws and regulations in the books. What's wrong with following the minimum requirements, acting quietly, and complying?
- History is littered with corporate initiatives and investments in green and healthy business ventures that failed.

But businesses should listen to their sustainability experts.

CSOs See What's Needed

Chief Sustainability Officers (**CSO**s) understand what is needed. They are mired in the details of external disclosure and reporting, tracking legislative and regulatory developments, diagnosing requirements of the ever-changing external reporting frameworks, and interacting with raters and rankers.

When they reflect on this, they have strongly declared what the C-suite and board must do.

In 2023, my team surveyed approximately 80 sustainability executives at mostly Fortune 500 companies. We asked how they believed their top executives viewed sustainability – and how they wanted those same executives to view sustainability in the next few years. (See Figure 3.)

The answers were striking, especially looking ahead.

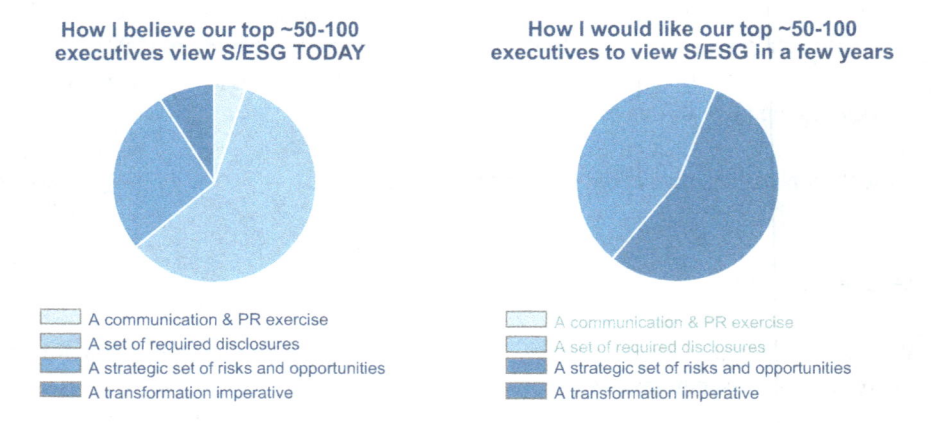

How I believe our top ~50-100 executives view S/ESG TODAY

How I would like our top ~50-100 executives to view S/ESG in a few years

- A communication & PR exercise
- A set of required disclosures
- A strategic set of risks and opportunities
- A transformation imperative

Figure 3: Every Company Needs to Transform

For companies to shift from the left side to the wishful right side of Figure 3 implies a *step-change in mindset.*

For any CEO, the right side of Figure 3 represents the perfect opportunity to signal the employees about the opportunities that lie ahead.

The problem for company executives and board members is that the image on the left pie chart will likely stay the same. The onslaught of regulations, disclosure requirements, and demands by investors and customers all point to increased disclosure. That requires companies to invest even more time and resources in data management, reporting, and verification. And that can reinforce the false idea that sustainability is mostly about compliance.

Climate Transition Plans are a Pipe Dream

Does your company have a net-zero target, as nearly half of large companies globally do? If so, how robust is your transition plan?

Less than half of 1 percent of 18,600 companies had credible climate transition plans as of early 2023, according to **CDP** (formerly the Carbon Disclosure Project).[14] Since 2023, the number has grown only slightly, remaining at about 1 percent. The key word here is "credible" – the ambitions simply can't be trusted.

Why? Perhaps because companies have been allowed to "choose their own adventure." Having a net-zero target has not been required by law in most jurisdictions.

The Clock Is Ticking on Climate Transition Plans

Companies will need to comply with disclosure requirements, which increasingly include expectations on transition plans. Investors won't look favorably on companies that don't meet the requirements. Companies will need robust, costed, data-based, and verifiable climate transition plans.

Core to every climate transition plan is a thought experiment: imagine how your business can look in a rapidly decarbonizing, resource-efficient future. This is a five-to-seven-year exercise: boards must drive the plans.

Chapter 4 provides a detailed template for CEOs and boards to assess the board's current *structure, fluency,* and *cadence* of steps that can enhance board oversight in the coming years.

Preview of Upcoming Chapters

Navigating Sustainable Growth: A Roadmap for Boards and Corporate Leaders includes insights I have gained from recent research on how to enhance board fluency, as well as many conversations with board members and CEOs. It also incorporates data and learnings from more than 200 companies that have leveraged ESG Navigator since 2018. This book is organized into three parts, plus detailed Appendices.

- **Part 1** sets the stage. Chapter 1 provides the *grounding*; Chapter 2 describes how investors will likely redefine and reward *sustainable growth*; Chapter 3 describes the *misalignment between boards and management*; and Chapter 4 describes how to assess and enhance *board sustainability oversight*.
- **Part 2** is a CEO guide to building a true sustainable growth strategy with over 300 examples of corporate best practices. It provides a simple, systematic structure to fully integrate sustainability into the core of how the company operates. An introductory chapter is followed by separate chapters addressing the four core components of sustainability: *Governance and Leadership*; *Strategy and Execution*; *Environmental Stewardship*; and *Social Responsibility*.
- **Part 3** is a call to action – offering key questions discussion in the boardroom (and during the strategic planning process), and some concluding thoughts.

The book appendices include:
- Appendix A provides **The Climate Story**, a brief primer about climate for executives and board members. Note that The Climate Story is available as a free pdf, accessible via www.The-Climate-Story.com.
- Appendix B contains a list of acronyms.
- Appendix C includes definitions of selected terminology.
- Appendix D provides a summary of how dozens of leading companies have collectively shaped ESG Navigator to meet their benchmarking, internal reporting, and strategic planning needs.
- Appendix E provides details of 100 Key Sustainability Indicators to assess company performance.

Notes

1 Segal, Mark, "ESG Issues to Increase Credit Risk in 2023" Moody's, January 10, 2023. https://www.esgtoday.com/esg-issues-to-increase-credit-risk-in-2023-moodys/
2 US energy facts explained, US Energy Information Administration, https://www.eia.gov/energyexplained/us-energy-facts/data-and-statistics.php

3 https://docs.google.com/spreadsheets/d/1j35F0WrRJ9dbIJhtRkm8fvPw0Vsf-JV6G95u7gT-DDw/edit?gid=647531100#gid=647531100

4 https://newsroom.accenture.com/news/2024/only-16-of-largest-companies-on-track-for-net-zero-goals-with-nearly-half-seeing-increased-emissions-accenture-analysis-finds

5 https://www.nytimes.com/2025/01/23/opinion/trump-china-ev-batteries.html?smid=

6 "America is losing the clean energy race to China," *Boston Globe*, June 16, 2024.

7 "2024 Outlook – Green tech, policy and climate finance to drive credit impact," Outlook, Moody's Investor Services, January 8, 2024.

8 Joyce Chen, "Rising Demands, Falling CEO Tenures," Equilar, July 21, 2023. [Note: Among S&P 500 public companies, the *average* CEO tenure also decreased over this period, though to a lesser amount. Since the *average* is influenced by a handful of long-serving CEOs (think Warren Buffett), *median* is a more accurate measure.]

9 https://www.axios.com/2025/01/03/activist-investors-27-ceos-2024

10 https://www.fcltglobal.org/resource/executive-pay/

11 23-09-28_FWC_2023_Top_250_Report.pdf (fwcook.com)

12 https://www.msci.com/documents/1296102/7330587/Research_Insight_Out_of_Whack.pdf/46baa603-a503-42c1-91c0-d0ef19b754b2

13 https://www.fcltglobal.org/resource/ceo-pay-executive-compensation/

14 "New CDP data shows companies are recognizing the need for climate transition plans but are not moving fast enough amidst incoming mandatory disclosure," CDP, February 16, 2023. https://www.cdp.net/en/articles/climate/new-cdp-data-shows-companies-are-recognizing-the-need-for-climate-transition-plans-but-are-not-moving-fast-enough-amidst-incoming-mandatory-disclosure

Chapter 1
Grasp Sustainability Fully

We want to be running toward new and emerging sustainability laws and regulations.

Mike Mabry, CEO, Global Resources International

Most people, including corporate leaders and board members, fail to grasp the magnitude, scale, and urgency of the societal transformation that sustainability represents. These two data points summarize the current situation:

- More than half (**59 percent) of companies believe they are meeting or exceeding expectations** on their sustainability strategy. (The balance sees room for improvement.)[1]
- As noted earlier, but worth repeating, **only about 1 percent of companies have credible climate transition plans**.

 Pause for Reflection

This data suggests that most company executives are kidding themselves.

Not deliberately. Most believe they *may* be able to address sustainability challenges while retaining their core business model and portfolio of businesses and offerings. They see the energy transition as a good thing. They take comfort in efforts to cut energy and water use, reduce waste, and grow the use of renewable and recycled materials.

That incremental approach fails to grasp what sustainability is all about.

Sustainability is about *transforming your company to seize the greatest set of business opportunities in over a century.*

In future chapters, I dive into how company executives, CEOs, and boards can position their company to thrive and profit from 'truly' sustainable growth. But first it is critical to have a shared understanding of the current sustainability playing field.

This chapter clarifies the terminology; addresses the ESG backlash; reviews the growth of sustainable investing; maps the regulatory landscape; and summarizes ESG reporting frameworks and ratings.

A reminder: this book focuses on *how* CEOs and board members should consider and act on these issues, not *why* they are important or *what* they mean for board members.

https://doi.org/10.1515/9783111548852-002

Which is it: Sustainability or ESG?

Yes. Both. Each term has limitations. Together, they can convey the right story if they position ESG or sustainability as a strategic, competitive issue.

The evolution looks like this:

- **Sustainability in the 1990s** = People, Planet, Profits. Sustainability became widespread in the 1990s, initially in Europe, meaning the triple bottom line. The big problem: it was silent on the most important piece, governance.
- **ESG circa the early 2000s** = Environment, Social, Governance. Coined by the United Nations in 2005 largely by and for investors, ESG added the critical missing "G" – the way we run our companies. But what happened to profits?
- **Sustainability Today** = sustainable growth redefined to include a new set of societal value metrics in addition to traditional metrics. (See Chapter 2.)

The right way to think about sustainability and ESG is the collective whole: people + planet + profits + governance. (See Figure 1.1.)

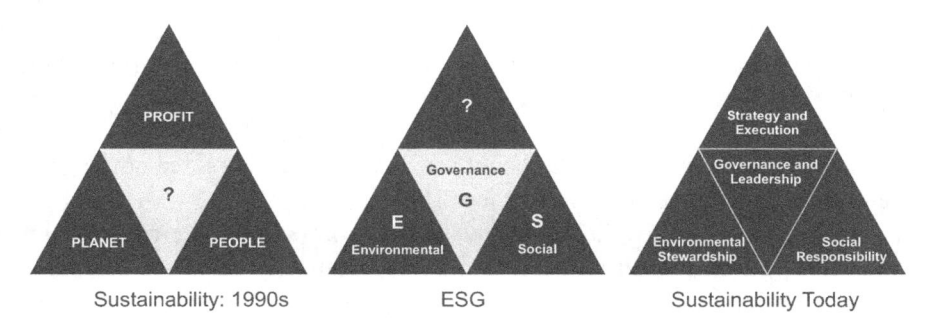

Figure 1.1: How to Think About Sustainability (vs. ESG) Today

Governance is the most important of the four components of sustainability – by far. A key focus of this book is how boards, CEOs, and their teams can lead with robust sustainability governance. I introduce this in Chapter 2 and dive into it in the balance of Parts 1 and 2.

The ESG Backlash

In mid-2022, a battle in the US pitted the oil industry and conservative politicians against liberals. Some of the backlash against sustainability terms – especially

ESG and its components such as diversity, equity, and inclusion (**DEI**) – is based on legitimate complaints, such as:

– **ESG investing**, where individual funds have been using various green, healthy, or sustainability labels including, but not limited to, ESG.
– **ESG ratings**, using varying methodologies and lacking consistency, provide a haven for greenwashing and an easy target for critics.

Most of the backlash, however, is a distraction motivated by political posturing, ignorance, or simply noise. Executives and boards need to block out the noise: step back, look at the data, see the middle ground, and move forward.

A good example of finding the middle ground relates to issues around DEI.

– Red state politicians call DEI "woke" and pull money from sustainability funds, arguing that ESG and DEI are spoiling the economy and the American dream.
– However, respected institutions, including McKinsey, Deloitte, MCSI, and the World Economic Forum all point to the value of diversity among boards and executives. A Moody's analysis of more than 3,000 companies worldwide showed that those with higher proportions of women on their board tend to receive higher credit ratings and, thus, enjoy a lower cost of capital than others.[2]

Company executives and boards should use data from Moody's and others, not newspaper editorial talking points, as justification.

At the end of the day, **the ESG backlash only points to the growing impact and scale of sustainability**. The backlash has forced asset managers and **ESG raters** to address key flaws. That's a good thing. Yet, that in no way diminishes the imperative for companies to embrace sustainability and transform to innovate and grow profitably.

The backlash will end soon. Watch, instead, for conservatives to call, resoundingly, to leverage climate and sustainability as a growth platform. Adaptation and resilience, especially where they overlap with national security, may yet become a conservative mantra.

Most board directors are unfazed by the backlash. Sixty-two percent told a recent survey that sustainability programs create long-term value. And 58 percent say sustainability issues have increased in priority for their boards.[3]

Sustainable Investing

Sustainable assets account for about 25 percent of total global assets under management (AUM), according to Bloomberg and the Global Sustainable Investment Alliance (Figure 1.2). This is a big deal.

Starting from boutique investors in the 1960s, sustainable investing grew to roughly one-third of total AUM by 2020 before a market adjustment. Then, with a combination of the COVID-19 pandemic and the ESG backlash, investors did a healthy reset.

It's worth noting that sustainable investing differs from green investing.

Sustainable Investing: Considers environmental and social impact in portfolio selection in addition to financial returns. It is normally associated with the transition to net-zero emissions or net-positive impact on biodiversity. Sustainable investing can include oil and gas owning portfolios managed with an ESG screen.

Green investing: Seeks to support business practices that have a favorable impact on the natural environment, including the conservation of natural resources.

A practical way to think about this: **sustainable investing is nothing more than a proxy for well-managed businesses**.

A Healthy Reset

Some critics were correct. Sharpening and regulating the criteria for what constitutes a true green, healthy, or sustainable fund is in everyone's interest. As a result, the sustainable investment industry is maturing. Shareholder interests are better protected. Figure 1.2 depicts how sustainable investment growth has unfolded.

The days are gone of investors slapping a green or ESG label on dozens of funds to attract investors. Tightening regulatory standards reflect that the industry has re-baselined, poised for future development. Changes originating in Europe have been spreading across the globe, moving the industry to more consistent and transparent standards.

Figure 1.2 depicts data for the US market for sustainable investments. The total as of the end of 2024 was $3,564 billion, representing 6.8 percent of total assets under management.[4] The global sustainable investing market size was estimated at USD 25.10 trillion in 2023 and is projected to grow at a CAGR of 18.8% from 2024 to 2030.[5]

Figure 1.2: Growth of Sustainable Investing[6]
Source: Morningstar Sustainalytics

The decline of sustainable investing in 2022, noted in Figure 1.2, is due to a maturing of the field and, in part, to the ESG backlash. At the same time, the picture is complicated by the decline in markets due to COVID-19. Here's the quick history:

- **1960s to 2000 – The Early Years:** Socially responsible investing (SRI), a niche movement whereby investors avoided 'sinful' investments (e.g., tobacco, firearms, or supporting South Africa's apartheid regime).
- **2000 to 2020 – Steady Growth:** Following the Kyoto Protocol (1997) and the United Nations Global Compact (2000), sustainable (and ESG) investing grew. The Paris Agreement (2015) and BlackRock CEO Larry Fink's 2018 letter urging CEOs to focus on the role of the company in society further accelerated growth. Fund managers placed the ESG label on many funds, aiming to cash in on increased awareness and demand for ESG investments.
- **2020 to 2024 – The Reset**: The various actions to sharpen and regulate sustainable investing have allowed customers to separate the truly sustainable funds from those comprising companies skilled at telling a good story.

BlackRock, Vanguard, and other major investors walk a fine line. On the one hand, they recognize both the risks posed by climate and other sustainability issues, and the business opportunities the green economy will unleash. On the other hand, they face complaints of over-emphasizing ESG factors.

Starting in 2022, major asset management firms BlackRock, State Street, Vanguard, and others scaled back the ESG label and enhanced internal scrutiny of what comprises a 'true' sustainability investment fund.

Shareholder Resolutions

Investor activism has grown steadily in recent years, and sustainability or ESG issues dominate their campaigns. Table 1.1 summarizes this globally.[7]

Table 1.1: Sustainability Shareholder Activity Globally

	2020	2021	2022	2023
Total number of campaigns	1,011	869	1,083	1,151
Total number of sustainability campaigns	727	669	889	940
Percentage: sustainability to total campaigns	71%	77%	82%	82%
Number of anti-ESG shareholder proposals (US)	0	21	53	91

Despite the rise in anti-ESG proposals, ultimately investors supported only 1.9 percent of them in 2024.[8] Therefore, *the overwhelming message is clear: sustainability is vitally important to executives, boards, and investors.*

Proxy Advisors

Investors, including hedge funds and mutual funds that own shares in multiple companies, pay proxy advisory firms to advise on shareholder votes. Two major proxy advisory firms, Institutional Shareholder Services (ISS) and Glass Lewis, are probing and reporting on how directors demonstrate their climate skills.

ISS is facing growing pressure to keep pace with rising climate change risks. In August 2023, a group of 36 investor clients, including UBS Asset Management, AXA, and a Swedish pension fund, called on ISS to introduce a new policy for the 2024 proxy season that fully integrates net-zero benchmarks and voting recommendations.[9]

Sustainable Investing Summary

Sustainability impacts trillions of dollars in terms of shareholder capital, brand, reputation, and the ability to access talent and capital. Many financial institutions have their own net-zero goals, exclusions policies, and caps to exposure on fossil fuels and other old economy industries.

The growth of sustainable investing, the large and steady volume of shareholder resolutions, and the increased activity of proxy advisors combine to offer a simple message to board members: **this is already big, and growing in scale, urgency, and importance.**

- Sustainable investing is a huge portion of total AUM globally. It will likely continue to grow in real dollars and as a percentage of the total.
- Sustainability topics increasingly dominate shareholder resolutions globally.

Investors are paying considerable attention to sustainability factors. That means **the board's ability to demonstrate effective sustainability oversight will increasingly be in the spotlight.**

Laws and Regulations

Most corporate sustainability activity and external ESG pressure on companies is about *disclosure*. As awareness of the importance of sustainability for long-term value increases, so do calls for companies to disclose their sustainability performance just like their financial performance.

Recent mandatory reporting frameworks, such as the **IFRS** Sustainability Disclosure Standards or the European Sustainability Reporting Standards (**ESRS**), are perceived as major new compliance burdens.

In fact, the **IFRS Foundation** and EU regulators were responding to company and investor demands. For decades, companies have responded voluntarily to information requests from customers, investors, employees, regulators, and more. Recent mandatory reporting frameworks seek to change this – for the benefit of companies and their key stakeholders.

Laws and Regulations in Context

Governments in 164 countries have enacted over 3,000 climate laws. In recent years, highly impactful legislation – specifically from the European Union and California – is changing the playing field.

Consider a basic bell curve with laggards on the left and leaders on the right. Regulations – much like industry associations – typically fall at about, or even to the left of, the midpoint.

Leading companies run toward the regulations as an opportunity to future-proof the company. They are happy to get on with strategic value creation while laggards struggle to comply. (See Figure 1.3.)

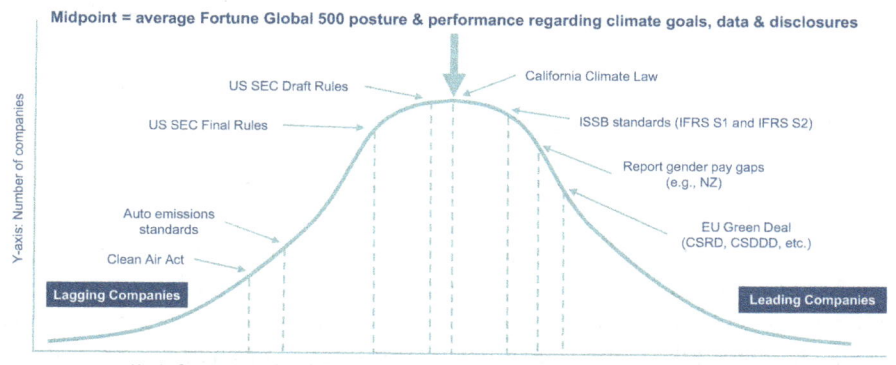

Midpoint = average Fortune Global 500 posture & performance regarding climate goals, data & disclosures

X-axis: Coverage regarding of sustainability and business integration.Company distribution across the bell curve is the company's stated climate and sustainability positioning, transformation ambition, long-term goals, and performance data.

Figure 1.3: Climate and Sustainability Regulations

In the US, much attention focused on the draft – then final – Securities and Exchange Commission (SEC) rules released in March 2024. This is understandable but mostly a distraction. *The SEC's rules, regardless of their uncertain future, barely approach the middle of the bell curve* (Figure 1.3).

US industry groups constantly push for weaker regulations. That's because regulations typically come along *after* US companies have already been addressing the regulated topics. The regulations then strive to set uniform standards and level the playing field.

US corporate leaders should watch state activity as a signal of future constraints and opportunities. At the end of 2024, a New York state law passed, modeled on the 1980 federal Superfund law, requiring big fossil fuel polluters to help pay for extreme weather damage.

EU Requirements: A Game Changer

The European Green Deal is a comprehensive, ambitious roadmap and action plan to transform the EU into a climate-neutral economy by 2050. Its scope includes climate change, biodiversity, environmental degradation, and "social fairness." Companies that conduct business in Europe or trade with EU member states are impacted.

This changes the game for virtually every large company. Core to the EU Green Deal is **CSRD** (the European Corporate Sustainability Reporting Directive):

- Requires detailed disclosures covering the full spectrum of business and sustainability topics.
- Includes 12 standards that address a company's impacts, risks and opportunities, strategy, targets and progress, products and services, business relationships, and incentive programs.
- Extends to direct and indirect business relationships across the value chain.

CSRD requirements will affect many US companies. The directive covers thousands of EU and non-EU businesses, initially large, listed companies. It also applies to most large, emerging market companies exporting to the EU. It also affects companies within the value chain of other companies doing business in Europe.

Consider the profound implications of the selected example CSRD requirements in Table 1.2.

Table 1.2: Selected European Sustainability Reporting Standards

Selected European Sustainability Reporting Standards
Climate Reporting Standards (reporting GHG emissions (Scopes 1, 2, and 3), plus: - Internal carbon pricing   - Transition plan for climate change mitigation   - Anticipated financial effects from material **physical risks** and transition risks   - Anticipated financial effects from potential climate-related opportunities
Selected Other Standards   - Resource inflows and outflows   - Transition plan and consideration of biodiversity/ecosystems in strategy and business model   - Managing material negative impacts on: own workforce; consumers and end users; value chain workers; and affected communities

The requirements in Table 1.2 fundamentally challenge companies to rethink their business models and strategic plans.

The unique aspect of the CSRD standards: they are still about sustainability disclosure, but **CSRD forces companies to review business models, product portfolios, planning, management, and strategy**. This leads to more useful data for investors chasing long-term sustainable growth.

In addition to CSRD, two other EU requirements will significantly impact multinationals:

- The European Corporate Sustainability Due Diligence Directive (**CSDDD**) puts sustainability due diligence into law. It applies to non-EU companies with significant revenue in the EU.

- The EU Carbon Border Adjustment Mechanism (**CBAM**) puts a fair price on the carbon emitted during the production of carbon intensive goods that are entering the EU, and encourages cleaner industrial production in non-EU countries.

Collectively, CSRD, CSDDD, and CBAM change the game. The period of strong emphasis on disclosure to satisfy external ESG ratings is over. Executives now must focus on strategy, management, and governance of sustainability impacts.

A US executive might ask: How can the EU regulate what we do here? Yet the US does the same thing, such as by regulating exports from Xinjiang due to human rights concerns. The message is: "If you want to do business with the US, you need to play by our rules." So it goes for the EU Green Deal: to do business in Europe, you need to play by their rules.

Under pressure from France and Germany, the EU may adjust the timing and the type of companies captured by the standards. However, the reporting requirements are likely to remain. The fundamental framework will continue to change the playing field.

Disclosure and Reporting Frameworks

For the past 25 years, companies have navigated a patchwork of reporting frameworks. While these frameworks began as voluntary, increasingly, they are intertwined with regulatory requirements.

Sustainability reporting frameworks have evolved in three broad waves. Figure 1.4 illustrates. (See Appendix B for a list of acronyms.)

The three waves of evolution in reporting reflect the broader awareness of how environmental and social considerations affect corporate value creation.

- **1997–2007** – is primarily about corporate accountability. The focus was on "corporate social responsibility (**CSR**)," as in business impacts on society and the environment. Impact-focused frameworks like the Global Reporting Initiative (**GRI**) and CDP dominated, with the focus squarely on emissions data.
- **2010–2020** – the awakening that sustainability matters also has financial consequences. Frameworks like the Sustainability Accounting Standards Board (**SASB**), integrated reporting, and the Task Force on Climate-Related Financial Disclosures (**TCFD**) ask companies to articulate how they address ESG challenges related to financial risk and opportunity. The Science-Based Targets Initiative (**SBTi**) asks companies to lay out their plans to develop a target for reaching, and validating, net zero.

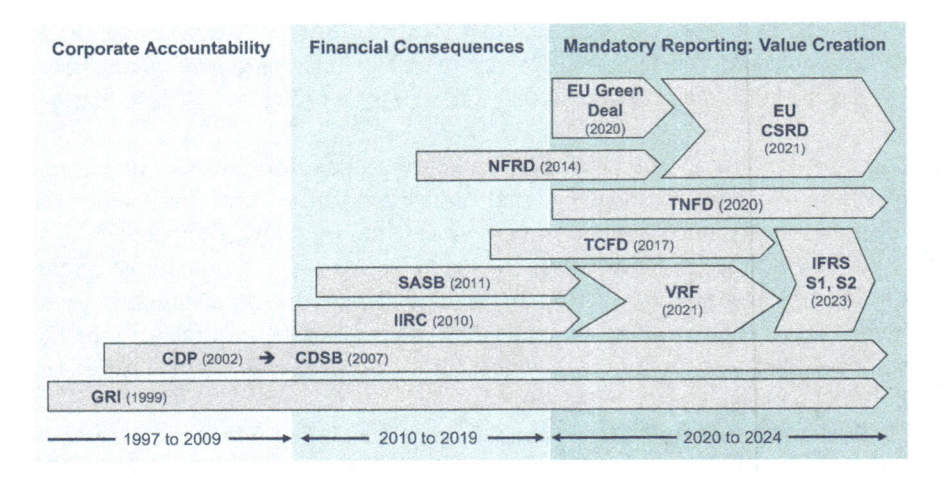

Figure 1.4: Sustainability Reporting: Evolution of Frameworks

–   **2021–2024** – the rise of mandatory sustainability reporting. The IFRS Sustainability Disclosure Standards and the ESRS focus on the context in which companies create financial value. Companies need to report on how ESG impacts, risks, and opportunities impact company strategy.

Even after 25 years, these reporting frameworks continue maturing. A key part of them today is a comprehensive double materiality assessment of company impacts as well as sustainability-related risks and opportunities:
–   **Assessing significant company impacts**: An 'inside-out' view of the company's impact on the economy, the environment, and society. For example, full GHG emissions from Scopes 1, 2, and 3 across the full value chain.
–   **Assessing significant sustainability-related risks and opportunities**: An 'outside-in' view of the impact of the external environment on the company's value creation. For example, the impact of a warmer climate, reduced access to fresh water, or increased vulnerability to adverse weather events on the company's ability to generate value.

Transparently reporting both perspectives is good business. It allows businesses to attract long-term, 'sticky' investors engaged in the company's long-term success. It also allows investors to better assess the inherent risks and understand when additional balance sheet capital is required.

Changing of the Guard

We have recently witnessed a *changing of the guard*. Now, instead of environmental and social non-governmental organizations (**NGOs**) pushing for consistency, investors are taking ownership of standardized sustainability data into their own hands.

Private equity giant Carlyle Group is working with its peers to adopt an industry-wide standardized sustainability data effort. The ESG Data Convergence Initiative (EDCI) aims to collect anonymized data annually from some 4,300 companies. It represents more than 400 major investors overseeing $28 Tn of assets worldwide.[10]

The ultimate goal – a single set of global standards, supported by accurate and consistent information disclosure from companies. ESG disclosure provides essential information for assessing the health of a business and its impact on the planet and society. Reporting should be prepared and published consistently and accurately. Eventually, we expect sustainability/ESG criteria to be fully integrated into global financial reporting standards.

Ratings and Rankings

ESG ratings have become mainstream. They are incorporated into risk calculations of asset managers, banks, and insurers.

Companies spend an inordinate amount of time disclosing data that will likely result in a favorable rating by the major ESG rating organizations, including CDP, MSCI, S&P Global, and ISS. Is this a good use of resources?

ESG ratings are important and widely used, yet deeply flawed:

- *Non-standardized criteria:* Assessment criteria and scorings are not standardized across rating agencies and methodologies.
- *Accountability:* ESG ratings are usually unregulated and unaccountable.
- *Ethical basis:* A wide range of companies, including tobacco and other 'sin' stocks, can be highly rated based on disclosure.
- *Private companies:* Companies that decline to disclose yet work ambitiously toward sustainable growth may be scored poorly.
- *Business model conflict:* Some ESG ratings are provided by companies that offer other services, such as credit ratings, benchmarking, and consulting services.
- *Subject to gaming the system:* Companies can 'game' the system by understanding the scoring methodology, then reverse engineer their activities, regardless of **materiality**.

– *Fifty percent only:* These ratings are usually based only on public information that companies disclose.

At best, ESG ratings and rankings represent only one side of the coin. They rarely peek behind the curtain and know the confidential information that companies do not disclose. The information ESG reporting frameworks request is important – but it is only half of how companies address global environmental and societal pressures.

While the ratings are deeply flawed, growing evidence shows that funds managed with screening for ESG risk and opportunity outperform their peers over the long term. In fact, research has found that actively managed integrated ESG investment strategies unlock long-term compound alpha opportunities. Additionally, avoiding ESG tail risks can improve the risk/return profile of a fund portfolio more than simply improving the average ESG score.

Summary

The overall direction is clear.

The growing connection, or interoperability, between regulations and disclosure standards offers CEOs and boards a chance to step back and see the larger view. Even companies viewing EU regulations as prohibitively costly will gain a clear picture of where this is likely to end up.

Companies globally must provide full, honest, transparent disclosure of sustainability and ESG information. That will be just as important as accurate, timely, and reliable financial information.

Companies must rethink how they can align with the clean energy economy and deliver 'truly' sustainable growth. This requires transforming the mindset – and the business itself.

To win in the marketplace, CEOs and boards should "run toward" climate and other sustainability regulations. That will help company leaders rethink and redefine the purpose, business model, investment priorities, and customer offerings.

Chapter 2 provides examples of sustainable growth metrics that leading companies are already using internally and disclosing externally.

Notes

1 "Sustainable Signals: Understanding Corporates' Sustainability Priorities and Challenges," Morgan Stanley Institute for Sustainable Investing, May 2024, p. 5.

2 Tyson, Jim, "Gender diversity on boards correlates with high credit quality," Moody's, CFO Dive, March 5, 2024. https://www.cfodive.com/news/gender-diversity-boards-correlates-high-credit-quality-moodys/709387/

3 "Top Concerns for Public Company Directors: AI, ESG, and Human Capital," NACD Directorship, Quarter Four 2023.

4 https://www.morganstanley.com/insights/articles/sustainable-funds-performance-second-half-2024

5 https://www.grandviewresearch.com/industry-analysis/esg-investing-market-report

6 Global Sustainable Investment Review, Global Sustainable Investment Alliance, 2012 to 2022. https://www.gsi-alliance.org/wp-content/uploads/2023/12/GSIA-Report-2022.pdf pg. 10–11

7 https://pages.marketintelligence.spglobal.com/Investor-Activism-Infographic-FY23-Demo-Request.html#:~:text=2023%20was%20another%20very%20busy,of%20campaign%20objectives%20in%202023

8 https://www.spglobal.com/marketintelligence/en/news-insights/latest-news-headlines/anti-esg-shareholder-proposals-boost-2024-proxy-engagement-deliver-few-results-82635562

9 https://www.reuters.com/sustainability/investors-call-iss-overhaul-its-net-zero-proxy-advice-2023-08-31/

10 "Private Equity's Green Starr," Bloomberg Business Week, March 11, 2024.

Chapter 2
Rethink Sustainable Growth

As an investor, I look to find well-run companies. Traditional financial fundamentals reflect what has been the case looking back. Coupling fundamentals with strong ESG signals reflect how companies are positioned for the future.
Bill Davis, Managing Director, Stance Capital

Every CEO sets job one as delivering sustainable growth and profitability. In this context, 'sustainable' means the ability to persist over time; to create businesses that deliver positive cash flows over the long term. My former employer, GE, did that under CEO Jack Welch. More recently, the revenue trendline from Microsoft is the dream of most CEOs. (See Figure 2.1.)

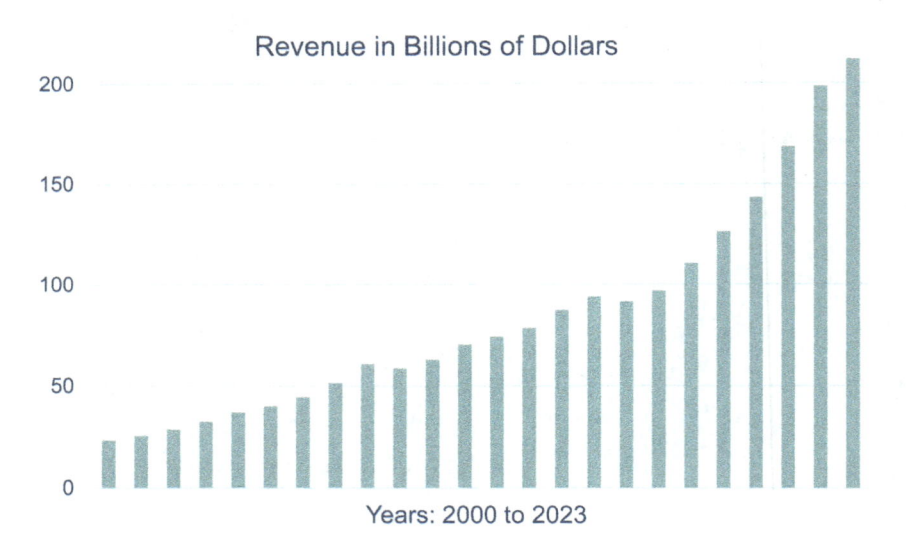

Figure 2.1: Microsoft Revenue Growth
Source: Microsoft

While this steady climb is a goal for virtually every company, it turns out to be an elusive one.

Most companies fail to deliver sustainable growth.

A 2024 Harvard Business School analysis of 10,897 publicly held US companies from 1976 to 2019 reported striking results:[1]

https://doi.org/10.1515/9783111548852-003

- More than three-quarters experienced little or no growth.
- Only 15 percent of the companies in the top quartile in 1985 could sustain their top-quartile growth for at least 30 years.

Why the major gap?

Most problems came from targeting growth in a highly reactive, opportunistic way rather than *systematically seeking new sources of growth and aligning resources accordingly*.

In seeking new sources of growth, **climate change (and sustainability broadly) represents the greatest set of opportunities in a century**.

Is Climate Material for our Company?

My answer is simple. Climate issues are dominant globally – recognized by governments, leading companies, and investors. Therefore, climate is material for virtually every company.

This point of view is validated.

 Pause for Reflection

Climate change will likely have material financial impacts on companies in 72 out of 79 industries, according to the SASB. That represents 93 percent of the US equity market, or $27.5 trillion.

But if companies manage climate and sustainability through the typical three-year strategic planning window, they will prolong risks and decrease growth opportunities.

The Five-to-Seven-Year Planning Horizon

How can a company appropriately consider the longer-term impacts of climate risk and opportunity in a business environment that prioritizes short-term results?

McKinsey research suggests the long-term focus pays off: **companies that plan and execute with a *long-term outlook of five-to-seven-years* substantially outperform peers, with 47 percent higher revenue growth** over 15 years.[2]

That should catch the attention of every CEO and board member as they manage the short-term/long-term conflict.

- **Short-term (zero-to-three-year) planning horizon:** The typical planning time frame for many companies and CEOs working to meet market expectations is three years, not the five-to-seven-year planning horizon.
- **Longer-term (four-to-seven-year) impacts:** Addressing climate change, access to clean water, resource **circularity**, and food security, among other factors, fall typically beyond the several-year planning horizon of most CEOs.

Boards must manage this inherent conflict.

 For Boardroom Discussion

The challenge for CEOs and boards is that the word 'sustainable' now requires a five-to-seven-year planning horizon:
- Recognizing the urgency, magnitude of action and the time required to address climate change and other sustainability issues.
- Re-evaluating the company purpose, business model, portfolio of businesses, and customer offerings to help customers address those trends.
- Anticipating how external stakeholders monitor the company's activities globally and impact the company – positively or negatively.

This is difficult. Business leaders want to preserve the economic landscape and societal norms of the old fossil-powered economy while re-designing and re-tooling it for a new zero-carbon world.

However, that incremental improvement is not working. For almost every company, the greater, necessary transformation requires shedding much of the old and welcoming the new. The impact of technologies such as AI and machine learning on internal operations and decision making can help. But they will not solve the climate challenge.

Board directors must courageously own the five-to-seven-year planning horizon and oversee a new set of sustainable growth metrics.

It is incumbent on the corporate secretary and senior sustainability executive to build the right board agendas that allow directors time to deliberate these issues.

If boards own the five-to-seven-year time horizon, when climate risks accelerate, they must have clarity about the business case for sustainability.

The Business Case for Sustainability

Investors want to spot tomorrow's winning companies. These companies:
- Manage costs and risks associated with climate and other environmental and social impacts better than peers.

- Invest in creating a portfolio of products and services that help customers de-carbonize, dematerialize, and succeed.
- Move toward net-positive impacts on the environment and society.

The business case has been studied for decades. While at Arthur D. Little, my colleagues and I first reported a simple framework (Figure 2.2) based on our work with Shell in the late 1990s.[3] Since then, many reputable institutions have followed suit. The business case is proven.

Figure 2.2: The Business Case for Sustainability
Source: Gilbert S. Hedstrom, Jonathan B. Shopley, and Colin M. LeDuc, "Realizing the Sustainable Development Premium," *Prism*, Arthur D. Little Journal, 2000

Much of the data disclosed on environmental and social impacts addresses the *left side* of Figure 2.2: it helps investors assess cost and risk. Many companies and boards spend most of their time and effort here.

However, leading companies have realized that the spotlight will turn toward the *right side* of Figure 2.2. They have begun to voluntarily disclose how they manage and position the company for the future.

Investors are watching: So are NGOs, whose criticism often affects share price and reputational risk.

Provide Investors What They Need

Investors seek reliable data on the sustainability of the companies they invest in. They look for businesses with a strong portfolio of products and services positioned to meet customer demands in a rapidly decarbonizing world that prioritizes resource efficiency and societal value.

They also want to peek behind the curtain to spot tomorrow's winning companies investing in green technologies and disruptive innovations that accelerate the pace of the carbon transition. Sounds simple, but it's not.

Two Major Roadblocks

Investors face two major roadblocks to spotting tomorrow's winning companies:
- **The data quality problem:** Data from company sustainability reporting is marginally better and more consistent across companies than five or ten years ago. Yet it remains far from robust. Investors are spending huge amounts to fix this.
- **The competitive insights challenge:** Investors want more than data about impact reductions, compensation, diversity, and the like. They want to understand which companies embed sustainability into corporate strategy, customer engagement, human capital management, and the innovation pipeline.

The *data quality problem* will gradually move to the background, as a combination of investors, regulators, and organizations involved in setting sustainability disclosure and reporting guidance converge on widely accepted disclosure standards.

The *competitive insights challenge* offers an opportunity for companies to *allow investors and lenders to peek behind the curtain.*

Peek Behind the Curtain

Investors scour data to identify a company's risk profile. They also want to know how a company plans to create a competitive advantage and win in the marketplace. The tricky part is that much of this "peek behind the curtain" information could be considered a competitive advantage, the company's 'secret sauce.'

This competitive insights challenge represents a fine line for companies: *How do we tell investors our strategy and unique competitive differentiators – without giving away secrets to our competitors?*

Table 2.1 shows examples of topics that are typically disclosed, and some that investors would love to know about but are generally not disclosed for reasons of confidentiality.

As Table 2.1 suggests, of all the actions companies undertake to address sustainability issues, they publicly disclose half.[4] The items they disclose are typically data aligned with external reporting frameworks and regulations. In Part 2, I share over 300 examples of how leading companies are disclosing data aligned with these and many other sustainability metrics.

Key to the board's role in the five-to-seven-year planning horizon is designing and implementing an updated set of sustainable growth metrics.

Table 2.1: What Investors Want: Disclosure vs. Confidential

Topic	Typically Disclosed	Typically Confidential
Governance	– Sustainability positioning – CEO/Chair letter – Board committees, charters, bios – Board and executive diversity – **Materiality assessment** – Goals, metrics, and progress – ESG ratings – Assurance and verification – Data, privacy, and cyber security policies	– C-suite and board deliberations about company purpose and long-term viability of core businesses – How sustainability is incorporated into **key business decisions** – Board agendas and time allocation in board meetings – Compensation incentives for sustainability deliverables – Implementation plans – Internal dashboards
Strategy	– General strategy statement – Enterprise risk management – Risk information – Product quality and safety	– Customer engagement – Product portfolio plans, R&D partnerships, innovation pipeline, and market expansion strategy – Strategic plans and discussions – **Scenario** planning detail – Revenue tracking detail
Environment	– **Scope 1, 2, and 3 GHG emissions** – Energy usage – Other operations' emissions, spills, water use, waste, etc. – Biodiversity policy – Product packaging	– Material sourcing information – Circular economy analysis – Product biodegradability, durability, recyclability, and traceability – Product end-of-life disposition
Social	– Workplace benefits, diversity, safety, health, wellness, etc. – Supply chain diversity – Human rights policy – Employee engagement – Sustainability skills, expertise	– Recruitment and retention data – Gender pay equity – Labor relations issues – Wages – Reliance on contingent workforce – Due diligence across the value chain

Tomorrow's Sustainable Growth Metrics

The metrics by which investors will measure and reward performance start with those used today. They will also include others that define the extent to which the company is making a *systematic, steady march toward a net-positive contribution to society.*

New Sustainable Growth Metrics

Taken together, we can imagine future disclosure metrics, including those described below and depicted in Figure 2.3.

- **Total carbon footprint:** Total GHG emissions for Scopes 1, 2, and 3 across the full value chain.
- **Resource inputs:** The extent to which resource inputs, including raw materials and process components, align with circular economy principles, such as renewable, recycled, **biodegradable**, or sourced from sustainable yield resources.
- **Resource outputs:** The physical impacts of products, packaging, waste, and other resource outputs on biodiversity and **ecosystem services**.
- **Product portfolio:** The amount and percentage of business activities by volume, revenue, and so forth, that produce positive impacts on natural capital – specifically full value chain GHG emissions.
- **Capital deployment:** The amount and percentage of capital expenditure, financing, or investment deployed toward climate-related risks and opportunities and supporting implementation of a company's energy transition plan.
- **Board and C-suite Diversity:** The percentage of board of directors and executive ranks by gender and other diversity metrics.

Each of these six sustainable growth metrics is addressed, at least in part, in key EU regulations. These include the ESRS and sustainability requirements under the IFRS. For example:

- **Total carbon footprint:** ESRS requires, among other things, absolute GHG emission targets, and whether they are based on conclusive scientific evidence. It also demands reporting on progress in achieving those targets.
- **Resource inputs:** ESRS requires, among other things, a list and prioritization of material resources; how the business affects resources and contributes to biodiversity; how the business plans to adapt its strategy and business model to preserve global resources; and the risks of not transitioning to a circular business model.
- **Resource outputs:** ESRS requires details related to products and services, including resource use, waste volumes, and financial impacts.
- **Product portfolio:** The EU disclosure standards refer to opportunities and require detailed information supporting that.
- **Capital deployment:** The ESRS E1 standard requires companies to disclose their climate-related impacts and risks, including their transition plans towards net zero. There is an expectation of disclosure of the investments and funding supporting the implementation of the transition plan.

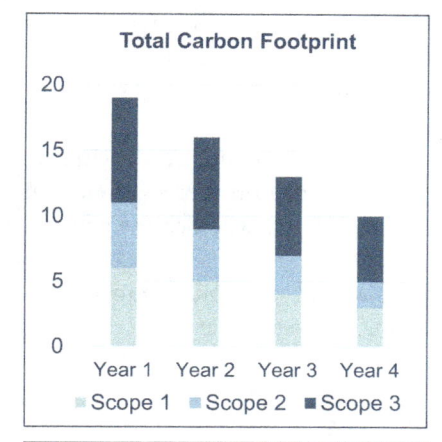

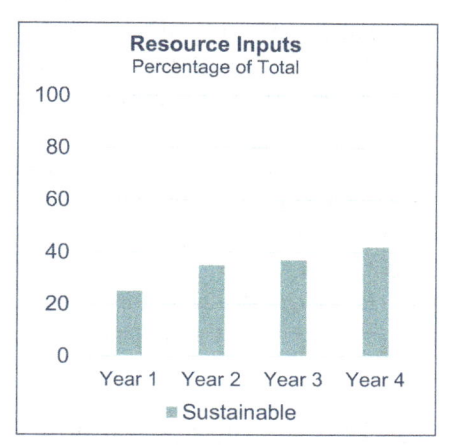

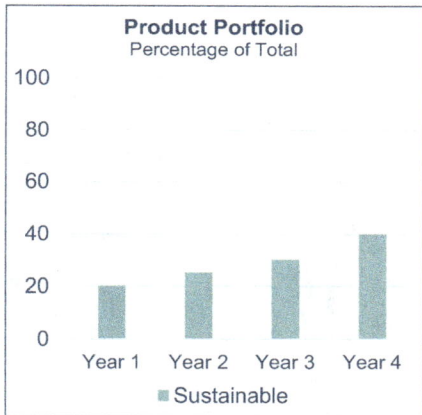

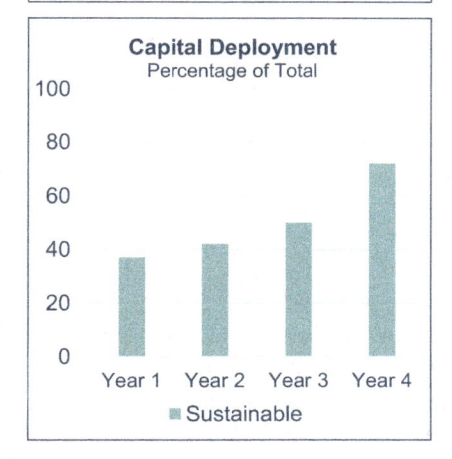

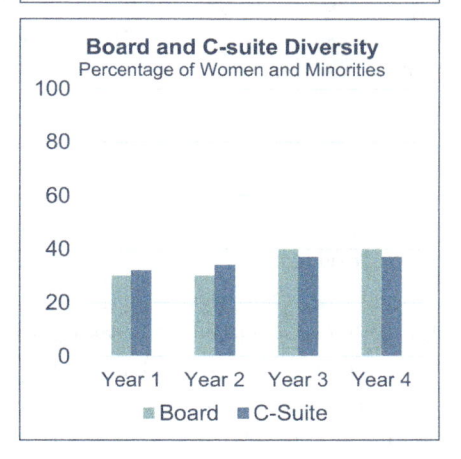

Figure 2.3: New Sustainable Growth Metrics

– **Board and C-suite diversity:** The EU Pay Transparency Directive requires information about the male-female pay gap and UK executive pay disclosure rules require CEO pay ratio disclosure for companies over 250 people.

In addition to these metrics, companies will need to measure and report climate-related physical and transition risks. To the extent that transition risk gets pushed out, as it may under the second Trump administration, this will increase physical risks.

The link is strengthening between confidential sustainability information that investors want to gain insight into and intangible asset value.

Build Intangible Asset Value: Hidden Gem

Across industries, intangible assets comprise approximately 90 percent of the S&P 500 total market value. (See Figure 2.4.[5]) We are not just talking about the massive brand value of Apple or Coca-Cola. Even in "hard asset heavy" companies, intangibles constitute at least 40 percent of total asset value.

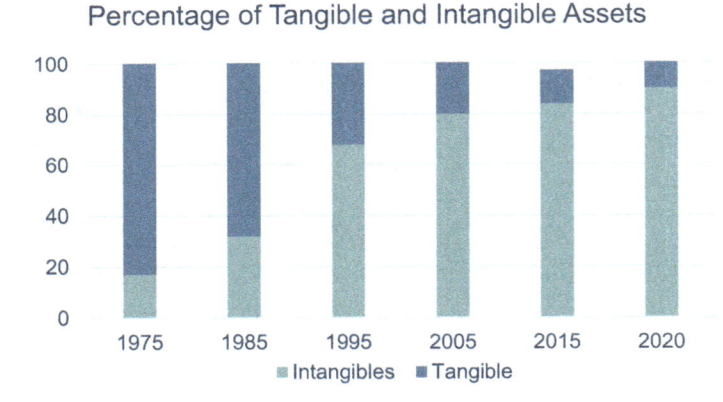

Figure 2.4: Growth of Intangible Asset Value
Source: Ocean Tomo

Intangible asset value has increased markedly in the past 50 years as brands have globalized and the data and knowledge economy has grown rapidly.

Intangibles are not easily measured. Listed entities often calculate intangibles by subtracting the company's book value from its market value. The key to enhancing intangible asset value lies with actions taken today that pay off in the future. That sounds like sustainable growth.

As standardization and regulation of sustainability data increase, companies could theoretically include reporting mechanisms and plans the company has put in place to become more sustainable in the coming years – in essence, creating an intangible sustainability valuation.

McKinsey found that companies delivering top-quartile growth in 2018 to 2019 invested 2.6 times more than their peers in intangible assets.[6] In addition:

 Pause for Reflection

According to McKinsey, "the evidence is stacking up in an age increasingly driven by innovation and knowledge that firms and sectors that invest most heavily in intangibles are reinforcing and deepening their competitive advantage and achieving the highest rates of growth in gross value added."[7]

Boards have a key opportunity to mine both tangible and intangible asset value.

Intangible assets fall into two categories:
- **Identifiable assets:** including software, patents, copyrights, trademarks, trade secrets, and recipes.
- **Unidentifiable assets:** core to a company and cannot be separated from its businesses, including reputation, brand, investments in human capital, customer loyalty, and innovation.

It is reasonable to assume that, going forward, the potentially strong connection between these unidentifiable assets and sustainability will drive market value.
- **Human capital:** investment in actions to attract and retain staff who increasingly care about climate and sustainability. Such investments include training and development, building knowledge and innovation skills, and promoting a winning culture aligned with making the world a better place.
- **Customer loyalty:** long-term investment in building deep customer and supplier relationships by not only delivering quality products and services at competitive costs, but also helping customers address their sustainability challenges.
- **Innovation:** investing not only in research and development but also in programs to build knowledge and innovation skills aligned with sustainability.

Investments in these three areas are highly interdependent. For example, companies investing more in employee training and creating innovative products and services are likely also helping customers reduce their negative climate impacts.

Importantly, these key factors that contribute to intangible asset value are closely aligned with those on the right side of Table 2.1.

Message for CEOs and Boards

If there is such alignment between the business case for sustainability and growing asset value, why the confusion, misunderstanding, and backlash?

Boards, CEOs, and C-suite executives cannot move forward to capture value from sustainability unless they start with three actions:

– Acknowledge the significant misalignment between boards and management.
– Strengthen board sustainability oversight.
– Conduct an objective, full assessment of where the company stands today.

Chapter 3 addresses the misalignment and Chapter 4 shows concrete ways to enhance board structure, fluency, and cadence. Chapter 5 then provides a simple toolkit for corporate leaders and boards to assess and improve.

Notes

1 Gary P. Pisano, "How Fast Should Your Company Really Grow?" Harvard Business Review, March-April 2024.
2 Barton, Dominic, James Manyika, Tim Koller, Robert Palter, Jonathan Godsall, and Josh Zoffer, "Where companies with a long-term view outperform their peers," McKinsey Global Institute, February 8, 2017 and "Putting stakeholder capitalism into practice," McKinsey & Company, January 2022.
3 Gilbert S. Hedstrom, Jonathan B. Shopley, and Colin M. LeDuc, "Realizing the Sustainable Development Premium," Prism, Arthur D. Little Journal, 2000.
4 ESG Navigator provides comprehensive ESG Ratings Maps that compare the methodology of major reporting frameworks and ESG ratings with the 100 Key Sustainability Indicators that have been shaped by industry leaders since 2018.
5 Annual Study of Intangible Asset Market Value, Ocean Tomo, A Part of J.S. Held, 2020.
6 "Unlocking growth through intangible assets: A Guide for people leaders," McKinsey, July 13, 2023
7 "Getting tangible about intangibles: The future of growth and productivity," McKinsey Global Institute, Discussion Paper, June 16, 2021.

Chapter 3
Align the Board and C-Suite

The hardest thing about sustainability is that we may not be around for the full impacts of climate change – but we must do this now.
Jo Mark Zurel, Chair, Board of Directors, Fortis Corporation

We've established that 'truly' sustainable growth going forward requires demonstrating strong financials and a track record of approaching zero, or even net-positive environmental **footprint** and positive social impact. It also entails helping your suppliers and customers to do the same.

Over the next few years, companies will need to reposition themselves to:
- *Win the war for talent* in an ever-globalizing world.
- *Engage customers* by walking the sustainability journey together and helping them rapidly decarbonize.
- *Apply the zero-waste philosophy* they have had in their operations to their full value chain.
- *Earn the trust* of today's and tomorrow's stakeholders – including increasingly educated, vigilant, and tech-enabled shareholders and NGOs.

For most companies, the shift from the old economy to the new clean energy economy requires nothing short of transformation.

Transformation: sweeping, dramatic change characterized by rapid, even disruptive, innovation that radically shifts the way things are done and motivates people to contribute their energy to win.

Companies that want to measure progress towards successful positioning to win in this new clean energy economy face **three major obstacles**.
- **Using the right rating scale:** Most rating scales assess companies' performance with a quarter of the companies in the top quartile. But that kind of scale does not work for measuring transformation. Most companies must transform. Over 150 major companies have used a rating scale that measures progress toward transformation. I introduce this scale later in this chapter and examine it in Part 2.
- **Recognizing the iceberg dilemma:** Virtually every rating scale available to companies relies on *data that companies disclose*. That is only the visible tip of the iceberg. It is not the full story, as illustrated in Table 3.1.

https://doi.org/10.1515/9783111548852-004

- **Conducting an honest assessment:** Executives can easily be seduced into thinking they are doing okay if their company receives a favorable rating relative to peer companies. A frank look in the mirror might reveal a different result.

Companies cannot measure progress on sustainability unless they have an objective and honest starting point. This requires that the CEO and board are aligned. That poses a stark challenge for many companies.

Fix the Misalignment Between Board and Management

Recent research by The Conference Board and PwC[1] points to serious gaps between how boards see themselves and how executives view them. The gaps relate to board structure, director sustainability expertise, and board meeting design. The gaps are illustrated in Table 3.1. A detailed toolkit to address the gaps is provided in Chapter 4.

Table 3.1: The Board/Management Misalignment

	Executives	Board
Board structure		
– Think at least one director should be replaced	89%	45%
Director sustainability expertise:		
– Boards have good risk management expertise	45%	82%
– Boards understand ESG risks	47%	82%
– Boards understand ESG opportunities	44%	77%
Board meetings design:		
– ESG receives sufficient board attention	29%	85%
– Climate receives sufficient board attention	35%	82%

The fact that boards and executives are misaligned on sustainability does not necessarily mean only one is correct. Healthy debates on priorities, timing, and cost are to be expected.

At a high level, it's useful to ask if your company is – and wants to be – a *Follower* simply engaging, accelerating, or leading in some areas, or a *Transformer*.

What is Your Company's Sustainability Position?

In December 2022, the NACD published as the cover story in its quarterly journal, *Directorship*, an article I wrote with Paul Camuti, executive vice president and chief technology, strategy, and sustainability officer at Trane Technologies, a global climate innovator with revenues near $18 Bn. In the article, "Transforming Board ESG Oversight,"[2] we introduced the idea of companies falling into one of two buckets. Most are Followers, but a growing number are Transformers.

Followers view climate change, global GHG emissions, biodiversity loss, social issues, and related ESG topics as potential problems. Most have not yet fully absorbed the opportunity to get ahead of the game. The more engaged Followers, by contrast, do these things:
– Monitor regulatory developments, engage with investors, track competitor actions, and understand workplace trends.
– Track climate disclosure requirements, especially from the EU and California.
– Read BlackRock CEO Larry Fink's annual letters to shareholders and engage in dialog with investors on ESG issues.
– Ensure company reports align with the latest external ESG reporting standards.
– Work on improving C-suite and board ESG expertise.
– Review their core businesses and approve strategies that reduce negative ESG impacts across the full value chain.

Some Followers monitor, and adjust as needed, to be a *Fast Follower*. In Figure 1, they sit at the right edge of the old economy image. They often believe that, perhaps with minor adjustments, the current business model, board oversight roles, and committee structure can guide future success.

Every board should carefully assess whether being a Follower is sufficient.

Transformers view sustainability, and especially climate change, as the defining issues of our day. They treat climate and biodiversity loss as "just transition" to a low-carbon economy, and related ESG issues at the core of the company's distinctive role in society:
– The CEO and management team place sustainability at the core of the company's purpose and strategy.
– They view sustainability as a disruptive driver of innovation.
– They see many other global challenges being tied to and exacerbated by climate change, such as food and freshwater insecurity, forced migrations, deforestation, supply chain disruptions, and health problems.

- They believe the global decarbonization challenge requires every company to radically reduce GHG emissions, not only in operations but across the full value chain.
- They see that we are past the "tipping point," and the race is on to transform companies for success in a decarbonized world grounded in societal value.
- They invest in creating a set of products and services that help customers radically reduce their GHG emissions.

Transformers want to lead with sustainability as a key differentiator. They sit squarely in the far right of Figure 1. They see corporate transformation as imperative, knowing this can only happen if the CEO and board take the lead. They adjust board oversight after a careful look in the mirror.

Lessons from Leaders

The board's ultimate purpose is to ensure the long-term viability and success of the company. Sustainability is fundamentally about understanding these increasingly material issues and navigating long-term change. That's why lessons from leaders, both successful ones and those who failed, can help.

Most of today's Transformers get to that place through the actions of visionary CEOs who set out to significantly reinvent their company – its overarching purpose, its business model, its portfolio of businesses and offerings, and its message to customers and the marketplace.

Transforming a company to align with the new clean energy economy is not tomorrow's opportunity. The signals of change are all around us.

Across industry sectors, the century-old fossil-fuel-based model of the industrial era is being shattered – not only by newer companies, but also by more traditional companies such as:
- **Enel**, founded in 1962 as Italy's electricity generation and distribution company, exploded on the global scene to become a world leader in renewable energy, operating in 30 countries. Since it privatized and listed in 1999, Enel has reached a market capitalization of $75 Bn and declares it wants to lead the transformation of the energy industry.
- **Mars,** a global food company with the footprint of a small country. Its tagline "The world we want tomorrow starts with how we do business today," and summary message "Family-owned. Future-facing. Purpose-driven," embed sustainability at the core. Mars supports these words with aggressive targets and execution plans. The company has action plans to eliminate its impact on

deforestation by its beef, cocoa, palm oil, paper, and soy supply chains. Top-tier financial performance enables it to do so, according to Mars.

- **Neste**, the Finnish oil and gas company, transformed from refining oil to producing sustainable energy. In addition to producing renewable diesel, the company is using renewable raw materials in its refineries, such as used cooking fat, waste fat from the food industry, and residues from vegetable oil production. Neste reached its target in 2017 to become the world's largest producer of renewable diesel. It also produces polymers and other chemicals from recycled and renewable materials. The company has a target to make production **carbon neutral** by 2035.
- **Novelis**, the world's leading producer of flat-rolled aluminum products, places sustainability at the core of its stated ambition, "To be the world's leading provider of low-carbon, sustainable aluminum solutions." The company aims to realize the benefits of a circular economy and fulfill its purpose of "Shaping a sustainable world together." The systematic focus on circularity and resulting GHG reductions are notable. Recycled aluminum inputs rose from 30 percent in 2011 to 61 percent in 2023. Today, Novelis is the world's largest recycler of aluminum.
- **Novo Nordisk**, the Danish multinational pharmaceutical widely recognized as a leader in stakeholder engagement, adopted the goal of zero environmental impact. Specific commitments address circular supply (reducing impacts across the supply chain) and circular products (designed to be reused or recycled).
- **Ørsted,** in 2008, was one of the most coal-intensive energy companies in Europe. In just ten years, it transformed from dependency on fossil fuels to becoming a renewable energy company. Over that decade, Ørsted reversed the ratio (85 percent to 15 percent) of fossil fuels to renewables in its heat and power production.
- **Schneider Electric** states upfront that we face a tectonic shift in energy transition and an 'electrical industrial revolution' catalyzed by digitization and circularity. It aims to have a **climate-positive** impact. The company's executive committee is highly diverse, with women making up over 40 percent. The 17-member supervisory board is one of the most diverse in industry: gender-balanced and with representatives from ten countries. As of May 2024, the average age was 57.5, nearly 6 years below the S&P 500 average.
- **Trane Technologies,** with a long history of climate leadership dating to 2015, when the CEO and senior business leader's personal KPIs became tied to the company's 2020 Climate Commitment targets. In 2019, the company's bold 2030 Sustainability Commitments included the SBTi-validated Gigaton Challenge to reduce emissions from products and services by 48 percent. It's a

first-of-its-kind, business-to-business commitment to significantly reduce customers' carbon emissions. In 2022, Trane Technologies' net-zero targets for 2050 were among the first in the world to receive SBTi approval.

– **Unilever** began a transformation during the 2008 financial crisis. In 2010, then-CEO Paul Polman launched the bold Sustainable Living Plan to double growth while cutting in half the company's environmental footprint. After his retirement and a turbulent period of investor scrutiny under Alan Jope, CEO Hein Schumacher laid out his focused Growth Action Plan to restore profitability. He has extended some sustainability targets, such as cutting plastics to 30 percent by 2026 instead of half by 2025. Nevertheless, Schumacher claims this change will make sustainability goals achievable, with a continued focus on decarbonization, nature, plastics, and livelihoods.

What do these leading companies have in common? In each case, a strong and visionary CEO led the charge. They may have started by viewing sustainability as a risk issue. However, they quickly moved beyond that, with the executive team and board collectively *embarking on a sustainable growth roadmap* that will drive the company toward the clean economy – and reap value for shareholders and society in doing so.

Look Around: Every Industry is Transforming

As Table 3.2 illustrates, every industry is undergoing transformation. Some sectors are taking baby steps while others are well along.

Table 3.2: Industries in Transformation

Industry	Yesterday's (Linear) Focus	Tomorrow's (Circular) Focus
Aerospace	More flights; more fuel and carbon	More connection; less carbon
Apparel	Sell clothing	Sell; lease; take back
Automotive	Sell cars and trucks	Sell mobility solutions
Chemicals	Make chemicals from hydrocarbons	Hydrocarbons, biomaterials, recycled products
Energy	More energy; more carbon	More energy; less carbon

Table 3.2 (continued)

Industry	Yesterday's (Linear) Focus	Tomorrow's (Circular) Focus
Food	More food that tastes good	More food; more health; less water; less waste
Hotels	Sell lodging from a facility	Sell lodging solutions
Industrial	Make; sell; and forget	Make; lease; take back; remanufacture
Information Technology	Entertain; save time; convenience	Help solve the world's toughest challenges
Mining	Mine ore	Mine landfills; take back; recycle
Pharmaceuticals	Sell drugs	Sell health solutions
Retailing	Sell stuff	Sell solutions
Waste Services	Sell waste hauling and disposal in landfills	Sell waste solutions; recycle, reuse; eliminate waste

Two industry sectors exemplify what transformative action to address climate change looks like:

– **Automotive:** Major auto companies across the globe are changing more in the recent five-to-ten-year period than they have in the past century. Yet they still use over 100 million tons of materials annually and contribute to over 10 percent of the world's carbon dioxide emissions, according to McKinsey.

– **Power generation:** Power companies' main assets are plants with a long useful life, which depreciate over many decades. The EU and US have been systematically closing coal plants and investing in renewable power generation for years. New coal plants are expected to be built in Asia, however, with China responsible for 95 percent of new construction in 2023.

One of the core sustainable growth concepts common to leading companies is the *transition from the traditional linear economy to a circular economy.*

Circular economy: An alternative to the traditional linear economy of "make, use, dispose." Instead, resources remain in use for as long as possible, extracting their maximum value while in use, then recovering and regenerating products and materials at the end of use.

Circularity: Organizational practices that optimize resource use and minimize waste throughout the full value chain.

Some may think the circular economy is unattainable; that we are locked into the old economy model. That is partially true, but the seeds of change are all around us. In Part 2, I walk through the four core parts of sustainable growth – governance, strategy, environment, and social – and provide over 300 examples of leading companies globally.

A Sustainable Growth Roadmap

How can a company measure progress and sustainable growth?

A proven way to create board and executive alignment is to establish a shared, robust view of how their company stacks up today. Don't reinvent the wheel.

Developing a Roadmap: By Industry, for Industry

At the beginning of this chapter, I noted three key obstacles to measuring progress toward tomorrow's sustainable growth:
- Using the right rating scale
- Recognizing the 50/50 dilemma
- Conducting an honest assessment

I was asked how to measure progress toward sustainability by boards of directors. After returning from living in Brussels and seeing how European companies were managing sustainability, several US boards asked me, during the executive sessions, whether I could develop a tool that could help them track progress. I initially created a pilot version and tested it with dozens of clients.

For the past fifteen years, I have had the privilege of working closely in collaboration with over 100 leading companies. Together, we created ESG Navigator – *by industry and for industry.*
- For ten years, I ran executive sustainability councils for The Conference Board. Collectively, about 100 sustainability leaders from 75 major companies participated in these councils, which met three times a year for several days. I designed and moderated the meetings.
- Since 2018, I have hosted monthly webinars for corporate leaders discussing how to navigate sustainability.

As I listened to companies' stories from 2008 to 2018, I quietly captured the learnings. Companies were being bombarded by outside groups telling them what and how to disclose. But *what they truly craved was a benchmark tool, built around actions that leaders take to create value from sustainability.*[3]

In Part 2 of this book, I introduce a powerful "snake chart" analytic used by companies to engage the CEO and board in discussions of sustainable growth. Then, chapters 6 to 9 walk through 100 KPIs illustrating what leading and transformative practices look like, plus over 300 best practices from global companies.

Leading with Board Sustainability Fluency

Nobody expects board directors to be technical experts in cyber security or sustainability. However, *board sustainability oversight will fall more and more in the public eye* – as will the need for directors to demonstrate a reasonable level of fluency in climate and sustainability.

 For Boardroom Discussion

Investors increasingly expect companies to prove that their board of directors has the relevant and current expertise to oversee corporate positioning and strategy within a rapidly changing external landscape.

I have been a student of corporate governance for over 30 years. Early in my career, I helped boards keep the company in compliance and the CEO out of the spotlight. In recent decades, I have been helping boards, CEOs, executives, and their sustainability teams navigate sustainability – and embrace the opportunities it opens for the future.

What does it look like when boards and management discuss the magnitude and scale of risks and strategic opportunities facing a company?

Over the decades, I have observed what works best and worst in corporate boardrooms. It often comes down to asking the right questions.

The Power of Asking the Right Questions

The power of a single question by a board member can change everything.

Should we be in this business?

Years ago, I participated in the board committee meeting of a major chemical company. The discussion about European regulations and company positions on chemical composition took a turn. At the time, the styrene business was a critical and profitable part of the company's portfolio. Yet the US Environmental Protection Agency listed styrene as a 'suspected carcinogen'.

At some point, an outside board member asked: **"Should we be in the styrene business?"**

The question was heresy. The room became silent. The company's CEO quietly said, "We will report back at the next board meeting."

That simple question triggered many months of analysis and discussion, forcing some uncomfortable conversations. Those conversations examined the possible implications of a company's operations on human health and the environment – *beyond what regulations required* at the time. They also questioned the potential impact on long-term value creation for the company.

In this situation, the board director asking the question had deep expertise in the subject matter. He was the former CEO of several major chemical companies.

I was not privy to the internal discussions that ensued. However, as a result of the board director's query about styrene, the board subsequently engaged in broader conversations about the long-term viability of different businesses. The company later sold its coal business, placed its oil business in a joint venture, and made other major portfolio changes.

Board members do not need to be experts of a topic to ask the right questions. That is why, in Chapter 10, I provide a detailed list of 15 key strategic questions directors can ask. For each of those questions, I offer several sub-questions.

To help board members build a base level of expertise in climate and sustainability, the next chapter provides ten best practices for companies to enhance board oversight of sustainability.

Notes

1 "Board Effectiveness: A Survey of the C-suite," May 2023, PwC and The Conference Board. https://www.conference-board.org/publications/board-effectiveness-2023
2 Gib Hedstrom and Paul Camuti, "Transforming Board ESG Oversight," Directorship, National Association of Corporate Directors, December 2022.
3 The Corporate Sustainability Scorecard was renamed ESG Navigator in 2020.

Chapter 4
Enhance Board Fluency and Oversight

If you have the right board, then you can build the required fluency in sustainability and ESG.
Wendy Kei, Chair, Board of Directors, Ontario Power Generation

It is asking a lot to expect the typical board to provide the oversight necessary to pivot from the old to the new clean energy economy model (illustrated earlier in Figure 1).

Most board members 'get' the importance of climate risk. They read about fires, floods, and other weather-related events. They understand the supply chain disruptions and increased property insurance costs. They see the growing body of non-financial reporting regulations in Europe and the US. They know every company bears some responsibility for its full value chain impacts – not just those of their own operations.

Many have decades of experience reducing operational pollution and managing social issues in the workplace and supply chain. They may view the growing pressures around carbon pollution as more of the same.

But they would be wise to hit pause.

Most likely, directors have been reacting without taking time to deeply understand the magnitude and scale of the issues. They likely listen to presentations about disclosures rather than stepping back to gauge the company's long-term viability, positioning, and strategy.

Hit Pause

Among 110,000 directors globally, from a sample of large global public and private companies across industries, *fewer than 1 percent have professional backgrounds in sustainability or ESG.*[1] This has the attention of major pension fund investors who want companies to appoint new directors equipped to manage climate-related challenges.[2]

The fact that most board members cut their teeth in the old economy of 'take, make, waste' is not necessarily a bad thing. After all, they are highly accomplished individuals with a capacity to learn and change.

Here's the rub: **most boards are ill-equipped to provide effective and robust oversight of climate and sustainability**.

https://doi.org/10.1515/9783111548852-005

That was my conclusion after a year of considerable research and data analysis. Many moments during my 15 years of running meetings of corporate sustainability leaders from major companies reinforced that.

Recent Research on Board Sustainability Oversight

During the past two years, I led an extensive project researching board sustainability oversight.[3] The goal was to identify best practices globally to address this question:

> *Does the board have the skills and expertise to guide the company in (1) critically assessing its current performance and the track it is on; and (2) creating the 'right' roadmap to a decarbonized future?*

This chapter provides board directors, CEOs, corporate secretaries, and chief sustainability officers with the simple tools to assess board sustainability oversight and map a path forward.

Ten Levers to Enhance Sustainability Governance

Based on our discussions with board members and top executives of leading corporations, as well as a detailed literature review, my colleagues and I have identified ten "levers" with best practices across three aspects of board oversight. (See Table 4.1.)

Table 4.1: Ten Board Levers to Enhance Sustainability Governance

Topic	Board Sustainability Oversight Levers
Structure	– Board committees, charters, and roles – Board evaluation process – Board diversity
Fluency	– Director self-learning – External advisors – Formal courses
Cadence	– Board calendar planning – Board meeting pre-reads and agendas – Board meeting location – Board dialog with company experts

For each of the ten board oversight levers, in the following pages, I offer recent direct quotes from board directors about their current situation and a simple, four-stage maturity scale to assess performance. The maturity scale ranges from Stage 1, the early engagement stage at which most companies are, to Stage 4, which defines ambitious and transformative leadership. This is the same rating scale that leading companies urged me to create in ESG Navigator.

Situation Today: *Board Structure*

A board is well-structured to provide robust sustainability oversight if it has a committee structure and charters that detail comprehensive oversight, a highly effective annual evaluation process, and multifaceted diversity.

Board Committees, Charters, and Roles: The existence of a board committee responsible for sustainability oversight is less important than the degree of attention the board focuses on sustainability. That said, the most common sustainability governance question I hear is often whether sustainability belongs to a separate, dedicated board committee.

My answer: it depends on where you are on the maturity curve. For companies early in their sustainability journey, a separate committee can focus resources and demonstrate to investors that you are serious about board oversight. For companies past Stage 2, the better solution is often to fold explicit responsibilities for sustainability into other existing committees. (The NACD *Directorship* article referenced in Chapter 3 "Transforming Board ESG Oversight," addressed this directly.)

Recent research from PwC shows boards spend insufficient time and focus on sustainability.[4]

- In 2023, only 54 percent of directors (down from 57 percent in 2022) say ESG issues and company strategy are linked.
- Only 48 percent say our board has discussed climate change in the past 12 months, down from 51 percent in 2022.

The increasing maturity is depicted below.

Board Committees, Charters, Roles

Engaging	Accelerating	Leading	Transforming
Board committee charters and roles focus on conventional environment, health, and safety (**EHS**) and public policy issues, with only summary reference to sustainability (**S**). No designated **S** leader.	Board committee charters explicitly discuss **S** oversight, noting where **S** issues are **material** in own operations. Designated committee or board member oversees sustainability.	Board committee charters (constantly reviewed) explicitly define **S** responsibilities and leadership, addressing material **S** issues across the value chain.	Every board committee incorporates relevant **S** topics, explicit and detailed in charters (updated frequently).

Board Evaluation Process: Most boards of publicly traded companies engage in a typically annual evaluation process. But a robust evaluation process will not happen without deliberate leadership from the CEO and board chair. Several board chairs and other directors reinforced this point:
- "Boards really don't like to do board assessments – beyond annual skills review. Some do not take it seriously."
- "Some directors start coasting."

These recent comments from board directors are backed by research from PwC. Over half (56 percent) of directors think there are inherent limitations to being frank in these assessments, and 60 percent of executives do not trust their boards to effectively self-assess their own performance. Likewise, 41 percent of directors think board assessments are too much of a check-the-box exercise.[5]

At the most basic level, the annual evaluation process might consist of a skills matrix – ensuring that current and future directors collectively have the right mix of capabilities. Beyond a skills matrix, the degree of formality and robustness of the evaluation process varies widely.

Boards at Stage 4 companies routinely conduct a thoughtful self-assessment of the effectiveness of their oversight and company performance on sustainability risks and opportunities, resulting in *a robust, multi-year acceleration plan to ramp up board fluency and maturity.*

Board Evaluation Process

Engaging	Accelerating	Leading	Transforming
A skills matrix and assessment mostly a "check-the-box" exercise.	Comprehensive view of board skills and experience represented and needed over next 3–5 years. Lacking a deep director dialog about "how we're doing."	Map board skills to issues that matter most to key customers and other stakeholders. Identify *5* skills needed: 3–5 years. Build cadence of learning and actions.	Institutionalize a process to guide the company's transformation. Examine scenarios and update annually – building knowledge and momentum.

Board Diversity: Board diversity, especially in gender, has been growing. Yet almost three-quarters of directors of Fortune 500 boards remain predominantly male, and nearly 80 percent are white.[6] Some key facts:
- From 2011 to 2021, the average percentage of women on S&P 500 boards nearly doubled. Yet, women comprise only a third of board seats.
- In early 2024, only about six percent of S&P 500 companies achieved or exceeded gender balance with at least 50 percent women. That's 29 companies.[7]
- The pace of board diversification is slowing. From 2022 to 2023, the growth of gender, racial, and ethnic diversity among directors grew only about 1 percent.[8]

Given all of this, it is unsurprising that only 19 percent of executives think their boards are diverse enough.[9]

Investors and many corporate leaders tout the benefits of a diverse board:
- As noted earlier, Moody's analysis shows that companies with higher proportions of women on their boards achieve higher credit ratings.[10]
- Companies with a gender-diverse board are more likely to be more open and honest about their ESG performance.[11]

During my recent research, board chairs of major North American companies shared the following comments directly and confidentially.
- "A highly diverse board in terms of gender, age, geography, and experience, is key to ensuring a high degree of sustainability fluency. Need at least two females on the board plus additional diversity to move the company."
- "I need our board to be prepared to answer tough questions about the role our company plays in society – when asked by the Gen Z and Millennials who will make up over 60 percent of the global workforce by 2025."

The range of practices today spans four stages of maturity.

Board Diversity

Engaging	Accelerating	Leading	Transforming
Board diversity (gender, ethnicity, religion, etc.) is cumulatively less than 20%. May or may not have a board diversity policy.	Board diversity (female and other underrepresented groups) is 20–30%. Board nomination and diversity policy is public.	Board diversity (female and underrepresented groups) is > 30%, with diverse experiences prioritized. Nomination policy aims for robust diversity.	Board reflects diversity of the workforce and market, with 50% female and underrepresented groups, and reflects highly diverse experiences.

Situation Today: *Board Fluency*

In late 2023, The Wall Street Journal noted that many company directors lack confidence in their board's ability to oversee sustainability. Most directors (83 percent) say these topics are key knowledge for directors, but less than half consider themselves to have advanced knowledge.[12]

Likewise, executives believe boards lack critical expertise.[13]

- Only 45 percent of executives say their boards have good risk management expertise.
- Many executives (39 percent) say their boards have poor ESG expertise; even more (47 percent) say they have poor climate expertise.

With markets and technology moving faster than companies realize, the mindset boards need is this:

> *If we were creating our company from scratch, knowing what we do about global climate and other demographic, societal, and environmental pressures, what would our blueprint look like?*

Companies can assess their readiness to draft that blueprint by examining these three levers: director self-learning, external advisors, and formal courses.

Director self-learning: Every director invests considerable time reading, talking with peers, and meeting with leaders. The challenge, highlighted in our recent research, is that most board directors may not actually want to dive deeply into sustainability. Board members recently told me:

- "Most directors who need (or want) to learn more about climate and sustainability may be embarrassed to ask."
- "The classic pattern is that most directors don't know much about sustainability; many ask poor questions; and maybe one or two know something."

- "I [board chair] find that a lot of directors that reach a certain age do not do any of this (self-education about sustainability)."
- "The trick is to get the ignorant and domineering directors to defer to the directors who know something about sustainability."
- "The solution is to get the Board Chair to say, "We want each director to elevate our degree of knowledge about sustainability."

Board education starts with improving an awareness of climate science. For Stage 4 Transformers, in the table below, the directors invest in learning about sustainability via expert panels, meetings with customers, investors, and outside experts.

Director Self-learning

Engaging	Accelerating	Leading	Transforming
Rely mostly on personal network and learning portal. View *S* as mostly risk and disclosure. Request *S* support if needed.	Seek opportunities to build own fluency. View *S* as strategy as well as disclosure. Some request *S* learning; 1–2 directors may speak on *S*.	Challenge company to think in terms of transformation. View *S* as critical strategic issues and opportunities. Director interest (passion) about *S* is spreading.	Meet with leaders in transforming companies. Engage *S* expert coaching. Many directors are passionate about *S*.

One board chair of a major North American gas and electric distribution company asks every director to report annually on outside sustainability education received (where 'education' is broadly defined).

External advisors: The scope and scale of climate risk and other sustainability issues touch virtually every business. The challenge for board members is gaining a full and balanced set of perspectives to prioritize actions and develop strategy. Recent quotes from directors:
- "Boards cannot address these and similar questions with pre-reads or training courses or consultant presentations. We need experts in sustainability with considerable board and governance experience to help us ensure the right perspective."
- "Boards need to have an outside sustainability expert advisor; otherwise, companies spin their wheels."
- "A leading practice would be to make private 1:1 coaching and mentoring available every three months, so directors can access a sustainability expert who is also deeply experienced in board governance."

At Stage 4, the board engages in special sessions on material issues across the value chain. They bring in respected sustainability experts with considerable board experience as ongoing advisors.

External Advisors

Engaging	Accelerating	Leading	Transforming
May have experts provide a "sustainability 101" or specific topic (e.g., compliance). General counsel or corporate secretary controls agenda item.	External *S* expert invited to engage on strategic *S* implications. Agendas allow for dialog and discussion with outside expert.	Ongoing engagement by *S* advisor with management team. Advisor meets annually with board or committee.	Ongoing participation at board or committee meetings. Directors are fully fluent and routinely access 1:1 coaching regarding nuances of *S*.

Formal courses: In some aspects of corporate governance, formal courses are well-established and widely accepted as good practice. In the sustainability realm, such courses are established in some regions (e.g., Canada, and Europe) but are in the early stages of maturity in the US.

Directors want to learn from peers, other directors further up the learning curve on a particular topic. They also seek out technical experts with extensive experience in the boardroom and on a material issue under consideration. Directors can access formal training in two ways:

- Participate in a formal course offered by third-party organizations. The key is to carefully assess the past experiences with the offering and whether participation is limited to sitting board members or open to corporate leaders who may periodically report to the board.
- Build a session tailored to the individual company. This can be organized via independent board organizations, such as the NACD in the US or the Institute of Corporate Directors (ICD) in Canada. Alternatively, company leaders can contract with independent experts in board governance and sustainability to conduct a session tailored to the company.

I recommend a course to directors only if it is well designed and taught by instructors who are *both* content experts *and* have extensive experience in listening and advising directors in full board and board committee meetings. In addition, course participants should be mostly or even entirely sitting directors. (Some courses by universities and others claim to target board members, yet they allow participation by a wide variety of individuals.) A few examples appear in the table below.

Wendy Kei, Chair, Board of Directors, Ontario Power Generation, tells me that "as part of personal development, boards should invest in continuing education courses for board members. This should include courses that advance the required fluency in sustainability, ESG and climate change."

Other recent direct quotes from board members include:
- "Most directors don't want to be told to take a course."
- "Board members need to understand how little they really know about sustainability."
- "Every board member needs a bit of general sustainability training. Without that, they have no self-awareness."

At Stage 4, we expect the board chair and several directors/management to periodically take the best courses available to learn or confirm the level of sustainability fluency. The table below shows the progression.

Formal Courses

Engaging	Accelerating	Leading	Transforming
Board directors self-select whether to attend courses on *S*.	Directors (or full boards participate in a *S* certificate program. Example: *NACD Virtual Briefing Desk*.	Directors participate in an interactive certificate program with peer-to-peer learning/cases. Example: *ICD Climate Course*.	Directors facilitate/teach in interactive certificate programs with other *S* experts. Example: Program tailored to company.

Situation Today: *Board Cadence*

When it comes to how directors spend their time on sustainability topics in full board and board committee meetings, it is very easy to get the Pareto principle (also known as the 80/20 rule of maximizing impact) wrong. Their agendas are likely full of information on pending or recent regulations, how they rate against their peers on sustainability disclosure, and potential reputational risks on the horizon.

But are they addressing the elephant in the room?
- What portion of the full value chain of the business is based on fossil fuels?
- What is the rapid decarbonization pathway which should deliver a competitive advantage over time?
- How would the company be viewed if it asked a group of leading customers, suppliers, and investors from Europe? Those companies may be feeling different pressures, including from insurance providers.

Boards can build a cadence of enhancing sustainability knowledge and fluency via four levers: board calendar and planning, board meeting pre-reads and agendas, board meeting locations, and dialog with company sustainability leadership and teams.

Board calendar and planning: The annual board calendar, with meeting dates, locations, and a broad-brush structure of agendas, is typically set for the remainder of the current fiscal year. The challenge, highlighted by board members, surfaces:

- "We need to build a robust cadence for the board to oversee sustainability; about six sessions a year with the board."
- "As part of the cadence, we need to institutionalize a process for long-term thinking – including scenario exercises; innovation workshops; strategy sessions; and **CapEx** planning cycle reviews (out five or more years)."
- "Scenario planning is key, leading to annual strategy meetings. Management drives 1.5°C and 2°C carbon scenarios."
- "Must be tightly integrated with business strategy. We moved our strategy discussions from 5 years to 10–15 years."
- "What investments do we need to make now to be the company we want to be when we grow up?"

As noted in the four-stage maturity path below, leading companies establish a *cadence* of enhancing sustainability knowledge and fluency over multiple years. They do this through a full board and committee annual plan that includes strategy and scenario sessions and special sustainability learning workshops. Here is the pathway:

Board Calendar and Planning

Engaging	Accelerating	Leading	Transforming
Focus is *S* risks (own operations and disclosure. Agendas: benchmarking, compliance, safety, goals, philanthropy, etc. Special engagement on strategy may be in addition.	Focus is on material issues (full value chain); impact on strategy. Full-time *S* leader shares performance vs. goals; emerging issues. Board may add an extra 1–2 hours 1–2x/year to address key *S* issue(s).	Focus is long-term strategy and net zero; deep dive climate risk/ opportunities by lines of business. Transformation case studies with scenarios. Debate and align on public policy. Board plans an extra 2–4 hours for special session(s).	Board does scenario planning (strategic implications of carbon scenarios). Agendas routinely include full value chain insights from experts and partners. Board spends an extra ½+ day of deep engagement and learning about a key *S* topic.

Board Meeting Pre-Reads and Agendas: In my experience participating in over 70 board meetings of major companies, directors want thoughtful information in advance so the conversation can be robust. Importantly, they want much of the meeting to be conversational, not just listening to presentations.

This is a challenge. Board packs are often 200 to 500 pages long. Consider these revelations from board members:

– "Risk people love to present data. Board members need to set the agendas to avoid overly focusing on details rather than discussing strategic implications."
– "I get very frustrated when most of our sustainability agenda time is spent listening to a presentation of slides we received in advance, and I [board chair] need to shut down board discussion because we ran out of time."
– "Our board meeting pre-reads are very robust. In the board meetings, we use no slides – 100 percent conversation."
– "I [board chair] have an advance call with every director. Our meeting time is mostly discussion."

The table below contrasts the Stage 1 approach (providing updates) with building a strong cadence of continued learning in Stage 4.

Board Meeting Pre-reads and Agendas

Engaging	Accelerating	Leading	Transforming
Goal: Brief on meeting content. Often a "grab bag" of *S* topics: trends, goals, compliance, ratings, etc. Occasional thought leadership.	Goal: Inform discussions. Insights on material *S* issues, aligned to strategy and innovation opportunities. Provide final *S* report (pre-launch). Frequent thought leadership.	Goal: Enable rich strategy and performance dialog. Comprehensive slides stand alone so meeting is a discussion anchored in strategy and **scenario analysis**. Provide draft *S* report for review. Provocative thought leadership.	Goal: Drive learning cadence. Meeting is dialog: latest signposts impacting strategy and scenario analysis; innovation pipeline; key business decisions/CapEx. Best external thought leadership pieces.

Board meeting locations: I confess that living in the Boston area, I enjoy being asked to participate in a January board meeting at a seaside resort in Florida. Board members like that also, especially when delivered by the company jet. But that is a Stage 1 practice.

The opportunity, highlighted in recent direct quotes from board members, is to use board meeting locations to significantly enhance the director's knowledge and fluency. As board members explained:

- "I [board chair] want to create an environment where the board and management team engage deeply on the right topics."
- "We should periodically meet at locations that represent our largest physical risks from climate across the full value chain."
- "Our last meeting was at a major supplier location; our next meeting is at the site of our largest customer."

The pathway from Engaging to Transforming is below.

Board Meeting Locations

Engaging	Accelerating	Leading	Transforming
Most meetings held at headquarters or resorts. Short tour if meeting held at a site.	Many meetings at HQ or resorts. 1–2x/year meet at a company site. Site meeting includes several-hour tour of operations.	Cadence of meetings at critical value chain locations (re **S** issues, footprint). High-impact learning on key material issues from local experts.	Meetings across value chain locations. Considerable pre-work and experiential learning during meetings.

Dialog with company staff: refers to the extent to which the board leverages internal sustainability experts prior to, during, and after board meetings and strategy sessions. This can be complicated, as these direct quotes from board members illuminate:

- "It's critical that the board spend time with the top, full-time sustainability leader. Otherwise, we risk hearing a sanitized view of what may be critically important details we should delve into."
- "CEO is comfortable with me [board chair] engaging directly with the C-suite and CSO. It is a fragile trust; I need to earn it."
- "CEO allows us to deal directly with his direct reports. I have quarterly 1:1 coffee with each director and C-suite member."

The Stage 4 practice means the board leverages internal sustainability experts, engaging with cross-functional and sustainability leaders prior to, during, and after board meetings and strategy sessions.

Dialog with Company Staff			
Engaging	**Accelerating**	**Leading**	**Transforming**
Goal: Inform board on ESG topics and strategy. Committee Chair has 1:1 conversation with CSO or equivalent with general counsel/ corporate secretary.	Goal: Discuss critical *S* issues at board meetings. Full-time *S* leader & team engage with board during tours.	Goal: Engage the board deeply on our top few *S* issues. Deep *S* engagement during annual strategy planning sessions.	Goal: Ongoing (formal and informal) dialog with board on our top few *S* issues. Deep engagement in annual scenario/strategy workshops/plans.

Board Action Plan

The ten levers for enhancing board sustainability governance offer the menu. Now, it is time to select your meal.

A few simple actions by the board can generate powerful, impactful results over the next two years. Some actions should be for the next fiscal year; others can be folded into the current, albeit full, board calendar.

Next Annual Cycle

Now is the time to look ahead to year-end, typically when the board approves the strategic and operational plans for the next year. Here are three ideas with high-impact changes for the *next* annual cycle:

– *Revamp the board evaluation process* to approach Stage 3 or 4 above. Ask tough questions about board sustainability fluency. Use the output of that evaluation for a robust discussion at an upcoming board meeting.
– *Hold a meeting at a supplier or customer location* – where your company's most material sustainability issues are most impactful.
– *Build a cadence in agenda topics.* Identify the three most material sustainability issues and build meeting agendas around enhancing knowledge about those issues.

Current Annual Cycle

Discuss and agree high-impact changes for *this* year. Recent examples provided by board directors:
- *Committee chairs meet face-to-face with the CSO.* Schedule a half-day for at least one board member to meet with the top full-time sustainability leader to discuss critical issues, challenges, opportunities, etc.
- *Committee chairs set agendas.* Don't settle for rubber-stamping the agenda. Consult with the CSO and set the agenda you want.
- *Meet with a decision-maker from key customers*, ideally in Europe or the UK.

At the end of each board meeting, the chair, or any director, should ask, "Which issues should we have on the agenda for our next meeting?"

Finally, the board should build a list of provocative, tough questions to ask during and between meetings. See Chapter 10.

Notes

1 "Sustainability in the spotlight: Has ESG lost momentum in the boardroom?" Diligent Institute and SpencerStuart, June 2023.
2 https://www.reuters.com/sustainability/boards-policy-regulation/woodside-investor-hesta-calls-appointment-climate-skilled-directors-2024-03-12/
3 This research (sponsored by Trane Technologies) was a follow-up to an article, "Transforming Board ESG Oversight", that I wrote with Paul Camuti, Trane's executive vice president and chief technology and sustainability officer. The article was the cover story on NACD's quarterly *Directorship* journal.
4 "Today's boardroom: confronting the change imperative," PwC's 2023 Annual Corporate Directors Survey, p. 7.
5 PwC 2023 Annual Corporate Directors Survey, p. 6.
6 "Amid Push to Diversity Corporate Boards, Change is Slow," The Wall Street Journal, October 2, 2023.
7 https://www.bloomberg.com/news/articles/2024-01-23/women-s-boardroom-gains-keep-them-decade-away-from-parity
8 "The Pace of Board Diversification is Slowing," NACD Directorship, Winter 2024, p. 15.
9 "Board effectiveness: A survey of the C-suite," PwC, April 2024.
10 https://www.cfodive.com/news/gender-diversity-boards-correlates-high-credit-quality-moodys/709387/
11 "Board gender diversity and ESG decoupling: Does religiosity matter?" Eliwa, Y., Aboud, A., & Saleh, A. (2023). *Business Strategy and the Environment*, 32(7), 4046–4067.
12 https://www.wsj.com/articles/many-boards-are-playing-catch-up-on-esg-and-green-issues-6de9552b
13 PwC survey

Part Two: **Integrate**

Chapter 5
Track Your Progress

Consider the story of one company that *figured this out*.

 Origin of the ESG Navigator Snake Chart

In 2018, **Fluor's** sustainability leader, Nancy Kralik, was a "one-woman-band," managing all aspects of sustainability and ESG for the largest publicly traded engineering and construction company in the Fortune 500. She managed preparation of the sustainability report, updated digital content, responded to external raters, and more.

In 2019, Nancy and her project engineer Lucy Brady realized that before they could track progress, they needed an objective assessment of where the company stood on sustainability. Using ESG Navigator, they gathered data from functional and business line leaders, then organized and assessed it.

To make sense of what they were seeing, they created a brilliantly simple analytical tool – later dubbed the '**snake chart**' – that summarized the data.

In 2020, Nancy shared her analysis and the snake chart with Fluor's C-suite and executive committee. The response was immediate and positive. They agreed to address the five gaps identified. A year later, she returned and showed the board the progress. She also identified new areas for improvement, noting additional headcount requirements. The CEO responded by increasing the headcount in Nancy's department from two to seven.

An unexpected benefit was gaining internal alignment across business and functional leaders. Each could see how sustainability impacted his or her department or business.

The core message from this story: *to gain traction in the C-suite and boardroom, measure your company's status and organize your analysis the way the CEO runs the company.* Don't just react to "outside-in" pressures and requirements.

How to Measure: Outside-In Versus Inside-Out

One of the major challenges with sustainability is: how do you measure this stuff?
Company executives are bombarded by pressures ***from the outside:***
- *NGOs* tell them what issues are most important and what to disclose.
- *Raters* tell them how they stack up against their peers, based on mandated disclosure.
- *Regulators* tell them what they are required to report.
- *Accountants* advise them how they need to prepare for external assurance.
- *Consultants* counsel them to upgrade internal systems, to track risk progress.

https://doi.org/10.1515/9783111548852-006

Corporate sustainability leaders spend most of their time on the outside-in stuff: tracking regulatory developments, preparing sustainability reports, supporting external communications, responding to ESG ratings agencies, and preparing reports for the C-suite and board.

As noted in the Introduction, Figure 3, they also understand that these external pressures must provide a basis for discussion about strategy.

 Pause for Reflection

Don't let outsiders dictate your sustainability strategy.
The work is necessary to comply with requirements or conform to industry expectations. But ignoring the bigger picture, for the sake of compliance, is the wrong approach. This work is mostly disconnected from corporate strategy – and from the drivers of value creation.

A 2024 Financial Times opinion summarized this, noting that **ESG as we know it is dead**. It is time to confront the uncomfortable truth: ESG as it stands – grounded in disclosures and voluntary market action – will not deliver the necessary change.[1]

A shift in corporate mindset is needed, viewing the sustainability agenda not simply as corporate responsibility, but as delivering a competitive edge.

What if you could take all of that *outside-in* stuff and convert it into **a simple, powerful *inside-out* roadmap**, fully integrating these external pressures with the company's strategy and business processes?

That's what Fluor did. Improving on an ESG Navigator platform, Fluor used its new tool for board reporting. At around this time, The Conference Board endorsed the platform, making it available to its members.

The Fluor Snake Chart

In 2020, during one of my monthly webinars, Fluor shared their story: how they conducted the company assessment, analyzed the data, and created the 'snake chart.' A similar example, but with 'dummy' ABC Company data, appears in Figure 5.1:

- The **white line** represents the benchmark group, which could be sectoral peers, sub-sector peers, a custom group, or all companies in the ESG Navigator database.
- The **yellow line** represents the company's candid self-assessment.
- The **dot color**, red or green. is driven by the gap from the benchmark group.
- The **dot size** is driven by elements flagged as most important.

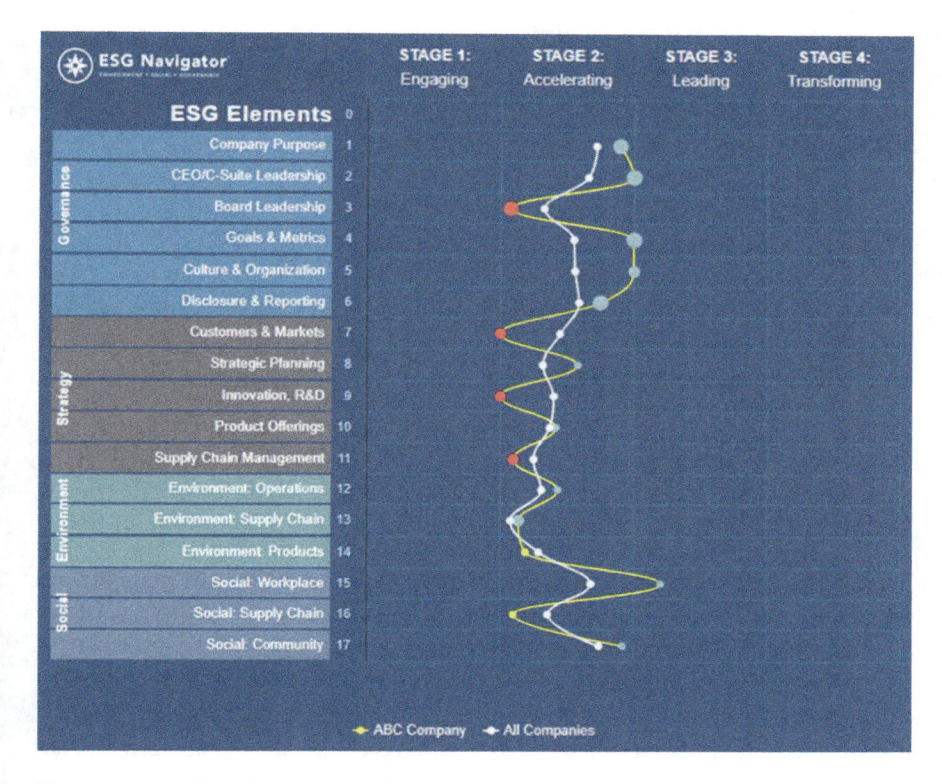

Figure 5.1: Example Snake Chart
Source: ESG Navigator

Around 30 sustainability executives from large, global companies participated in this 2020 webinar. They loved the Fluor story and especially the snake chart. They asked me to build this powerful analytic into the platform so that they could benefit from it – and help further shape it.

Not a Typical Rating Scale

Why did the snake chart Fluor create appeal to so many companies?

The answer is twofold. First, it was a simple, graphic depiction of how a company stacks up, **suitable for the CEO and board**. Second, the rating scale was **designed for measuring transformation – not for patting ourselves on the back** as we prolong business as usual. Executives need a rating scale that measures transformation.

The typical ESG rating scale works by dividing peers equally into four quartiles of performance. All very neat but missing the mark for measuring transformation. The platform Fluor and many other companies used is a much tougher rating scale that identifies where progress is being made.

Engage → Accelerate → Lead → Transform

The ESG Navigator platform Fluor used is based on incremental maturity towards a **full sustainable growth business model**. Companies rate their own performance confidentially on 100 KPIs from stage 0.5 to stage 4.0. The results roll up to the snake chart.

Engaging (Stage 1)

Stage 1 companies engage with sustainability issues in a variety of ways that do not change their company or their businesses fundamentally.

The chief EHS officer often drives sustainability efforts in collaboration with the officer(s) leading human resources, corporate citizenship, and philanthropy. Environmental stewardship and social responsibility are considered the "right thing to do." Environmental management is largely about risk management. Social responsibility is about, workplace, community responsibility, and philanthropy.

Stage 1 companies are committed to compliance – not just with laws, regulations, and internal company standards, but also increasingly with expected industry codes of practice, including sustainability reporting guidelines. Stage 1 companies implement programs to reduce energy use, GHG emissions, and waste in their operations. They respond to environmental and social pressures throughout their supply chain.

Stage 1 companies typically support positions endorsed by their major industry associations. These companies may partner with external stakeholders on selected initiatives. Many Stage 1 companies publish flashy external EHS or sustainability reports.

In summary, Stage 1 companies **"dabble in sustainability" while continuing with business as usual** – making and selling their traditional products. They may do many 'good' things, yet the board has not recognized the full impact, scale, and potential of sustainability, and the CEO is generally shy of mentioning it at all.

Accelerating (Stage 2)

Stage 2 companies explicitly recognize the potential significance of sustainability – and launch a few key initiatives to position the company as a leader on a business-critical aspect of it. In some cases, Stage 2 companies set forth CEO-driven and bold sustainability positioning and goals. Many companies have done this with their GHG reduction goals.

The business model of Stage 2 companies is largely unchanged. Those in the manufacturing or process industries still largely operate in the traditional, linear, "take-make-waste" model. Those in the lighter footprint and service sectors tend to focus on the environmental and social impacts of their own operations, rather than on the full value chain.

The CEO and other senior executives may weave sustainability into public statements and speeches. The company also sees sustainability issues not only as a source of risk, but also as a source of potential opportunity. The company stakes out a position that addresses a material environmental or social issue that is business-critical to the company and its industry, such as electronic waste, human rights in the supply chain, or conflict minerals.

In summary, Stage 2 companies have well-defined environmental and social management programs: materiality assessment, risk assessment, footprint reduction, external reporting, and more. Such companies build a culture that values sustainability. For example, they may roll out 'Sustainability 101' trainings and hold quarterly ESG company-wide meetings. However, those activities tend to be *bolted onto* rather than *woven into* **core business processes and business decisions**.

In other words, these companies have not fundamentally changed their business models.

Leading (Stage 3)

Stage 3 companies begin to transform their business portfolios to leverage sustainability opportunities. They make strategic choices to divest or gradually phase out "old economy" businesses and invest in cleaner, greener, or socially beneficial enterprises, A Stage 3 company, internally and externally, appears to be open, transparent, innovative, and critically aware of risks and opportunities.

Moving beyond a few key CEO-driven sustainability initiatives, the Stage 3 companies embody economist Joseph Schumpeter's concept of "creative destruction." For instance, the CEO may update the company's vision, mission, and values to align directly with how sustainable growth will be measured going forward (as discussed in Chapter 2).

Companies moving significantly into Stage 3 consider sustainability key to their long-term viability and value creation. Sustainability represents one or more platforms for top-line growth. They **anticipate customer needs** and future differentiators, as Toyota did with the Prius more than two decades ago.

Most Stage 3 companies see the transition to a low-carbon economy as the century's biggest industrial challenge. They invest heavily in renewable energy and want to join the clean technology revolution. They see massive growth opportunities in areas such as clean transport and smart cities, and they promote freshwater access and other such activities.

In summary, CEOs of Stage 3 companies take a long-term view, with a focused strategy that places global environmental and social drivers at the core. They begin the hard work of **weaving material ESG issues into the fabric of every critical business process, key business decision, and investment**. For all but the newest and greenest companies, this requires significant effort, as anyone close to the transformation of the leading companies mentioned in Chapter 3 can attest.

Stage 4 – "Transforming"

Stage 4 companies are evolving as models of twenty-first-century sustainable growth corporations. They sustain a steadfast focus on long-term profitability and growth while also rapidly decarbonizing and maximizing resource efficiency across the value chain.

In Stage 4 companies, **sustainability is fully integrated** within all aspects of the business, starting with the vision, mission, culture, business model, and goals. The company has a roadmap for sustainable growth and profitability, which explicitly reflects responsibility to future generations. This commitment extends far beyond the CEO.

Those in the manufacturing or process industries, historically reliant on physical resources, integrate into the circular economy, defined in Chapter 3.

No major company is fully Stage 4, but a growing number of companies have Stage 4 attributes. Some are young, innovative, sharing-economy ventures; others are well-known names in transition, such as *Enel, Mars, Neste, Novelis, Ørsted, Schneider Electric, Trane Technologies*, and *Unilever*.

Enhancements to the Snake Chart

The Fluor story and Figure 5.1 depict company performance across two dimensions: the maturity scale just discussed and the four major building blocks of sustainable growth:
- Governance and Leadership
- Strategy and Execution
- Environmental Stewardship
- Social Responsibility

Shortly after we incorporated the snake chart into ESG Navigator, webinar participants said they wanted to track their progress year-over-year. Figure 5.2 illustrates the next iteration of the snake chart.
- The **white line** represents the benchmark group (see Figure 5.1).
- The **yellow line** represents Company ABCs candid self-assessment.
- The **dotted yellow line** represents a prior year's data (selected by the user).
- The **dot color** (red or green) is driven by the gap from the benchmark group.
- The **dot size** is driven by elements flagged as most important.

Members appreciated the insights this tool provided but wanted to clearly set goals and summarize priority focus areas for the CEO and board.

Goals and Customer Expectations

With companies feeling growing pressure from customers—especially in Europe and the UK—they also wanted to depict *customer expectations*.

 DuPont's Snake Chart Addition: Customer Expectations

In 2023, **DuPont** shared with 40 sustainability leaders how they used ESG Navigator to map customer expectations. DuPont asked its commercial leaders to assess how it was doing on key sustainability indicators relating to customer engagement, innovation, product environmental impacts, product offerings, and strategic planning. The company manually plotted the results on its own snake chart.
   A year later, DuPont shared an update, noting a powerful interaction with the CEO and board.

Once again, members requested platform enhancements. Figure 5.3 depicts an example of the snake chart with customer expectations and goals.

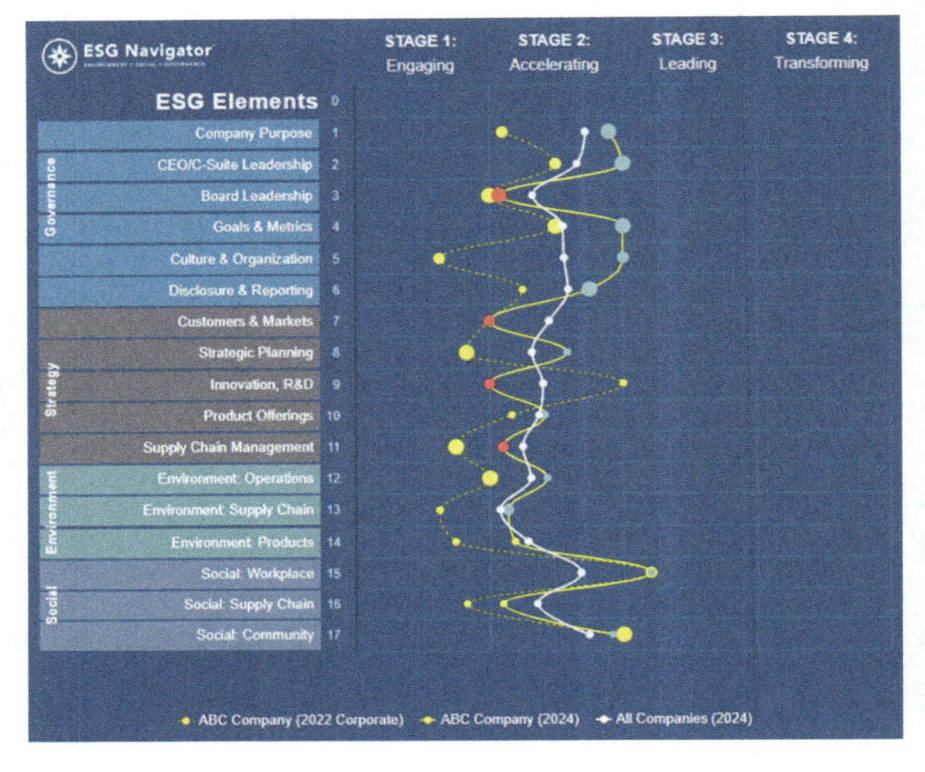

Figure 5.2: Snake Chart – Year-over-year Progress
Source: ESG Navigator

- The **white line** represents the benchmark group (see Figure 5.1).
- The **yellow line** represents ABC company's candid self-assessment.
- **Solid diamonds** represent goals.
- **Hollow diamonds** represent customer expectations.
- The **dot color**, red or green, is driven by the gap from the benchmark group.
- The **dot size** is driven by elements flagged by the company as most important.

The aggregate score for each element in the snake chart is a summary of typically five or six individual KPIs, which roll up to the snake chart score. There are 100 KPIs in total.

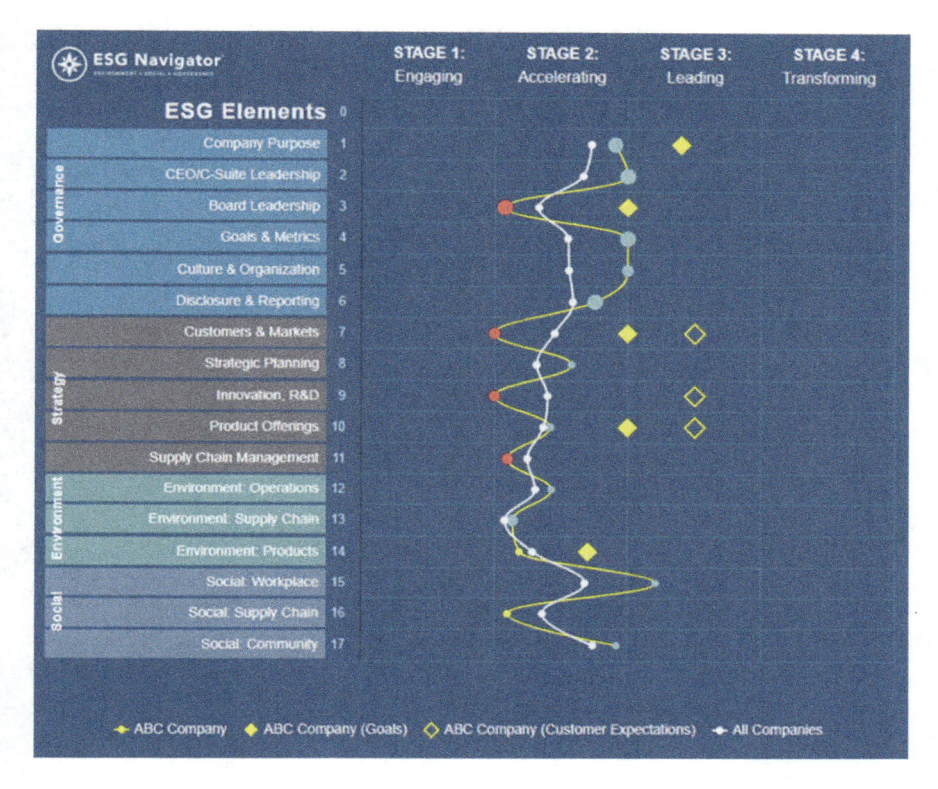

Figure 5.3: Snake Chart with Customer Expectations and Goals
Source: ESG Navigator

100 KPIs: "My Library" for Leading Sustainability Executives

Each of these 100 KPIs, known as **KSIs**^{TM} includes a short description of each of the four stages of sustainability maturity. These are sufficiently detailed so an executive can easily score his or her company's performance relative to each indicator from 1 to 4.

In 2018, when the first 60 companies used ESG Navigator to self-assess their sustainability performance, the platform had over 150 KSIs. After several iterations based on significant input from corporate sustainability leaders, the number dropped to 100 in 2022, where it has remained.

For sustainability executives, the Stage 4 (Transforming) descriptors (Appendix E) help them 'peer around the corner' to understand the ultimate target, and what sustainable growth means going forward.

 ESG Navigator is "My Library"

IBM's recently retired CSO, Wayne Balta, agreed to be the inaugural chair of The Conference Board's Sustainability Innovation and Growth Council when I launched it in 2012. He and his colleague Edan Dionne, VP of Sustainability, long viewed ESG and sustainability as an opportunity for competitive differentiation. They used ESG Navigator not so much as a rating tool as a repository.

Edan confirmed: "**ESG Navigator is my library**. It organizes current and emerging ESG topics in one place, helping me assess the relevance of these topics to our business. It also helps me peer around the corner, to see where sustainability is heading and identify improvement opportunities."

Balance of Part 2

The next four chapters diagnose the four main components of sustainability depicted earlier in Figure 1.1 and illustrated in the snake chart figures:
- Chapter 6: Governance and Leadership
- Chapter 7: Strategy and Execution
- Chapter 8: Environmental Stewardship
- Chapter 9: Social Responsibility

Each chapter details the ESG Navigator KSIs that leaders from over 100 companies and outside experts have helped to fine-tune for more than two decades. I include how the KSI characterizes a leading or transformative practice.

The next four chapters share over 300 corporate best practices, organized by the 100 Key Sustainability Indicators that leading companies have shaped over the past decade. The best practices are drawn from over 125 companies across most industry sectors and major geographies.

For more information about the maturity model, see Appendix D. The full list of 100 KSIs with Stage 1 and Stage 4 descriptors is in Appendix E.

Note

1 Lindsay Hooper, "ESG is dead. Long live ESG," Financial Times, September 19, 2024.

Chapter 6
Getting Governance Right

Consider the story of one company that is *getting sustainability governance right*.

 A Half-Day Boardroom Scenario Session

At the request of the CEO of a major North American utility, I led the board through a one-hour discussion of "Sustainability and the Future." The conversation continued over dinner.

Having an outside 'expert' speak to a board is not unusual. However, what happened next, in my decades of working with large company boards of directors, was unprecedented.

The next morning, the company's sustainability director (not the CSO or a top consultancy) led the full board and executive team in a three-hour scenario planning exercise. The goal was to determine how the company would fare in potential future worlds involving the extremes of: (1) global attention to climate change and (2) technology developments.

For several hours, the board and C-suite engaged energetically in small group exercises with report-outs and open discussion. This was in sharp contrast to the typical, highly orchestrated board meeting.

The board then met in executive session as the rest of us left the room. When we returned, the Chair said that this had been the best use of time he could remember at any board meeting. Quite a statement! He summarized next steps, noting that the board decided to add a similar extra half-day to their next full board meeting.

The core message is this: **it is possible for a sustainability director to change the boardroom conversation** – and dramatically.

At a Glance – The "G" in ESG

In the previous chapter, I discussed how Fluor and DuPont used a powerful 'snake chart' to convey performance to the CEO and board. In both cases, their message was: if you want to make progress on sustainability, you must **lead with governance.**

Governance essentially defines *"how we run the place."* It's how a company generates sustainable long-term returns. As the glue that holds every aspect of sustainability together, it is **by far the most important and least understood component of sustainability**.

Until companies get governance right, they find it difficult to get anything else right. This is true with creating successful products, robust brands, and strong financial results. It is also true with sustainability.

As introduced in Chapter 1, Figure 6.1 reminds us that governance is at the heart of everything that improves the positioning and performance of sustainable growth.

https://doi.org/10.1515/9783111548852-007

Figure 6.1: Sustainability: Governance

Governance: The leadership structures, policies, processes, and practices affecting the way the CEO, board, and senior management team run a corporation. It includes the organization, culture, and goals. It also covers the relationships between various stakeholders: shareholders, employees, suppliers, customers, banks and other lenders, regulators, the environment, and, importantly, the community at large.

Governance: Core Elements

The core elements of sustainability governance have largely remained unchanged in 25 years. They are:

- **Company Purpose**: How do sustainability and the drive to deliver long-term value to society integrate into our company's core purpose – not just statements of vision, mission and values, but also the supporting actions?
- **CEO and C-suite Leadership**: How deeply engaged are our CEO and C-suite in spreading the sustainability message, stimulating robust board of directors' discussions, and building accountability and sustainability leadership?
- **Board of Directors Leadership**: What oversight structure, processes, and systems support our board of directors' commitment and engagement with sustainability?

- **Goals and Roadmap**: How robust are our company's sustainability goals for material issues across our value chain, driving footprint reduction and value creation?
- **Culture and Organization**: How does our company's culture and organization promote integrating sustainability into executive compensation and job descriptions, resulting in actions from the C-suite to the shop floor?
- **Disclosure and Reporting**: To what extent are our sustainability disclosure and reporting transparent, robust, and aligned with financial reporting?

For each of these elements, the KSIs depicted in Figure 6.2 reflect how companies measure performance.

Company Purpose	CEO/C-suite Leadership	Board Leadership	Goals & Roadmap	Culture & Organization	Disclosure & Reporting
Purpose, Vision, Mission	Public Positioning	Full Board Oversight	Goals and Roadmap: Near-Term	Compensation and Goals	Annual Reporting
Operationalizing Sustainability	Financial Strategy	Committees, Charters, and Roles	Goals and Roadmap: Long-Term	Organization	Disclosure of Impacts and Strategy
Public Commitments	Engagement with Investors	Sustainability Fluency	Materiality Assessment	Accountability and Leadership	Assurance and Verification
Long-term Viability of Core Businesses	Collaboration with Key Customers	Meeting Agendas	Tracking Footprint Reduction	Reward and Recognition	Transparency and Marketing
Key Business Decisions	Messaging to Employees	Time Commitment in Meetings	Tracking Revenue		Public Policy (e.g., Lobbying) Alignment
	Engagement with NGOs	Board Diversity	Accounting for Material Risks, Externalities		
			Ratings and Rankings		

Figure 6.2: Governance KSIs
Source: ESG Navigator

Governance KSIs

The governance KSIs from Figure 6.2 are not a list of topics imposed by outsiders. Instead, they reflect how companies manage sustainability. Each of the individual KSIs has been shaped, refined, vetted, and honed "by industry, for industry" since 2015.

Bear in mind that for each KSI, companies can measure and map their progress across a maturity path that measures performance across four stages of maturity. (Additional information about the governance KSIs is in Appendix E.)

Below (Table 6.1) is an example of a full four-stage rating scale for a single KSI: Company Purpose, Vision, and Mission.

Table 6.1: Example KSI Detail: Governance

Company Purpose, Vision, Mission

Engaging	Accelerating	Leading	Transforming
Sustainability (*S*) is viewed as CSR and/or an extension of EHS and philanthropy. Company purpose, vision, and mission can enable *S*, but the extent of *S* ambition is not explicit.	*S* is *part of* how the company sees its role in society and is explicitly highlighted. Employees, customers, and investors view company as committed to *S*. Corporate values are like peers.	*S* is integral to vision and mission and *near the core of* how the company sees its role in society – creating value for all stakeholders. Actively pursues road to net zero. *S* statements and company values stand out among peers.	*S* is the North Star *at the core* of the company's distinctive role in society. Every strategic and key operational decision is guided by purpose, with *S* driving a goal of net-positive impact.

In the pages that follow, I walk through each of the governance KSIs depicted in Figure 6.2, posing a question to illustrate world class, followed by several best practices examples.

It is worth noting that **best practices today, while world leading, may not necessarily yet be a transformational, Stage 4 action**. Think of Stages 1, 2, and 3 as "good, better, best." Think of Stage 4 as what's expected of leading companies in the near future. In some, but not all cases, a best practice today meets the full Stage 4 descriptor. (See Appendix E.)

Purpose

A company's purpose conveys what it stands for, where it wants to go, and what it aims to do. But as the five supporting KSIs below illustrate, a company's true purpose is reflected in how the board and executive team manage on a day-to-day basis.

Company Purpose, Vision, and Mission (KSI 1.1)

To what extent is sustainability the North Star? Is it core to the company's distinctive role in society? Is every strategic and key operational decision guided by purpose and driving toward net-positive impact?

Purpose: The fundamental reason for an organization's existence. It answers, *"Why do we exist?"* It emphasizes what binds employees to one another and to the communities we interact with.
– **Ecolab**: "To make the world cleaner, safer and healthier – helping businesses succeed while protecting people and vital resources."
– **Nestlé:** "To unlock the power of food to enhance quality of life for everyone, today and for generations to come."
– **Trane Technologies**: "We boldly challenge what's possible for a sustainable world."
– **VF Corporation**: "We power movements of sustainable and active lifestyles for the betterment of people and our planet."

Vision: The future aspirations of the organization. It answers, *"Where do we want to go?"* It focuses on what the company seeks to achieve long term.
– **IKEA**: "To create a better everyday life for the many people."
– **Ørsted:** "To create a world that runs entirely on green energy."
– **Tesla**: "To create the most compelling car company of the twenty-first century by driving the world's transition to electric vehicles."

Mission: The organization's core activities and focus. It answers, *"What do we do, for whom, and how do we do it?"* It outlines the primary objectives and strategy of the business.
– **BNP Paribas**: "To contribute to responsible and sustainable growth by financing the economy and advising clients according to the highest ethical standards."
– **Interface:** "Endeavoring to become the first name in industrial ecology, a corporation that cherishes nature and restores the environment."
– **Seventh Generation**: "Nurturing the health of the next seven generations by providing effective, safe, bio-based products."
– **Starbucks**: "To inspire and nurture the human spirit – one person, one cup, and one neighborhood at a time."

Operationalizing Sustainability (KSI 1.2)

To what extent are the CEO and C-suite driving deep integration of sustainability into core business processes, cascading via individual performance goals throughout the company's regions, businesses, and organization?

- **AXA,** a founding member of the Net-Zero Insurance Alliance (NZIA), has committed to transitioning its underwriting and investment portfolios to net zero by 2050. AXA also prioritizes low-carbon technologies and nature-based solutions. It achieved a near 50 percent carbon intensity reduction of its corporate portfolio as of 2023 – greatly surpassing the 25 percent reduction target for 2025.
- **Marks & Spencer** reset its 2007 Plan A in 2024 with a singular focus on becoming a net-zero business across its value chain by 2040.
- **Neste** began its transformation from a regional oil refiner into a global leader in renewable fuels in the early 2000s. The company continues to increase its share of renewable and circular solutions, working with suppliers to reduce emissions.
- **Puma** cut its carbon footprint by a third from 2017 to 2024 while doubling annual revenue and promoting product recycling and refurbishment.
- **Tesco,** the first business globally to set a zero-carbon goal in 2009, was later the first FTSE 100 Company to set science-based, 1.5°C carbon reduction targets. It issued £1 Bn in sustainability-linked bonds in 2023, tying financial performance to reducing Scope 1 and 2 emissions.

Commitments by Board and/or C-Suite (KSI 1.3)

To what extent do the CEO and full board of directors personally and visibly commit to bold sustainability action (e.g., decarbonization, investment in natural capital, enhancing societal value, etc.)?

- **Iberdrola,** the Spanish electric utility, began transforming over 20 years ago. Executive Chairman Ignacio Galan aggressively supports renewable energy, efficient storage, and smart networks to avoid future shocks, promoting a self-sufficient energy system.
- **Ørsted** was an oil and gas company in 2009 called DONG Energy, with 85 percent of its production from fossil fuels. In 2009, the CEO and board implemented a transformation roadmap. In 2017, Ørsted divested its oil and gas business. In 2024, shuttered its last coal-fired power plant as it became the world's largest developer of offshore wind power.

- **Sims Limited** of Australia, the world's largest metal recycler, had the first board to sign a sustainability commitment in 2015.
- **Trane Technologies'** board personally signed a similar commitment in 2021.

Long-Term Viability of Core Business(es) (KSI 1.4)

How is the company – and its individual businesses – positioned to thrive and profit as climate impacts grow and customers increasingly value decarbonization, resource efficiency, and social equity?

- **Chubb** stopped insuring new coal-fired electric generating plants in 2022. It also ceased investing in companies with more than 30 percent of revenues from thermal coal mining or energy production from coal.
- **Veolia**, the French utilities company, has developed extensive waste-to-energy projects, significantly reducing landfill use and GHG emissions.
- **Xylem**, the world's largest pure-play water technology company, in 2023 acquired Evoqua, a leader in mission-critical water treatment solutions, creating a global platform to solve critical water challenges at scale.

Key Business Decisions (KSI 1.5)

How robustly do material sustainability issues incorporate into key boardroom decisions (e.g., acquisition or divestiture, product launch, major capital investment, leadership change, or a company transformation)?

- **Amgen**, the CA-based pharmaceuticals company, requires all capital projects to include projected carbon emissions.
- **Dow's** Valuing Nature goal was the first corporate commitment to factor nature into its business decisions. Under this goal, Dow is more than halfway toward $1 Bn of net present value through business projects that simultaneously benefit the bottom line and natural ecosystems.
- **Hyundai**, the world's number three car company by sales, has steadily ramped up its commitment to electrification. While many car manufacturers backtracked from EV commitments, Hyundai plans to offer 21 different EV models and double the number of hybrid electric models by 2030.

CEO and C-suite Leadership

It's fascinating that in the critical area of CEO and C-suite leadership, neither the major sustainability disclosure regulations nor the ESG reporting frameworks and ratings cover a single KSI to a significant degree. The KSIs, after all, simply represent actions companies take on their own to create value from sustainability. The six KSIs related to CEO and C-suite leadership are detailed below.

Public Positioning (KSI 2.1)

How often has the CEO publicly commented on material sustainability issues facing the company, highlighting its responsibility in addressing those challenges?
- **Fortescue**, a global mining company, is an unlikely climate advocate. CEO Andrew Forrest has boldly stated: "There is no way to keep the goal of limiting warming to 1.5°C alive without ending the use of fossil fuels and accelerating the rollout of renewable energy and green technology."
- **Apple** CEO Tim Cook is a vocal advocate for sustainability, committing Apple to achieve a carbon-neutral supply chain and products by 2030.
- **Microsoft** CEO Satya Nadella has pledged to make Microsoft carbon negative by 2030 and to remove its historical carbon emissions by 2050.
- **Salesforce** CEO Marc Benioff has made substantial public commitments to climate action, pledging biodiversity protection and aggressive emissions-reduction targets.
- **SC Johnson** CEO Fisk Johnson has publicly crusaded to contain the plastic-waste crisis. That's even while his company, the maker of Ziploc bags, has featured at the center of the plastics debate.

Financial Strategy (KSI 2.2)

How directly is the company using financial practices and tools to promote and drive achieving climate and other sustainability targets?
- **Citi** committed to $1 Tn in sustainable finance by 2030, using ESG criteria in assessing lending decisions, directing financing towards sustainable projects and environmentally responsible industries.
- **Constellation Energy**, the largest US producer of carbon-free energy, issued the first corporate **green bond** ($900 M) to finance nuclear, clean hydrogen, energy storage systems, wind repowering, and carbon-free energy solutions for its customers.

- **Societe Generale**, a French multinational financial services company, set a $521 Bn sustainable finance target from 2024 to 2030, with 80 percent for environmental and 20 percent for social activities.

Engagement with Investors/Owners (KSI 2.3)

To what extent do the CEO and CFO use investor meetings to educate investors about climate change and other material sustainability issues, positioning the company for long-term value creation?
- **American Airlines** CEO Robert Isom outlined, at its 2024 Investor Day, plans for delivering long-term growth while reducing carbon emissions, modernizing its fleet, optimizing technology, and adapting to consumer trends.
- **Caterpillar** CEO Jim Umpleby listed sustainability as priority 3 of 4 in the brand's "2023 Investor Presentation," viewing increasing demand for renewable energy and infrastructure presents an opportunity to grow.
- **Solvay's** CEO, CFO, and other leaders meet with institutional investors, ESG research providers, and proxy advisors at least annually.

Collaboration with Key Customers (KSI 2.4)

How much time do the CEO and C-suite members spend each year engaging with customers in various markets at the forefront of sustainability trends, with a goal to create sustainably advantaged products and services core to the growth strategy?
- **Salesforce** CEO Marc Benioff hosts the annual "Dreamforce" customer conference, fostering community among users and ensuring they are aware of how Salesforce can be used in pursuit of a sustainable future.
- **Tata Steel** engaged with UK customers to obtain commitments to buy green steel from an electric arc furnace, enabling it to proceed.

Messaging to Employees (KSI 2.5)

To what extent do the messages from the CEO to employees via town hall meetings, site visits, and so forth link sustainability to corporate strategy?
- **Cummins'** Jennifer Rumsey, in her first two years as CEO, engages employees deeply on the environmental and social dimensions of sustainability, saying climate challenges will be the company's "moment to shine" and issuing the company's 2024 Human Capital Management Report.

- **Hershey**'s CEO Michele Buck launched "Empowering Internal Change Agents" to identify non-executive employees at all levels who stood out for their big and bold ideas. She tasked them with tackling challenging initiatives and goals.
- **Logitech's** Hanneke Faber reinforced messages to employees during her first year as CEO with action: achieving gender parity on the leadership team; providing carbon labels on 66 percent of products (with a goal of 100 percent in 2025); setting ambitious Scope 3 goals and designing products for sustainability.

Engagement with NGOs (KSI 2.6)

How many hours per year does the CEO personally engage with leaders of NGOs focused on the company's material sustainability issues?
- **Apple's** Tim Cook, partnering with Conservation International, has emphasized transparency and international cooperation in addressing climate change.
- **Dow** was the first major company to establish an external sustainability advisory board comprised of a cross-section of outside leaders to advise senior management. **DSM, DHL Group, Mercedes-Benz, Merck, Tetra Pak**, and **Trane Technologies** also currently leverage such advisory bodies.
- **Walmart** CEO Doug McMillon announced to investors in 2024 that the company met its Project Gigaton goal, launched in 2017, six months ahead of schedule. The company established a long-term partnership drawing on the science expertise of" the Environmental Defense Fund in 2005. EDF helped set the goal to reduce, avoid, or sequester 1 gigaton of emissions from its supply chain, evaluate pathways to reduce emissions, and analyze supplier data.

Board of Directors Leadership

Chapter 4 provided detailed information on how to enhance the board's understanding of sustainability. Listed below are the six KSIs with company examples where available. (For example, companies do not share board agendas or time spent on certain topics in board meetings.)

Full Board Oversight (KSI 3.1)

To what extent and frequency is the full board actively involved in discussions on sustainability issues, risks, and opportunities? Does the annual board self-assessment build a robust cadence for learning about climate and other material environmental and social issues?

– **Trane Technologies** illustrates how a board with multifaceted diversity spends sufficient time on sustainability. The full board and each board committee have explicit climate and sustainability responsibilities. Meeting agendas drive deep engagement with material risks and opportunities, continually enhancing the board's oversight capabilities. Trane Technologies' board achieved gender parity in 2023, one of 29 S&P 500 companies at the time.

– **Weyerhaeuser** places world-class expertise in climate and biodiversity, which are material sustainability issues, at the core of board oversight. Larry Selzer, CEO of The Conservation Fund, has served on the board since 2016. He sits as one of four outside directors on the Governance and Corporate Responsibility Committee. Selzer brings deep expertise in biodiversity and climate, coupled with decades of partnering with CEOs of major corporations on natural capital projects.

Committees, Charters, and Roles (KSI 3.2)

To what extent does each board committee charter detail specific climate and sustainability oversight responsibilities?

– **Arkema**, a French specialty materials manufacturer, assigns oversight to its Board Innovation and Sustainable Growth Committee.

– **Colgate-Palmolive's** board oversees critical sustainability issues as a full board and in committees. The Enterprise Risk Management Committee oversees the climate- and plastic-transition risks. The Personnel and Organization Committee added sustainability as a component of annual executive incentives in 2023.

Sustainability Fluency (KSI 3.3)

How fluent is the board collectively, and are directors individually, on material sustainability risks and opportunities across the value chain, and to what extent are board directors engaging in structured learning between board meetings? (See Chapter 4.)

– **Fortis'** Board Governance and Sustainability Committee charter explicitly calls out monitoring external engagements, emerging trends, risks, and issues related to sustainability. The board chair requires each director to report annually on sustainability education received.

- **J.M. Huber**, the century-old producer of consumer and industrial items, provides quarterly updates to Corporate and Business Sector Boards, with specific educational topics at each board meeting. During 2024, the topics were decarbonization strategies, what CSRD means for the company and the changing global regulatory landscapes.
- **Wendy Kei**, Board Chair of Ontario Power Generation, personally serves as director in residence during a four-hour session of the Institute of Corporate Directors Board Oversight of Climate Change course. She asks other board directors and members of management to take courses and to invest time to build climate fluency.

Meeting Agendas (KSI 3.4)

To what extent do board meetings involve sustainability learning, such as scenario planning with business leaders to discuss full value chain sustainable growth risks and opportunities? (See Chapter 4.)

Time Commitment in Meetings (KSI 3.5)

To what extent is the time spent on sustainability at every meeting significant, more than 12 hours per year in full board or board committee meetings? This may involve deep dive sessions, deliberating the long-term viability of businesses under different scenarios. (See Chapter 4.)

Board Diversity (KSI 3.6)

How closely does the board reflect the diversity of the workforce and the market, targeting gender equality, representation from diverse groups, and highly diverse life experiences?
- **Citi** increased the gender diversity of its board from 50 percent in 2021 to 58 percent in 2022. A woman chairs the Nomination, Governance, and Public Affairs Committee, and at least one female board member sits on each of the six board committees.
- **General Motors** has one of the most gender-diverse boards, with 58 percent women. Women also chair most GM's board committees.
- **Honeywell**'s board composition is 42 percent ethnically or racially diverse, and 33 percent are women.

- **Schneider Electric**, a global leader in energy and automation with $38 Bn in revenue, headquartered in France, has a highly diverse board. The 14 directors who are of non-French nationality represent 11 countries. The company has been recognized as a top European company for women on boards.

Goals and Roadmaps

The seven KSIs defining how companies manage and track sustainability progress, along with selected company examples, appear below.

Goals and Roadmap: Near Term (KSI 4.1)

Are goals highly rigorous, such as having third-party **science-based targets** for a net-zero statement? Are they supported by a detailed roadmap linked to longer-term targets?
- **Apple** reaffirmed its commitment in 2024 to achieving carbon neutrality across its entire supply chain and product life cycle by 2030, using recycled and renewable materials, clean electricity, and low-carbon shipping.
- **BT Group** committed in 2023 to achieve net-zero carbon emissions across its operations by 2030.
- **Heineken** expanded its long-standing 'Brew a Better World' program in 2023, setting targets for 2030, including carbon-neutral production, water usage, and sustainably sourced materials.
- **Marks & Spencer** launched Plan A 2030 in 2023 to become a net-zero business across its entire value chain, focusing on circular economy principles, sustainable sourcing, and waste reduction.
- **Puma** set a new goal to cut absolute Scope 1 and 2 emissions by 90 percent and Scope 3 emissions by 33 percent by 2030.
- **Starbucks** announced in 2024 its commitment to achieve carbon neutrality across its global operations by 2030.

Goals and Roadmap: Long Term (KSI 4.2)

How robust is the company's roadmap detailing how it will reach long-term targets, such as driving net-positive impact across the value chain?

- **Aldi** announced a goal to reach net-zero GHG emissions across its entire value chain by 2050, validated by the Science-Based Targets initiative (SBTi).
- **Diageo** is four years into a ten-year action plan to reduce the company's material impacts.
- **Sony** continued its "Road to Zero" in 2024, aiming to achieve a zero environmental footprint by 2050, focusing on reducing GHG emissions, conserving resources, and promoting biodiversity.
- **Unilever** introduced its Climate Transition Action Plan in 2023, aiming to achieve net-zero emissions across its value chain by 2039.

Materiality Assessment (KSI 4.3)

To what extent does the company conduct rigorous double materiality assessments and act on the results? Have they assigned direct accountability and ownership of this process at board level?

- **Ford**'s Integrated Sustainability and Financial Report 2023 places its double materiality assessment directly up front, showing how the most material issues directly impact the company's strategy, aspirations, and concrete actions on its "Road to Progress."
- **General Mills** provides an excellent example of operationalizing the results of a robust (double) materiality assessment. The CSOs informs her board each year of the top three material issues for the board. In 2023, she worked with the CEO and board to address full value chain issues related to regenerative agriculture.

Tracking Footprint Reduction (KSI 4.4)

Does the company measure cuts in footprint, aligned with circular economy principles and with well below 2°C goals?

- **IKEA** reduced its climate footprint by 24.3 percent in 2023 compared to its 2016 baseline while growing revenue over 30 percent.
- **LEGO** achieved "the corporate sustainability holy grail" in 2023: decoupling growth from the use of fossil fuels and carbon footprint.
- **L'Oréal** enhanced its Sustainable Product Optimization Tool (SPOT) in 2024 to analyze 14 criteria (including GHG, water, and biodiversity) across the product life cycle. The methodology was approved by independent scientific experts and independently verified.
- **Mastercard** decreased its GHG emissions by 1 percent in 2023 while growing revenue 13 percent.

Tracking Sustainability Revenue (KSI 4.5)

What portion of the company's revenue over the next three and five years will come from products and services, that support customers' sustainability efforts?
- **Kingfisher's** "Green Star Products" accounted for 47 percent of home product sales in 2022, with a goal of comprising 60 percent of sales in 2025.
- **Philips** is on track in 2024 to meet its target of 25 percent of income generated from business activities that align with circular economy principles.
- **Siemens** progressed during 2023, with 65 percent of its relevant product and service families reflecting RED (Robust Eco-Design) principles, toward a 100 percent goal by 2030. They reported in 2024 that 25 percent of total revenue is EU Taxonomy-aligned, and 68 percent is Taxonomy-eligible. (The EU Taxonomy Regulation, published in 2020, defines which economic activities are environmentally sustainable).

Accounting for Material Risks, Externalities (KSI 4.6)

How robustly is the company accounting for its full value chain impacts, positive and negative, on the environment and human health?

Starting in 2026, the European CBAM will impose carbon-related tariffs on imported goods in certain sectors. Creating an internal price for carbon is generally a Stage 2 (Accelerating) practice – which 2,000 companies follow, according to the CDP.
- **Allbirds** and **REI** joined 20 consumer brands launching the Climate Label in 2025. It requires participants to set an internal carbon fee on their Scope 1, 2, and 3 emissions.
- **Amgen**, the CA-based pharmaceuticals company, had the highest published internal **carbon price** as of 2023, sitting at $1,600 per metric ton CO_2, according to CDP and Reuters. All capital projects and purchases seeking investment must include projected carbon emissions.
- **Holcim Group**, the Swiss building materials maker, has assessed and disclosed ESG impacts through an Integrated Profit & Loss statement since 2014, showing a total contribution to society of 5.9 Bn Swiss francs in 2023.
- **Mayr-Melnhof Karton,** the packaging company based in Austria, was one of few companies awarded an A rating by CDP among 15,000 scored, recognized for transparency and performance on climate.
- **Puma** enhanced its environmental P&L (EP&L) methodology in 2023, adding primary data for Tier 1 and Tier 2 suppliers. The EP&L began in 2011 to incorporate a monetary value on the environmental impacts along its supply chain.

Ratings and Rankings (KSI 4.7)

Is the company well positioned in rankings by the most respected ESG raters and respected by peers and NGOs, for its governance and strategy?
- **Danone** attained a triple-A rating (AAA) from CDP, gaining the top score in climate change, forest preservation, and water security categories.
- **Nvidia** appears on both Forbes and Fortune's lists of "Best Companies to Work For" in 2024 lists and is number 2 on Glassdoor's annual list of "Best Places to Work." It is number 18 in JUST Capital's 2024 "America's Most Just Companies."
- **Sekisui House:** In 2023, the Japanese building and real estate company received a AAA from CDP, appeared on the 2023 Bloomberg Gender Equality Index for the third consecutive year, and received a AAA from MSCI.

Culture and Organization

Below are the KSIs related to culture and organization, along with selected examples.

Compensation and Goals (KSI 5.1)

How robustly are the material sustainability impacts (including carbon reduction) built into executive compensation plans and performance incentives that cascade throughout the organization?
- **Akzo Nobel's** long-term incentive program, detailed in its Remuneration Policy for the Board of Management, links 34 percent of compensation and incentives to ESG metrics, with 33 percent each to EBITDA and to ROI.
- **Lego** ties part of salaried employees' bonuses to its annual carbon reduction goals.
- **Mars** connects 20 percent of overall executive remuneration to sustainability goals as of 2024 and is cascading net-zero goals to business leaders, helping the company decouple growth from its carbon footprint.
- **Mayr-Melnhof Karton** created a CO_2 bonus, linking employee remuneration to CO_2 reduction targets.
- **Trane Technologies** ties executive and manager incentives to company performance and to progress against the company's 2030 commitments.

Organization (KSI 5.2)

To what extent does the CEO personally drive action on material environmental and social risks and opportunities, appointing several C-suite members on an executive sustainability council that meets at least quarterly?

- **BNP Paribas**, the French bank, has a robust and comprehensive organizational structure that weaves sustainability into the fabric of the company. Separate executive committees oversee sustainability finance strategy, investment research and screening, infrastructure, and regulatory activities.
- **Colgate-Palmolive** assigns the group president and CSO as sponsors for climate transition and plastic-transition risks. A senior manager oversees mitigation, management, and board reporting.
- **DuPont's** sustainability organization includes strong CEO leadership and board oversight. A dedicated board committee oversees sustainability, with each of the other committees having explicit sustainability duties. The full board integrates ESG risk into company strategy.

Accountability and Leadership (KSI 5.3)

Does a single C-suite member lead sustainability, with explicit responsibilities for all C-suite members and senior leaders?

- **AstraZeneca's** CSO is also EVP of global operations and IT. He oversees the company's Ambition Carbon Zero program and the goal of halving overall emissions by 2030 and cutting it 90 percent by 2045.
- **DuPont's** VP of Sustainability reports to the Chief Technology and Sustainability Officer and chairs the Sustainability Leadership Council under the guidance of executive sponsors.
- **Mars'** CSO is also the company's Chief R&D and Procurement Officer, a remit that balances long-term sustainable growth with short-term financial impacts.
- **PepsiCo's** CSO reports directly to the CEO, guiding the company's efforts in climate action, sustainable agriculture, and circular economy initiatives.

Reward and Recognition (KSI 5.4)

How comprehensively do the CEO and C-suite recognize sustainability excellence in high-profile ways, perhaps awarded annually by the CEO and/or board of directors?

- **Arkema**, a French specialty materials manufacturer, empowers employees to act on climate via grassroots projects. It recognizes winners at Go for the Planet, an awards ceremony with a bimonthly newsletter.
- A **Dell** employee was recognized by Forbes' 30 Under 30 for sustainable materials engineering work. Dell's celebration of her achievements and external recognition helped foster a culture to inspire young women.

Disclosure and Reporting

Regulatory developments, such as the EU's CSRD, are driving more detailed disclosure requirements and laying the foundation for transparency.

Companies often generate unintended consequences from their commercial business activities. In 2024, **Morgan Stanley** learned a tough lesson. It abandoned a 2030 goal set in 2019 to underwrite 50 million metric tons of plastic pollution prevention. Activists called out the company for omitting this from its 2023 sustainability report.

Below are the six KSIs related to disclosure and reporting, along with selected best practice examples.

Annual Reporting and Financial Disclosures (KSI 6.1)

Does the annual report have sustainability information fully integrated, such that sustainability issues are woven into business strategy and core business processes, aiming for net-positive impact?

- **Akzo Nobel** prepared its integrated annual report as a baseline to align as closely as possible with the upcoming CSRD.
- **BP** reports ESG metrics in its annual report, incorporating TCFD framework and WBCSD's scenario catalog. For two decades, the company has published ESG data alongside financial data in its annual report.
- **Heineken's** combined 2024 financial and sustainability annual report details insights into the company's EverGreen strategic priorities.
- **Norsk Hydro's** Integrated Annual Report 2023 covers a broad range of metrics, tracked over multiple years, with granularity by business, region, and facility.

Disclosure of Material Impacts and Strategy (KSI 6.2)

How comprehensive is the company's disclosure regarding full value chain impacts (positive and negative), quantifying where possible?
- **3M's** 2024 Global Impact Report included a balanced mix of input, output, and process metrics with multi-year data, including breakdowns by region.
- **Seventh Generation** publishes a Climate Fingerprints Report showing a commitment to transparency and comprehensive environmental responsibility. By addressing the indirect emissions resulting from its financial activities, the company sets a precedent.
- **Veolia** aims to be the benchmark company for ecological transformation solutions for water, waste, and energy management.

Assurance and Verification (KSI 6.3)

To what extent is the company's reporting on sustainability data aligned with credible ESG reporting frameworks and assessed, audited and verified with the same rigor financial data?
- **Nestlé** works with independent auditors to verify its ESG data and provide limited assurance. It provides a methodology document on its website describing each material KPI under review.
- **PepsiCo** has used third-party assurance for sustainability metrics since 2008. It continually updates and increases metrics that receive third-party assurance.
- **Xylem**, the US water technology provider, obtained limited independent assurance of its 2023 sustainability report. It reports according to GRI, SASB, World Economic Forum Sustainable Value Creation Core Metrics and Disclosures, and the UN Global Compact Principles.

Transparency and Marketing (KSI 6.4)

Has the company earned recognition for leading on transparency, addressing the **GRI reporting principles** or equivalent, and encouraging increased transparency across its value chain and among industry peers?

Greenwashing is rampant. In the first lawsuit of its kind, the state of California alleged in 2024 that **ExxonMobil** had engaged in a decades-long campaign of deception that caused and exacerbated the global plastics pollution crisis.

Companies with a strong sustainability story have also faced criticism, including: **Danone** (carbon-neutral claims on its Evian Spring Water); **Clorox** (garbage bags made of recycled ocean plastic); **Coca-Cola** and **Nestlé** (claims that plastic water bottles are 100 percent recycled).

- **3M's** 2024 Global Impact Report lists material KPIs across a wide range of ESG issues, with data spanning several years and independent assurance.
- **PepisCo,** nominated in Reuters' 2024 Sustainability Awards in Transparency and Reporting category, and for the fifth year, to Governance Intelligence's Best ESG Reporting for large-cap companies.
- **Unilever** CEO Hein Schumacher demonstrated transparency in 2024 that when the initial sustainability targets were set, it underestimated the required scale and complexity. He noted that the company is now in a better position to provide and maintain investments in achieving several feasible targets.

Public Policy Alignment (e.g., Lobbying) (KSI 6.5)

To what extent does the company engage only with industry associations that take a leading position on major issues, such as supporting net zero? Has it stopped supporting those that, for example, lobby against decarbonization in line with the Paris Agreement?

- **IKEA** lobbied the Canadian government to end its tax on second-hand goods as it rolled out its Ikea Preowned pilot program in 2024.
- **PepsiCo** joined coalitions, including the US Climate Action Partnership, signed the American Business Act on Climate Pledge, and was a founding member of the US Climate Leadership Council. PepsiCo withholds funding from certain initiatives that do not align with its positions and urges peers to align with the Paris Climate Accord.
- **Salesforce** Marc Benioff signed an open letter ahead of COP29 alongside 116 other CEOs, requesting policy changes to drive climate action. The company joined Business for Nature in 2022, calling for world leaders to require organizations to address and disclose nature-related dependencies. It's also pushing for stronger regulation of AI emissions impacts.
- **Unilever** threatened in 2024 to leave any trade association not aligning with its pro-Paris Agreement policy, asking whether the organizations help or hinder regulations and standards toward net zero emissions. The company previously left the US Chamber of Commerce for its notorious hostility to climate policy.

Chapter 7
Strategy and Execution

Climate has been a material issue for many companies for decades. Consider one story from years ago.

 Provocative Boardroom Sustainability Discussions

Over years as an outside advisor, I met with the Board Committee of Ashland Inc. a dozen times. I participated in each full meeting and often in executive session with the outside directors.

Ashland exemplified the toughest corporate audience for discussing climate and sustainability: headquartered in Kentucky, the center of the US; carbon-intensive businesses; and a US-centric leadership team. The company included Ashland Petroleum, Ashland Chemical, Valvoline, and Arch Coal.

But Ashland's board had diverse perspectives and life experiences. They asked tough questions.

At one meeting in the late 1990s, they discussed mountaintop removal in the coal industry and climate change. Outside directors asked me to brief the CEO and company presidents on climate trends and risks.

It did not go well. The Arch Coal president interrupted me every few minutes. Then, when I was ready to run for the exit, he cornered me and asked for my slides.

Without divulging confidential conversations, the diverse views on the Ashland board allowed the dialog to probe the deepest questions including, "Why are we in this business?"

The key message is for companies to **"Uber yourself before you get Kodak'ed."** To do so, C-suite and board conversations need to explore *how to transform the company to be a leaner, fitter, and less carbon-intensive twenty-first-century winner.*

At a Glance: The Missing "S" in ESG

The mainstream investment community began to latch on to sustainability in 2005 through the lens of ESG. That made sense because *governance* was not only missing from the earlier *People – Planet – Profits* characterization of sustainability; it is also the most important part.

But what happened to *profits*? A company cannot be "sustainable" unless it generates sustained profits.

For nearly 20 years, it has been striking that ESG, as a descriptor of sustainability, has remained inherently silent on corporate strategy and execution. As Figure 7.1 illustrates, the ESG characterization of sustainability misses the vital dimension of weaving ESG issues into corporate strategy and execution.

https://doi.org/10.1515/9783111548852-008

Figure 7.1: Sustainability: Strategy

This is one of several reasons the **ESG acronym has outlived its usefulness**. Instead, as discussed in Chapter 2, the proper focus today is 'truly' sustainable growth.

Strategy: Core Elements

Michael Porter argues that *strategy is about being different*. The core elements of strategy, as impacting sustainable growth, define key areas of differentiation:

- **Customers and Markets**: How are we working with key customers to reduce their full life-cycle impacts and create sustainable solutions?
- **Strategic Planning**: To what extent are sustainability considerations fully embedded in our company's strategic and operational planning processes?
- **Innovation, Research and Development**: How are sustainability issues integrated into innovation research, processes, and investments – ultimately aimed at helping customers and delivering value to society?
- **Product Offerings**: How deeply are sustainability risks and opportunities embedded in our evolving portfolio of products and services?
- **Supply Chain Management**: How robustly are we managing sustainability risks associated with the company's overall approach to supply chain management?

Within each of these elements, a series of KSIs depicted in Figure 7.2 reflects how companies incorporate sustainability into strategy.

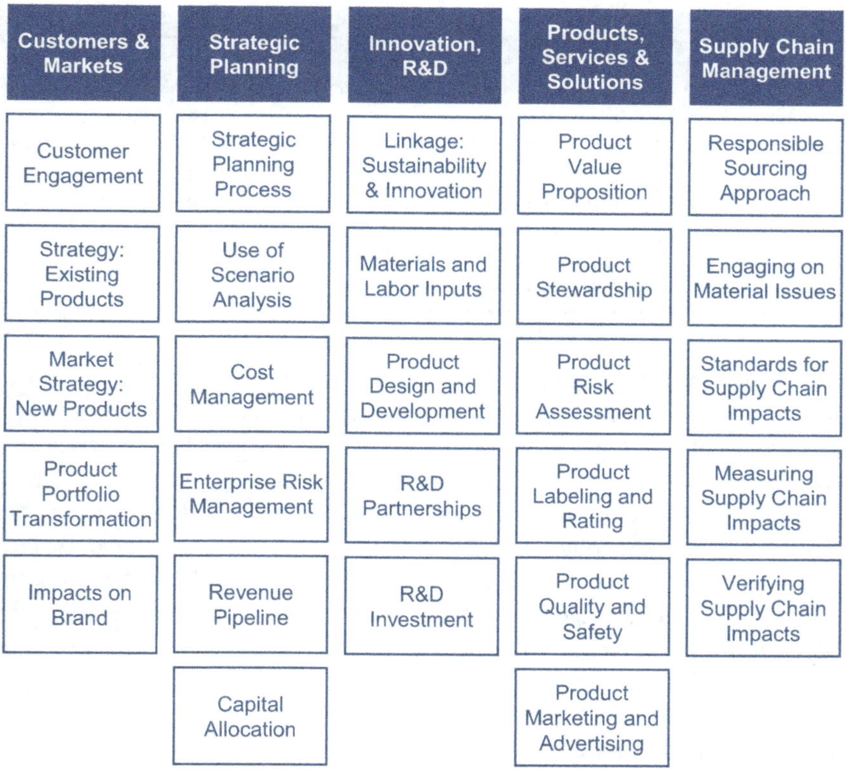

Customers & Markets	Strategic Planning	Innovation, R&D	Products, Services & Solutions	Supply Chain Management
Customer Engagement	Strategic Planning Process	Linkage: Sustainability & Innovation	Product Value Proposition	Responsible Sourcing Approach
Strategy: Existing Products	Use of Scenario Analysis	Materials and Labor Inputs	Product Stewardship	Engaging on Material Issues
Market Strategy: New Products	Cost Management	Product Design and Development	Product Risk Assessment	Standards for Supply Chain Impacts
Product Portfolio Transformation	Enterprise Risk Management	R&D Partnerships	Product Labeling and Rating	Measuring Supply Chain Impacts
Impacts on Brand	Revenue Pipeline	R&D Investment	Product Quality and Safety	Verifying Supply Chain Impacts
	Capital Allocation		Product Marketing and Advertising	

Figure 7.2: Strategy KSIs
Source: ESG Navigator

Strategy KSIs

Bear in mind that for each KSI, companies can measure and map their progress across a maturity path that measures performance across four stages of maturity. Below (Table 7.1) is an example of a full four-stage rating scale for a single KSI: Market Strategy: Existing Products and Services.

Table 7.1: Example KSI Detail: Strategy

Market Strategy: Existing Products and Services			
Engaging	**Accelerating**	**Leading**	**Transforming**
Sell existing portfolio of products and services into traditional markets and market segments. Expand into new markets motivated by traditional business factors (e.g., regulations, economics).	Develop or expand product and service offerings with enhanced sustainability features in existing markets or market segments (e.g., by geography, customer base, demographic).	Grow sales of sustainability attributes and products systematically. Implement an exit strategy for selling products and services with negative impacts.	Launch industry breakthroughs with new sustainability features. Differentiate from competitors based in part on these features.

The following pages walk through each of the strategy KSIs depicted in Figure 7.2. Each KSI starts with a question to help the reader gauge how close a company is to a transformation (Stage 4) position, followed by several best practice examples.

The best practice examples, while world leading, may not necessarily yet be Stage 4 (transformational) actions. Think of Stages 1, 2, and 3 as "good, better, best." Think of Stage 4 as what will be expected soon of leading companies. In some, but not all cases, a best practice today meets the full Stage 4 descriptor. (See Appendix E.)

Customers and Markets

Below are the KSIs related to how company leaders engage with customers to shape future offerings and drive sustainable growth.

Customer Engagement (KSI 7.1)

How robustly is the company engaging with customers to jointly create or expand the market for sustainable offerings that meet rigorous criteria for sustainability attributes?
- **Alaska Airlines** started using sustainable aviation fuel (SAF) in 2011. It allows customers to choose to offset their flight's carbon emissions by purchasing SAF credits equivalent to 5–20 percent of their estimated CO_2 emissions.

- **Allianz**, one of the world's leading insurers and asset managers, is decarbonizing its portfolio and helping clients transition to greener energy. They incentivize customers to file claims to repair rather than replace items and to use sustainable rebuilding materials. In 2025, it expects all large oil and gas clients to have made net-zero commitments for 2050.
- **BT Group** customers are curbing emissions by using BT Group's AI-enabled Carbon Network Dashboard.
- **Nestlé** is expanding its portfolio to include more high-protein food and beverages in response to customer needs in food-insecure regions globally.
- **Subaru** inspires customers at retail locations to place hard-to-recycle items in designated bins, reducing landfill impact. It has kept 13 million pieces of waste out of landfills since 2018.

Market Strategy: Existing Products and Services (KSI 7.2)

To what extent has the company launched product breakthroughs with sustainability features to differentiate it from competitors?
- **E.ON** partnered with Ripple Energy in 2024 to allow customers to purchase shares in wind or solar energy production using a co-operative model, applying savings from renewable energy generation to their energy bills.
- **Munich Re** is decarbonizing its portfolio by underwriting clean energy. It will no longer insure new oil and gas exploration, extraction, and production. It has committed to fully exit thermal coal insurance by 2040.
- **VF Corporation**, owner of the Smartwool brand, introduced a 'circularity first' sock in 2023, combining repurposed yarn with responsibly sourced Merino wool.

Market Strategy: New Products and Services (KSI 7.3)

To what extent is the company reimagining the market to advance the decarbonization and dematerialization of its sector, mapping investments to most material issues across the value chain?
- **Barclays** launched a Green Home Mortgage initiative in 2023, offering lower interest rates for energy-efficient homes.
- **Honeywell's** digital transformation improved productivity and offered a new customer value proposition around operationalizing sustainability.
- **Hyundai** launched hydrogen-powered heavy-duty trucks in 2023, using fuel cell technology as an alternative to diesel engines.

- **Novozymes** introduced 'Bio-Solutions' in 2023 to enhance crop yields without synthetic fertilizers and produce detergents requiring less water and energy.
- **Rolls Royce** advanced the development of its all-electric aircraft to advance zero-emission flight and electric propulsion technology.
- **Siemens** launched the Decarbonization Business Optimizer in 2024 to help building owners and operators reduce their facilities' emissions.

Product Portfolio Transformation (KSI 7.4)

How aggressively is the company transforming its portfolio of products and services to embrace sustainability, leading as the market grows while exiting less sustainable products and services?
- **Aurubis** of Germany, the world's second largest copper producer, developed hydrogen-capable anode furnaces which reduce 5,000 tons of CO_2 annually. Until hydrogen is cost-competitive, the efficient new furnaces still help to decrease CO_2 emissions because they use ~30 percent less natural gas.
- **AXA** is committed to net-zero emissions across its insurance, reinsurance, and investment portfolios by 2050, aligning with the Paris Agreement. It prioritizes low-carbon technologies and nature-based solutions to combat climate change and enhance biodiversity. By 2022, AXA reduced its general account portfolio's implied temperature rise to 2.5°C, below the market average of 2.7°C.
- **CIBC**, the Canadian financial institution, by 2023 was halfway to its goal of mobilizing $300 Bn in sustainable financing by 2030.
- **Neste** started transforming from a regional oil refiner to a global renewable fuels leader in the early 2000s. It continues to increase the share of renewable and circular solutions while working with suppliers to reduce emissions.
- **Siemens** increased the portion of its relevant hardware, software, and service portfolio that incorporates its RED approach to 54 percent of the entire portfolio in 2024.

Sustainability Impacts on Brand (KSI 7.5)

How extensively is the company's brand tied directly to driving **total societal value**, often aligned with one or more of the UN Sustainable Development Goals?
- **Allbirds'** commitment to carbon-neutral products and eco-friendly materials has helped it become a market leader in sustainable footwear. Its many low-carbon, sustainable materials include merino wool and eucalyptus fibers.

- **Chemours**, a DuPont chemicals spin-off, delivered half its 2024 revenue from offerings that make a specific contribution to the UN Sustainable Development Goals (**SDGs**).
- **Ørsted** rebranded following its transformation to a renewable energy company. Its aim is to "create a world which runs entirely on green energy, giving back to nature and society more than it takes."
- **SC Johnson** CEO Fisk Johnson views ingredient transparency as vital to building trust in its brands. The maker of Windex, Shout, and Raid has implemented world-leading innovative sustainability measures in its supply chain and manufacturing.

Strategic Planning

When surveyed, most CEOs say they have a sustainability strategy. Yet dig a little deeper and that "strategy" likely includes the basics of sustainability reporting, some footprint reduction goals, a materiality assessment, and scattered programs and initiatives. Most companies lack a process that goes further by hard-wiring the environmental and social issues most material to corporate strategy.

The KSIs below offer positive examples.

Strategic Planning Process (KSI 8.1)

How robustly do climate and other material issues drive strategic planning, resulting in a horizon of at least five years and a bold roadmap to decarbonize, reduce footprints, and enhance societal value?

- **Allianz** published its first Net-Zero Transition Plan in 2023. It commits to transition and climate stress-test its portfolios to net-zero GHG emissions by 2050.
- **CIBC** reduced by 22 percent its operational emissions intensity for Scopes 1 and 2, of its oil and gas portfolio clients in 2023, moving toward 30 percent by 2030. This is part of its roadmap toward net-zero emissions from financing and operational activities by 2050.
- **John Deere** aims to connect 1.5 million agricultural, construction, and forestry machines to its digital platforms by 2026, helping users manage critical operations, monitor job quality, and analyze seasonal results.
- **Fortescue** outlined its ambitious climate transition plan in 2024, eliminating fossil fuels by 2030 without relying on carbon offsets or carbon capture, and calling this "Real Zero."

- **HSBC**, the London-headquartered bank, launched a comprehensive net-zero transition plan to phase down financing carbon-intensive sectors, in line with keeping global temperature rise below 1.5°C. It keeps 2030 targets for oil and gas, power and utilities, transport, thermal coal mining, and steel manufacturing and plans to disclose progress annually.

Use of Scenario Analysis (KSI 8.2)

To what extent has the company used robust scenario analysis to explore business risks and opportunities in a variety of plausible futures, building on yet separate from its climate scenario analyses?

One board member told me recently that *she expects management to conduct detailed climate scenarios; the board works through business scenarios.*

- **Shell** has used scenario planning for decades to identify business risks and opportunities. It is informed by data, using models and insights from leading experts.
- **Sony** publishes advanced planning scenarios with associated risks and countermeasures such as reducing product weight and packaging, using plastic alternatives, increasing product lifespans, and leveraging automation.

Cost Reduction (KSI 8.3)

Has the company employed impact-weighted accounting or full-cost accounting across the full value chain to cut waste relentlessly and achieve full life-cycle cost savings?

- **Ford's** "Creating Value and Positive Impact" graphic in its Integrated Sustainability and Financial Report illustrates how the company aligns financial performance with sustainability. It links cost impacts, capital investments, and their effects on customers, employees, investors, suppliers, communities, and the planet, showcasing Ford's holistic approach to creating sustainable value.
- **Herman Miller**, the office furniture maker, follows sustainable manufacturing practices to reduce fuel usage and repurpose wood waste. It pledges to achieve zero waste with 125,000 tons of product returned for recycling each year, a 50 percent increase in local renewable energy used, and 100 percent of items approved by Design for the Environment.
- **LyondellBassell**, a multinational chemical company, delivered $400 M of recurring annual EBITDA in 2023 by cutting costs and emissions.

Enterprise Risk Management (KSI 8.4)

How directly do material sustainability issues fully integrate into the company's enterprise risk management process – as stand-alone risks as well as potentially having a multiplier effect on other business risks?
- **Allianz** enterprise risk management includes climate risks, using scenario analysis to inform business strategies and investment decisions. This approach aligns financial stability with environmental resilience.
- **Chubb's** enterprise risk framework encompasses climate risk and integrates into all levels of business, from C-suite and board, down through all levels of employees.

Revenue Pipeline (KSI 8.5)

To what extent do sustainability drivers dominate growth options – with the company on track to generate most sales from sustainability-advantaged products and services?
- **DuPont** continued progress towards its 2030 goal to design 100 percent of products and processes using sustainability criteria. As of 2024, 80 percent of the portfolio meets its Portfolio Sustainability Assessment methodology covering four categories: water stewardship, climate action, circular economy, and safety.
- **HP** produced 60 percent of 2023 revenue categorized as sustainable, defined by the Corporate Knights Sustainable Economy Taxonomy.
- **Siemens** reports revenue from its RED portfolio and tracks products and services with regulated substances, aiming to reduce their negative environmental impacts.

Capital Allocation to Address Material Impacts (KSI 8.6)

To what extent do the company's capital expense practices align with those of a company rapidly transforming to achieve net-positive impact?
- **Dow** is building the world's first net-zero hydrogen-powered plastic facility in Canada, set to produce recyclable virgin plastic with zero CO_2 emissions in 2027.
- **Enel**, a leading energy company, has committed over 60 percent of its capital expenditure to renewables and decarbonization initiatives, expanding solar, wind, and hydroelectric projects.

- **Honeywell** reports that 60 percent of 2024 new product R&D investment was directed toward sustainability-oriented outcomes.
- **Iberdrola** a global renewable energy company, allocates 75 percent of its capital expenditure to green initiatives, such as wind farms and grid modernization.

Innovation, Research and Development

Leading and transforming companies see innovation as core to their future and see sustainability as the main driver of innovation. Below are the innovation KSIs along with selected examples.

Linkage between Sustainability and Innovation (KSI 9.1)

How aggressively does the company link sustainability as a driver of long-term growth, with a goal of decoupling sales growth from full value chain impact?
- **Johnson Controls** in 2024 opened a new Innovation Center with 250 employees focused on smart building technologies and sustainable solutions.
- **LEGO Group** increased the renewable materials in its products by over 80 percent during the first half of 2024 compared to 2023. (In 2023, it abandoned an initiative to recycle plastic bottles into bricks due to technical challenges.)
- **L'Oréal's** annual Brandstorm competition has provided coaching and training to more than 700,000 people under the age of 30 since 1992. The annual event encourages young people to create sustainable and inclusive beauty products.

Materials and Labor Inputs (KSI 9.2)

How aggressively has the company implemented processes to eliminate high-hazard materials and labor inputs and to maximize natural and highly recycled or recyclable materials?
- **Keurig Dr Pepper** announced a plastic-free, compostable, and plant-based innovation in 2024. Its K-Rounds, plastic-free coffee pods with a plant-based coating can withstand high-water-pressure espresso machines.
- **LG Chem** commenced large-scale production of biodegradable plastics in 2023.
- **VF Corporation** is scaling regenerative natural rubber for products across its apparel brands.

Product Design and Development (KSI 9.3)

Are sustainability issues, risks, and opportunities woven in, formally and at an early stage, at each step of the product development process? Does a risk assessment underlie the "go/no-go" decision?
- **Adidas** launched the first recyclable running shoe, "made to be remade" from ocean plastic. With **Allbirds**, its "Futurecraft.Footprint" uses recycled polyester, a wood pulp-based material, and recycled rubber.
- **Cisco** claims that 96 percent of new products and packaging incorporate Circular Design Principles.
- **Dell's** design guidelines aim to reduce the size and number of components, the amount of material, and the complexity of system assembly.
- **Interface** designs modular carpet tiles using fully recyclable materials. The company's ReEntry program takes back used carpets to recycle into new products.
- **Levi Strauss**, to promote circular fashion, integrated Circulose material made from recycled fibers into its WellThread collection, designed for recyclability.
- **Schneider Electric's** Green Premium products since 2008 have provided transparency to customers about hazardous substances, environmental impact, and equipment end-of-life, offering digital, verified product footprints.
- **Volvo** partnered with Swedish steel manufacturer SSAB to create a recycled steel (SSAB Zero) using fossil-free electricity and biogas. It slashes CO_2 by 80 percent compared to conventional steel making.

R&D Partnerships – Driving Sustainability Benefits (KSI 9.4)

Has the company been aggressively seeking sustainability-related R&D partnerships that could make a significant positive business and societal impact?
- **Cargill** partnered with **KOTUG International** to deploy the world's first zero-emission, fully electrified pusher boats and barges for inland shipping in 2024.
- **Colgate-Palmolive** teamed up with **Uber Freight** to test autonomous truck shipments in 2023, increasing efficiency and reducing fuel consumption.
- **Dow** joined **Procter & Gamble** in 2024 to develop a dissolution technology for transforming rigid, flexible, and multilayer plastic packaging into recycled polyethylene for use in packaging.
- **General Mills** has partnered with **Ahold Delhaize** to expand regenerative agriculture for wheat and oats.
- **Schneider Electric** teamed with **KB Home,** the large US builder, to launch the first energy microgrid communities in 2022.

R&D Investment in Sustainable Products and Technology (KSI 9.5)

Has the company been making major investments in disruptive technologies, perhaps partnering with key customers, to reduce the full value chain footprint?
- **BASF** invested half of its 2023 R&D in a Sustainable-Future Solutions portfolio, assessing and ranking products against sustainability R&D guidelines.
- **E.ON** is developing large-scale battery storage systems. It's integrating them into former coal plants and other preexisting energy infrastructure.
- **Enel** launched the Flexibility Lab to develop and integrate flexible, digital energy solutions into the grid, testing them in real-world conditions. It's collaborating with local utilities, start-ups, and technology providers.

Product Offerings

Leading companies drive revenue growth through sustainable products and services. Where feasible, they shift from selling products to services and solutions, benefiting from recurring revenue streams and long-term customer relationships. Below are the KSIs along with selected examples.

Product Value Proposition (KSI 10.1)

To what extent is the company systematically moving to products supporting net zero and to services and solutions – with a core value placed on driving toward a **closed-loop** supply chain?
- **Bundles**, a Netherlands-based provider of subscription and pay-per-use services for home appliances, is making products accessible with free maintenance and repair services.
- **Novozymes** promotes biotechnology as scalable, sustainable alternatives to traditional industrial processes.
- **Philips Lighting**, now known as **Signify**, offers Light as a Service. Customers lease lighting systems while the company retains ownership and responsibility for maintenance, upgrades, and end-of-life recycling.
- **Suez**, the French global leader in water and waste management, deploys technologies that transform waste into biogas and electricity, reducing emissions.
- **Xerox**'s Managed Print Services model, wherein customers pay for printing services per-use basis, supports its long-standing vision of waste-free products from waste-free factories.

Product Stewardship (KSI 10.2)

Does the company systematically review and assess the environmental and social impacts of its offerings, quantifying benefits and purposefully growing green or healthy products and services?
– **SC Jonson's** proprietary Greenlist tool evaluates and scores its product ingredients based on impacts on human health and the environment. It prioritizes safer, more sustainable ingredients in product development to ensure high standards for safety and environmental responsibility.
– **SABIC's** product stewardship program consistently ranks highly for reducing hazardous chemicals and promoting safer alternatives and for transparency.

Product Risk Assessment (KSI 10.3)

Does the company use formal sustainability risk mapping to drive portfolio changes within and across product lines?
– **J.M. Huber** completed life-cycle analyses for more than 90 percent of its Huber Advanced Materials product portfolio by 2023, sharing the results with customers.
– **Whole Foods** publishes a long list of hundreds of other banned ingredients, even including synthetic dyes approved by the FDA for food, drugs, and cosmetics.

Product Labeling and Rating (KSI 10.4)

Does the company use industry-leading product labeling and rating, supporting portfolio changes across businesses?
– **Allbirds** was the first fashion brand to label the carbon footprint of each product, promoting transparency and encouraging consumers to consider environmental impacts in purchasing.
– **Clorox** uses SmartLabel, a "one-stop-shop" digital platform where customers scan a barcode on over 450 products to access an ingredients list, potential health hazards or notifications about ingredients of concern. Information about disposal and recycling is also included.
– **Danone** introduced transparency in its product labels, including information on carbon footprint and sourcing, earning the company recognition from the World Wildlife Fund.

- **Whole Foods** began displaying the Sourced for Good seal on products in 2021. It reflects product sourcing, Fair Trade Certification, and environmental impact. It requires all organic products to be USDA stamp-approved (inspected and deemed safe for consumption by the USDA).

Product Quality and Safety (KSI 10.5)

Are product quality and safety standards across the portfolio fully aligned with **sustainability principles**, such as circular economy?
- **John Deere** is known for its durable and reliable products in agriculture and construction equipment.
- **Toyota**'s comprehensive safety governance framework includes advanced testing procedures, continuous safety evaluations, and proactive risk monitoring. Additionally, the company invests globally in driver education programs and safety awareness initiatives.

Product Marketing and Advertising (KSI 10.6)

Has the company earned a reputation for full transparency – that is, communicating the full life-cycle impacts, challenges, and successes in product advertising, labeling and marketing?
- **Eileen Fisher** offers insights into its garments' sourcing, production, and recycling processes. Through initiatives like the "Renew" program, the brand promotes circular fashion and educates customers on sustainable practices.
- **Patagonia** provides detailed information about the sourcing, production, and environmental impact of its apparel. Through the "Footprint Chronicles," the company offers transparency regarding the life cycle of its products, including challenges and areas for improvement.
- **Seventh Generation** discloses comprehensive information about product ingredients, sourcing, and environmental impacts. Its transparency in labeling and marketing reflects a commitment to consumer health and sustainability.

Supply Chain Management

For many companies, a major portion of negative environmental and social impacts occurs in the supply chain. This section addresses the overall corporate management of the supply chain. (Chapter 8 has a section on specific environmental supply chain issues. Chapter 9 has the same for social issues.)

Below are the KSIs with selected examples.

Responsible Sourcing Approach (KSI 11.1)

Has the company implemented sustainability into buyer performance goals and incentives, embedding responsible sourcing policies, standards, and processes throughout?

– **Apple** aims to ensure ethical sourcing through its Supplier Code of Conduct, as well as audits, capacity-building, and resource tools to empower workers.
– **Danone** has committed to a clean supply chain by 2025. They work with the Earthworm Foundation to ensure traceability of palm oil and trace all palm oil back to the plantation where it was grown.
– **Nike** includes stringent supplier standards regarding wages, working hours, and conditions, regular audits, targeted worker training, and capacity-building.
– **Toyota** aims to reduce emissions from suppliers, logistics, and dealers 30 percent by 2030 compared with the 2019 baseline.

Engaging on Material Supply Chain Issues (KSI 11.2)

How robustly does the company engage in ongoing dialog with supply chain partners to map sustainability issues and risks, foster peer learning, and focus on growth opportunities?

– **Bristol Meyers Squibb** created a supplier decarbonization accelerator program to help its suppliers set and meet their decarbonization goals. It includes webinars, resources, and free meetings with a sustainability advisor.
– **Dell** maintained its CDP "Supplier Engagement Leader" status in 2024. It was recognized for assessing climate performance within business strategy, science-based target reporting, Scope 3 emissions accounting, and supplier engagement.
– **Patagonia** achieved Regenerative Organic Certification for its cotton supply chain in 2024, emphasizing practices that restore soil health, promote animal welfare, and improve the livelihoods of farmers.

Standards for Supply Chain Impacts (KSI 11.3)

Has the company established robust controls and systems – and imposed non-negotiable sustainability requirements for demonstrated impact reduction – across the full supply chain?

- **Bayer** requires all suppliers to avoid conflict metals and minerals. Suppliers of strategic importance must present an EcoVadis rating or a comparable audit result.
- **Ecolab** requires suppliers to disclose sustainability progress via CDP supply chain and establish science-based targets or similar for carbon reduction.
- **Microsoft,** in its 2024 Environmental Sustainability Report, announced a new requirement for select high-volume suppliers to use 100 percent carbon-free electricity for Microsoft-delivered goods and services by 2030.

Measuring Supply Chain Impacts (KSI 11.4)

To what extent does the company measure, track, and report material sustainability impacts throughout the supply chain, with a goal of net-positive impacts?

- **BASF**, as a founding member of Together for Sustainability, aims to standardize supply chain audits. Following audit failure, supplier relationships are terminated if there is no improvement.
- **Cisco** claims that 90 percent of its component, manufacturing, and logistics suppliers by spend have a public, absolute GHG emissions-reduction target.
- **H&M** has initiatives focused on sustainable materials, ethical labor practices, and circular fashion. The company aims to transition to a circular business model by 2040 that minimizes waste and resource use.
- **Nestlé** has implemented its "Nestlé in Society" strategy, which includes commitments to sourcing sustainably, reducing environmental impact, and promoting responsible labor practices throughout its supply chain.

Verifying Supply Chain Impacts (KSI 11.5)

Has the company conducted third-party audits of suppliers in higher-risk countries, as defined by Human Rights Watch or a similar list – and published the results?

- **Patagonia**, as a founding member of the Fair Labor Association, subjects its supply chain to random audits, and shares the results publicly.
- **Ford** uses third-party assessments to evaluate supplier compliance, including material sourcing and mining practices.

Chapter 8
Environmental Stewardship

Consider the story of one company that struggled decades ago with getting environmental stewardship *right.*

 Almost Kicked Out of Oklahoma

I was almost kicked out of Oklahoma for mentioning climate change to a top executive of a major oil and chemicals company.

As the senior advisor to the CEO's business transformation team, I focused on his desire for the company to lead on environment.

Interviewing the Senior Vice President of Strategy in a corner office, I asked him what a leadership posture on climate change looks like. I noted that the company's major competitor had an aggressive public posture on carbon-related risk and opportunity.

He glared and said, "Don't ever mention climate change around here."

Our team then tried a different angle, interviewing the company's UK production manager. We were surprised what we learned.

Six weeks later, we invited the production manager to join a presentation to the Executive Leadership Team. He revealed that the company's European headquarters had crafted a public position statement, similar to the competitor's, on climate change.

The CEO and SVP were shocked. Nobody in Oklahoma City had seen that document.

As this story shows, **sustainability involves tough and evolving conversations**. If company leaders do not have those conversations, they are probably dancing around the edges of the core sustainability issues.

At a Glance: The "E" in ESG

Every company is responsible for the full environmental impact of its products and services across the value chain. *Starbucks* is responsible for the water and pesticides used to grow its coffee beans, as well as the labor practices involved. *PepsiCo* and *Tesco* own the ecological impact of producing the food and beverages they sell.

Environmental stewardship depicted in Figure 8.1 (similar to Figure 1.1) has long dominated the sustainability headlines in the United States.

https://doi.org/10.1515/9783111548852-009

Environment: Core Elements

NGOs tend to think of sustainability by issue, such as carbon, water, and waste. However, most companies assign accountability for specific issues the way they run the company: operations, sourcing, production, distribution, sales, customer service, and so forth.

Figure 8.1: Sustainability: Environment

Environmental issues across the value chain fall into three buckets:
- **Environmental Footprint – Operations**: How deeply and robustly are we managing and reducing the environmental risks associated with our wholly owned (and >50 percent owned joint venture) operations globally?
- **Environmental Footprint – Supply Chain**: How deeply and robustly are we managing and reducing the environmental risks associated with the company's full supply chain impacts?
- **Environmental Footprint – Products and Services**: How deeply and robustly are we managing and reducing the environmental risks associated with our product and service offerings?

The value chain structure makes sense. One company's products are another company's source materials. *Walmart's* supplier requirements are a product issue for suppliers including *Dell, HP, Procter & Gamble*, for example, which must reduce or take back their packaging material.

For most companies, most of the full life-cycle environmental impacts occur in only: (a) one or two areas of environmental impact, such as carbon/GHG; toxics, water; and (b) one key part of the supply chain, such as the supplier, own operations, product use, and disposal.

Within each of these elements, a series of KSIs s depicted in Figure 8.2 reflects how companies address environmental stewardship.

Environment: Operations	Environment: Supply Chain	Environment: Products
GHG Emissions: Scope 1	Approach to Supply Chain: Environment	Responsibility for Product Use and End of Life
GHG Emissions: Scope 2	Materials Sourced: Human Made	Product Traceability
Non-Carbon Emissions	Materials Sourced: Biological-Based	Product Carbon Impact
Buildings and Equipment	GHG: Scope 3	Product Durability
Water Management	Supply Chain Impact: Biodiversity	Product Biodegradability
Biodiversity and Land Management	Supply Chain Impact: Water	Product Recyclability and Reusability
Waste Management	Supply Chain Impact: Waste	Product Water-Use Efficiency
		Product Packaging

Figure 8.2: Environment KSIs
Source: ESG Navigator

Environment KSIs

Bear in mind that for each KSI, companies can measure and map their progress across a maturity path that measures performance across four stages of maturity. Additional information about the environment KSIs appears in Appendix E.

Below (Table 8.1) is an example of a full four-stage rating scale for a single KSI: Materials Sourced: Human-Made (e.g., chemicals, metals, plastics, etc.).

Table 8.1: Example KSI Detail: Environment

Materials Sourced: Human-Made (e.g., chemicals, metals, plastics, etc.)

Engaging	Accelerating	Leading	Transforming
Adopt some resource efficiency efforts, with a focus on compliance. Source about 10–20% recycled content.	Eliminate prioritized list of toxics and "de-select" hazardous materials. Source 20–50% recycled content.	Apply green chemistry principles aggressively, eliminating toxics and high S/ESG risk product inputs. Source 50–75% recycled content.	Approach closed loop with 75–100% recycled content. Align with green chemistry principles.

In the pages that follow, I walk through each of the KSIs depicted in Figure 8.2, posing a question to help gauge how close a company approaches a Transformation (Stage 4) position, followed by several best practice examples.

The best practice examples, while world leading, may not necessarily yet be a Stage 4 action. Think of Stages 1, 2, and 3 as "good, better, best." Think of Stage 4 as what's expected of leading companies soon. In some, but not all cases, a best practice today meets the full Stage 4 descriptor. (See Appendix E.)

Environmental Footprint: Operations

Below are the seven KSIs with selected examples.

GHG Emissions: Owned/Controlled Sources (Scope 1) (KSI 12.1)

How close is the company to carbon neutrality or better, without using unbundled renewable energy credits or low-quality carbon offsets?
- **Meta** achieved its goal of supporting its global operations with 100 percent renewable energy in 2020. It continues to invest in renewable energy projects to maintain this commitment.

- **Microsoft** committed to shifting to 100 percent renewable energy by 2025 and has been carbon neutral across its global operations since 2012. It continues to invest in renewable energy projects.
- **Amazon**: As part of its net-zero carbon commitment for 2040, it is on a path to power its operations with 100 percent renewable energy by 2025. It's already the largest corporate purchaser of renewable energy globally.

GHG Emissions: Energy Purchased (Scope 2) (KSI 12.2)

How close is the company to sourcing 100 percent renewable energy?
- **Google** advanced its commitment in 2024 to operate on 24/7 carbon-free energy by 2030, sourcing carbon-free energy for its data centers and offices worldwide.
- **Microsoft** committed $10 Bn in 2024 to develop 10.5 gigawatts of renewable energy to power its data centers and address the significant energy demands from AI. It's the largest corporate clean-energy initiative globally.
- **Vodafone** achieved 100 percent renewable electricity usage across its European network in 2023, supporting the net-zero emissions target for 2040.

Non-Carbon Emissions (KSI 12.3)

To what extent does the company achieve zero discharge of hazardous substances and 100 percent fully benign emissions?
- **Decathlon** is a member of the Zero Discharge of Hazardous Chemicals (ZDHC) Program, by which it commits not to emit hazardous chemicals into the environment. The French sporting goods brand integrates sustainable chemical management practices across its value chain to ensure safer products for consumers and reduced environmental impact.
- **H&M Group** has been a proactive member of the ZDHC Program since 2011, and in 2022 achieved 99 percent compliance. The company has set a goal to achieve 100 percent toxic-free fashion by 2030, aligning with its ambition to become fully circular.

Buildings and Equipment (KSI 12.4)

How aggressively is the company moving toward net-zero energy in all owned or leased buildings within the next five years, working toward **LEED** (Leadership in Energy and Environmental Design) certification for their buildings?

- **Aldi**, America's fastest-growing grocery chain, became the first US food retailer to commit to phasing out super-polluting chemical refrigerants, aiming for natural refrigerants in all its stores by 2035.
- **Starbucks** aims to design, build, and operate 10,000 greener stores globally by 2030, collaborating with the World Wildlife Fund to develop and implement standards for things including recapturing residual water from ice machines, switching to LED lights and Energy Star certified appliances, and tailoring waste disposal practices to the local municipalities' systems.

Water Management (KSI 12.5)

How close is the company to achieving **water neutrality** in all operations – and managing for net **water positive** impact on stressed aquifer supply?

- **BMW** is pioneering reverse osmosis technology. In 2023 it reduced water consumption by 15.9 million gallons at a key site. In addition, dry separation, using limestone instead of water, resulted in major water and energy savings.
- **Coca-Cola's** Water Stewardship goal by 2030 seeks to return 100 percent of the water used in its production to nature and communities. It integrates water-risk assessments and community partnerships to ensure accountability and transparency in water management.
- **Heineken** had water-replenishment programs at 28 of 32 sites in water-stressed areas in 2023, targeting balanced use and reduction in water-stressed areas by 2030.

Biodiversity and Land Management (KSI 12.6)

How aggressively is the company reducing nature-related impacts, restoring and protecting habitat, and investing in natural capital?

- **GSK** committed to positive biodiversity at sites it owns by 2030, with biodiversity action plans in place at all sites by 2025. The biopharma company has pledged that all agricultural, forestry, and marine-derived materials will be sustainably sourced and deforestation-free by 2030.

- **L'Oréal** plans to assess all its buildings and industrial sites for biodiversity impacts by 2030, aiming for positive impact against a 2019 baseline. Additionally, the L'Oréal Fund for Nature Regeneration supports projects restoring degraded land in forest and marine areas.
- **Mahindra Group**, a global federation of over 100 companies in more than 20 sectors, was among the 130 companies in 2024 calling upon global leaders to prevent biodiversity loss ahead of COP16.
- **Ørsted** is partnering with World Wildlife Fund to achieve net-positive biodiversity impact with all new renewable energy projects from 2030 onwards.

Waste Management (KSI 12.7)

How close is your company to achieving zero waste to landfill, 100 percent recycling, and zero hazardous waste?
- **3M**, while still generating 56,600 metric tons of hazardous waste in 2023, achieved zero waste to landfill at half its manufacturing sites, with transparent reporting.
- **Eli Lilly** repurposed, recycled, or reused over 97 percent of its plastic waste in 2023, nearing 100 percent by 2030.
- **Subaru** products have all been manufactured in zero-waste-to-landfill plants since 2004, being the first US auto-maker to do so. Plastic makes up only around 2 percent of its waste, but it continues to develop new recycling technologies.

Environmental Footprint: Supply Chain

Below are the KSIs with selected examples.

Approach to Supply Chain Environmental Impacts (KSI 13.1)

To what extent is the company partnering with suppliers to drive the supply chain environmental footprint toward zero?
- **Dell** partners with high-emitting suppliers to assist in cutting emissions, improving data accuracy, investing in automation, completing emissions forecasts, and performing hot-spot analyses.
- **H&M** reached 85 percent sustainably sourced materials in 2023, including 25 percent recycled materials.

- **Nike** partnered with **Apple** in 2023 to launch the Clean Energy Procurement Academy, helping suppliers reduce emissions.
- **SC Johnson's** Greenlist program remains a rigorous, science-based process. Each ingredient in its products undergoes a four-step evaluation to assess potential impacts on human health and the environment.

Materials Sourced: Human-Made (KSI 13.2)

How close is the company to achieving closed-loop sourcing?
- **Dell** committed that half of all product content, and all packaging content will be made from renewable or recycled materials by 2030.
- **Novelis** has achieved an average of over 60 percent recycled content across all its product lines, the highest percentage in the aluminum flat-rolled products sector.
- **Puma** has scaled up its textile-to-textile recycling, producing more than a million replica soccer club jerseys in 2024 from 100 percent recycled materials.
- **SC Johnson** is expanding its concentrated refill options to help customers reduce plastic waste by nearly 80 percent. It is committing to 100 percent recyclable, reusable, or compostable packaging by 2025, tripling post-consumer recycled content.

Materials Sourced: Biological Based (KSI 13.3)

How close is the company to sourcing all biological based materials (e.g., from agriculture, forests, and fisheries) from responsible and/or certified sources? This includes growing the percentage of bio-based source materials, if proven to be preferable?
- **B&Q**, the Kingfisher subsidiary, sourced 99 percent of its wood and paper responsibly in 2024.
- **Mars** is paying higher rates to farmers who produce milk with lower emissions, knowing that this helps transition to better methods and technologies.
- **Mondelez' Cocoa Life** program trains cocoa farmers in sustainable practices to improve crop resilience, combat child labor, promote gender equality, and conserve forests to tackle deforestation. It seeks to reach 300,000 farmers by 2030.
- **Natura & Co** actively preserves 1.8 m hectares of land in the Amazon, equivalent to half of the Netherlands. The cosmetics group aims to contribute to the

preservation of 3 m hectares by 2030. It fosters collective efforts to ensure zero deforestation in the Amazon.

–   **Whole Foods** supports climate-smart, biodynamic and regenerative agriculture to improve soil health, biodiversity, and carbon capture. From 2025, all produce and floral suppliers must adopt Integrated Pest Management, prioritizing natural pest control to reduce chemical use and support pollinator health.

Scope 3 GHG Emissions (KSI 13.4)

How successful is the company working with suppliers, customers, and others to meet a science-based target to cut Scope 3 GHG emissions?

–   **3M** received SBTi validation in 2024 for its target to reduce Scope 3 emissions by 42 percent by 2030 against 2021. With more than 60,000 products and a vast supplier network, 3M developed its own methodology to measure supply chain emissions. This accounts for variations among products, suppliers, and estimation methods, ensuring more precise tracking.

–   **Kingfisher** requires its top 100 suppliers, responsible for the largest share of its Scope 3 emissions, to develop an SBTi-aligned roadmap and decarbonization plan by 2028. By 2030, the next 450 suppliers must establish similar targets, while remaining vendors must implement an emissions-reduction plan.

–   **PepsiCo** has committed to reducing its Scope 3 emissions by 40 percent by 2030, using a 2015 baseline. This belongs to the PepsiCo Positive (pep+) climate action strategy, striving for a 75 percent reduction in Scopes 1 and 2 emissions by 2030, and net-zero emissions by 2040.

Supply Chain Impact: Biodiversity (KSI 13.5)

How close is the company to 100 percent sustainable sourcing to restore, preserve, and enhance biodiversity, with independent verification?

–   **IKEA** is developing a science-based biodiversity performance framework with indicators and goals. It worked with WWF-India in 2023 to develop three biodiversity parks to restore cotton ecosystems using regenerative agricultural practices that support pollinator habitats.

–   **Wilmar**: The Singaporean food processing and investment holding company with over 300 subsidiaries implemented a No Deforestation, No Peat, No Exploitation (NDPE) policy across its supply chain in 2023. Its goal is to eliminate deforestation, protect peatlands, and uphold human rights in palm oil production. Wilmar collaborates with suppliers and stakeholders.

Supply Chain Impact: Water (KSI 13.6)

How close is the company to achieving water-neutral status across the supply chain?
- **Diageo** implemented a comprehensive water stewardship strategy in 2023. It improved efficiency, replenished water in stressed areas, and advocated for responsible water use. The goal is to have a water-positive impact by 2030.
- **Heineken** has pledged to fully replenish the water it uses in water-stressed areas by 2030, returning an equivalent volume of water to local watersheds through restoration projects and sustainable practices. This is part of its "Every Drop" water strategy, supporting UN Sustainable Development Goal 6 to ensure clean water access.
- **Keurig Dr Pepper** has committed to replenishing 100 percent of the water used in its beverage manufacturing in high water-risk communities by 2025. It seeks to achieve a net-positive water impact by 2050.

Supply Chain Impact: Waste (KSI 13.7)

What measures has your company taken to collaborate with suppliers, resulting in demonstrated zero waste to landfill or equivalent?
- **Google** collaborates with suppliers through strict sustainability guidelines, including waste diversion and recycling practices. Suppliers are encouraged to implement circular economy principles, such as repurposing materials in electronics and furniture.
- **Toyota** requires suppliers to comply with its Green Supplier Requirements, mandating waste minimization, recycling, and sustainable practices. It encourages suppliers to adopt environmental management systems, focusing on reducing waste and enhancing recycling initiatives.

Environmental Footprint: Products and Services

Every company is responsible for the full environmental impact of its products and services across the value chain. Below are the KSIs along with selected examples.

Responsibility for Product Use and End-of-Life (KSI 14.1)

To what extent has the company implemented robust systems ensuring end-of-life responsibility that approaches closed-loop and preserves or restores ecosystem services??
- **BMW's** closed-loop recycling system for high-voltage batteries recovers 100 percent of core raw materials.
- **Dell** commits by 2030 to reusing or recycling an equivalent weight of disposed products for every product customers purchase.
- **H&M** introduced garment collection and recycling programs in 2023. It's goal is to become fully circular and climate-positive by 2040.
- **REI** runs REI Used Gear, where customers can trade in used outdoor gear and clothing for store credit.
- **Steelcase**, a leading office furniture manufacturer, collaborates with partners to extend product lifecycles through reuse, donations, and recycling. Its Eco'Services initiative diverted 3,600 tons of furniture from landfills in 2023.
- **Timberland's** Timberloop take-back program expanded in 2023 into 13 countries in Europe, the Middle East, and Africa.

Product Traceability (KSI 14.2)

How robustly has the company implemented systems to ensure that all high-risk source material inputs are **traceable** from raw material extraction to product end-of-life?
- **3M** requires materials and suppliers from at-risk regions to submit to rigorous screening. For example, every 3M Post-it Note must be traceable, ensuring that virgin wood fiber is harvested in a way that maintains or enhances high conservation values, free of deforestation.
- **Patagonia** uses 100 percent traceable down, sourced as a by-product of the food industry, and certified to the Global Traceable Down Standard.
- **Volvo** issued the world's first electric vehicle (EV) passport in 2024 a model for tracking the origins and carbon footprints of battery components.
- **Volkswagen**, since 2021, has published a Raw Materials Traceability report. In 2024, it covered 18 raw materials and their respective suppliers.

Product Carbon Impact (KSI 14.3)

To what extent has the company implemented systems ensuring that all products and services pose minimum carbon impact and maximum energy efficiency?
- **Adidas** has set a goal to reduce emissions per product by 15 percent by 2025 against 2017. In 2023, the average GHG emissions per product decreased by 3 percent compared to 2022.
- **Interface** has claimed that all of its flooring products are carbon neutral across their entire life-cycle since 2018.

Product Durability (KSI 14.4)

Has the company built a robust product life-extension business whereby it sells highly durable products and shifts from selling products to selling services and solutions where possible?
- **Airstream** designs its motorhomes and trailers using high-quality materials to last for generations.
- **Filson** offers a lifetime guarantee on much of its rugged outdoor gear and apparel. High-quality materials include heavyweight cotton and waxed canvas.
- **Miele** of Germany designs high-end, easily repairable domestic appliances with long lifespans. Instead of moving down-market to boost sales, the company's focus on high performance and durability justifies premium prices.
- **Patagonia's** Worn Wear program is one of the few refurbishment programs in the clothing industry to scale successfully.
- **Yeti** designs coolers and outdoor gear to last a lifetime. With quality materials and rigorous testing, it offers customers a warranty on many products.

Product Biodegradability (KSI 14.5)

To what extent are all product offerings biodegradable, if applicable – with biodegradability calculations validated by highly respected rating agencies?
- **IKEA** plans to use only renewable and recycled materials, removing all single-use plastic products globally by 2030. The company phased out all single-use plastics from its home furnishings in 2020.
- **Pela**, founded in 2011 in Canada, produced the world's first compostable smartphone case. It has expanded into other sustainable lifestyle products, including eyewear and phone grip accessories.

Product Recyclability and Reusability (KSI 14.6)

Has the company achieved recyclability and reusability for its entire portfolio of offerings?
- **HP** has implemented a closed-loop recycling process for ink cartridges. It collects, disassembles, and recycles cartridges to create new ones.
- **Desso**, part of the $3 Bn Tarkett conglomerate, produces EcoBase carpet backing, which incorporates 75 percent recycled content from bottled water waste. It's certified **Cradle-to-Cradle** Gold for circularity and Platinum for material health.
- **Eileen Fisher** has offered gently used items for resale since 2009, taking back over 2 million pieces to renew or upcycle in its Waste No More line.
- **IKEA** is supporting the reuse of its products with its Ikea Preowned pilot program.
- **Terracycle**, which specializes in recycling challenging materials, such as coffee capsules, toothbrushes, and snack wrappers, partners with manufacturers to create new products and materials from waste.
- **Tesla** launched a comprehensive battery recycling program in 2023, developing efficient recycling processes, and collaborating with partners to establish recycling facilities.

Product Water-Use Efficiency (KSI 14.7)

Has the company been improving water-use efficiency during the customer use of its products and services– and is it designing all offerings for minimum water use?
- **Holcim Group** developed Hydromedia, a sustainable water management system made from permeable concrete that rapidly absorbs stormwater off streets and parking surfaces, reducing flood risk.
- **Levi Strauss & Co.** in 2024 expanded its Water<Less techniques to reduce water usage during apparel finishing. The company collaborates with suppliers to promote water conservation throughout its supply chain.

Product Packaging (KSI 14.8)

Has the company implemented renewable, recyclable, and/or reusable options approaching 100 percent of total packaging?
- **Coca-Cola** in 2023 delivered 14 percent of its beverage volume in reusable packaging, with a 2030 goal to reach 25 percent.

- **Aldi's** US supermarkets ceased offering plastic shopping bags in 2024. It has committed to 100 percent reusable, recyclable, or compostable packaging by 2025.
- **Dell** surpassed 96 percent of packaging made from recycled, renewable or reduced carbon-emission materials in 2024.
- **Dow** has achieved 79 percent recyclable or reusable packaging as of 2024. Its goal is 100 percent.
- **Samsung** introduced eco-friendly packaging for its Galaxy smartphones in 2023, replacing plastic components with recycled and biodegradable materials.
- **Tesco** introduced a zero-waste packaging initiative in 2023, offering products in reusable containers to reduce single-use plastic. Customers can return the containers for cleaning and reuse.

Chapter 9
Social Responsibility

Consider a complex situation where environmental and social issues are intertwined.

 A Corporate Policy Can Shut Down an Operation

I spent two weeks in Papua New Guinea as a member of a high-level audit team, charged with assessing the environmental status of one of the largest copper mines in the world.

The controversial Ok Tedi mine sits in one of the most remote places in the world, about 6,000 feet above sea level, in a rainforest area on geologically "new" soil, which was easily eroded. It was in the crosshairs of NGOs.

The environmental issues at the open pit mine were extensive. Thirty staff environmental scientists and experts had commissioned ecosystem studies about the impacts of tailings runoff into the Fly River, one of the most fertile fishing grounds in the South China Sea.

We toured the site extensively; reviewed compliance records; took helicopter rides up and down the river systems; and met with local community groups. After 12 days, we came to a surprising conclusion: on paper, the Ok Tedi mine appeared to be largely in compliance with New Guinea laws and regulations.

Around a conference room table that evening, however, I noticed the Corporate Environmental, Health, and Safety Policy on the wall. We read the words carefully, including a "commitment to protecting human health and the environment." After some heated discussions, our team concluded that the site complied with regulations but did not conform with its Policy, intended to protect investors from risks.

Our report made it to the highest levels of the company. Not long after, BHP began divesting itself of the Ok Tedi mine and taking major financial charges against operations.

The message: **social issues are complex and intertwined with environmental issues**. Tradeoffs must often be considered. Availability of fresh water may be primarily an environmental issue in the suburbs of Los Angeles yet considered a social issue in water-stressed regions.

At a Glance: The "S" in ESG

From its beginning, the SRI movement had social issues at its core, as the name implies. Early and long-standing leaders such as Calvert focused as much or more on social issues as on environmental matters.

Social issues are owned not only by the parent company but also throughout the value chain. Every company that purchased copper sourced at Ok Tedi owned

https://doi.org/10.1515/9783111548852-010

the social and environmental issues in Papua New Guinea. In other high-profile examples:

- **Nike** owned the child labor issues in Nike, Inc. v. Kasky lawsuit that reached the US Supreme Court in 2003.
- **Apple** owned the **Foxconn** labor and environmental abuses a decade ago.
- **Dell, Google, Microsoft, Tesla**, and **Apple**, are fighting a lawsuit that would make them own alleged human rights violations for mining in the Democratic Republic of Congo.

Since the 1990s, social issues have been a core part of sustainability and ESG (Figure 9.1).

Figure 9.1: Sustainability: Social

Social: Core Elements

Social responsibility issues broadly fall into three buckets:

- **Social Performance – Workplace:** How does our workplace environment and supporting programs, incentives, and initiatives engage our employees and others in sustainability issues?
- **Social Performance – Supply Chain**: How deeply and robustly are we managing and reducing the social risks associated with the full supply chain impacts?

- **Social Performance – Community**: What types of policies, programs, partnerships, and investments are we making to benefit the communities in which we operate and society at large?

Within each of these elements, a series of KSIs depicted in Figure 9.2 reflect how companies address social responsibility issues.

Social: Workplace	Social: Supply Chain	Social: Community
Workplace Environment	Approach to Supply Chain: Social	Philosophy Regarding Community
Diversity, Equity, and Inclusion	Human Rights	Engagement with Communities and NGOs
Recruitment and Retention	Labor Relations	Social Investment
Safety Programs and Performance	Supply Chain Diversity	Community and Stakeholder Partnerships
Health and Wellness	Supply Chain Capacity Building	Infrastructure Development
Training and Staff Development		Community Job Creation
Employee Engagement		

Figure 9.2: Social KSIs
Source: ESG Navigator

Social KSIs

Bear in mind that for each KSI, companies can measure and map their progress across a maturity path that measures performance across four stages of maturity. Additional information about the environment KSIs are in Appendix E.

Below (Table 9.1) is an example of a full four-stage rating scale for a single KSI: Workplace: Training and Staff Development.

Table 9.1: Example KSI Detail: Social

Training and Staff Development			
Engaging	**Accelerating**	**Leading**	**Transforming**
Provide basic safety, ethics, diversity etc. training for all employees. Provide sustainability (*S*) skills training and career development.	Provide *S* short course for all staff. Promote career mobility (e.g., rotating jobs) and *S* learning. Provide, measure, and report *S* skills development.	Provide *S* employee training to help reduce footprint. C-suite engages in sustained *S* learning and skills development. Include *S* training in leadership development.	Invest in robust *S* training tools and infrastructure so that all staff are aligned with company ambitions. Provide high-profile *S* learning for high-potential employees.

The following pages walk through the social responsibility KSIs depicted in Figure 9.2. Each KSI starts with a question to help the reader gauge how close a company is to a transformation (Stage 4) position, followed by several best practice examples.

The best practice examples, while world-leading, may not necessarily yet be a Stage 4 (transformational) action. Think of stages one, two, and three as good, better, best. Think of stage 4 as what's expected of leading companies soon. In some, but not all cases, a best practice today meets the full Stage 4 descriptor. (See Appendix E.)

Social Performance: Workplace

Below are the KSIs with selected examples.

Workplace Environment (KSI 15.1)

To what extent does the company earn a reputation for highly valuing human capital – where employees are truly living the company purpose and driving the achievement of robust sustainability goals?
- **Cisco's** Digital Well-being Hub holistically studies the ways in which people engage with technology – and its impact on various aspects of their health, using AI to detect early signs of burnout in employees, and embed well-being strategies directly into the workflow.

- **L'Oréal** USA developed an internal global pay measurement tool to consistently measure and monitor equitable pay across its workforce. In 2021, they began to assess intersectional gender equity, including factors such as race, ethnicity, and sexual orientation.
- **Marriott International** employees overwhelmingly (90 percent) say it is a great place to work, compared to less than 60 percent at a typical US-based company. Marriott International pledged to hire over 3,000 Ukrainian refugees globally by 2026.
- **Nvidia**, on many 2024 best companies to work lists, provides new hires with a welcome grant of $25 to donate to the charity of their choice and connects employees with volunteer opportunities.
- **Valmont**, a US producer of products for the infrastructure and agriculture markets, launches cross-functional employee "Green Teams" to monitor energy and resource use and improve conservation performance.

Diversity, Equity, and Inclusion (KSI 15.2)

To what extent is the company pushing the boundaries of its industry sector with highly diverse C-suite and staff – and extending its policies to business partners, viewing diversity as promoting business value?

- **H&M** achieved 64 percent of leadership positions and 57 percent of board members held by women in 2023.
- **Hershey's** achieved gender parity among employees in 2023, two years ahead of the 2025 goal and were named a 2022 Best Company for Women by Forbes.
- **Intel** achieved gender pay parity globally in 2019, and racial/ethnic pay parity in the US in 2022.
- **Nike** reported 50 percent women in the workforce and 45 percent in leadership positions while achieving 100 percent pay equity across all employee levels in 2023.
- **Schneider Electric's** Executive Committee (44 percent women) is one of the most gender-balanced senior management teams among large French companies.
- **Starbucks** and **Target** received A+ grades in the 2–24 Racial and Gender Pay Scorecard for disclosures of median and adjusted pay gaps, along with annual commitments to conduct and publish pay equity analyses.

Recruitment and Retention (KSI 15.3)

To what extent does the company's mission, positioning, leadership, and commitment engage the workforce, resulting in a reputation as an employer of choice in recruitment and retention?

- **Alaska Airlines** Annual incentive payout benefits and travel perks bring total payouts for Air Group Employees to $200 M for 2023. Performance-based payouts are "determined by our performance towards specific company-wide goals for safety, guest experience, sustainability and profit."
- **Target** pays for undergraduate and associate degrees for full-time US employees and offers them the chance to apply for Target's sophomore internship program.

Safety Programs and Performance (KSI 15.4)

To what extent have the CEO and C-suite been driving a safety culture that is pervasive and consistently reinforced, earning widespread recognition?

- **Caterpillar** has achieved a 25 percent improvement in recordable injury frequency (RIF) from 2018 to 2023. The company aims for a 50 percent reduction by 2030.
- **DuPont's** commitment to safety, including robust EHS practices, is embedded in company culture, core values, and stakeholder engagements. An Operational Excellence (OpEx) framework of processes and tools manages the work.
- **South32** is developing a critical-minerals mine in the US using remote-automated equipment, creating safer new jobs for the host community in a local control center vs. underground.

Health, Wellness, and Sustainable Lifestyles (KSI 15.5)

To what extent does the company provide formal health and wellness programs to all employees and business partners, including robust mental health programs?

- **Google** increased paid parental leave in 2022 to 24 weeks for birthing parents and 18 weeks for non-birthing parents.
- **Intuit** offers a 401(k) plan with a 125 percent match up to 6 percent of eligible pay, and an Employee Stock Purchase Plan with a 15 percent discount.
- **SAP** offers US employees extensive benefits, including family planning, caregiver support, virtual physiotherapy, financial advising, and free lunches at some locations.

Training and Staff Development (KSI 15.6)

How is the company investing (tools, infrastructure, etc.) to ensure staff understand and are aligned with company ambitions – with high-profile learning for high-potential employees?
- **Danone** launched DanSkills in 2024, open to all employees, to be deployed in 55 countries. Danone provided 1 million training hours annually for 'jobs of the future' in 2024.
- **Johnson & Johnson** makes 'Sustainability & My Job' training available to all employees and includes sustainability in finance and supply chain programs.
- **Starbucks** has partnered with Arizona State University for over a decade, allowing US employees to pursue tuition-free first-time bachelor's degrees.
- **Trane Technologies**' Sustainability Ambassador Network provides all employees on-demand learning pathways, virtual Roundtable events, sustainability challenges and newsletters. The Ambassadors share and implement best practices across the global network.

Employee Engagement (KSI 15.7)

How is the company engaging staff, monitoring, tracking, and supporting employees working on high-impact projects with major sustainability value contribution?
- **Subaru** assists its employees with recycling personal hazardous waste, recycling 31,000 pounds of such waste in 2023.
- **Trane Technologies** measures employee pride, energy, and optimism through its Employee Engagement Index. In its 2023 survey, the company maintained or improved scores on 97 percent of questions, achieving an overall engagement score of 80 out of 100, reflecting the company's commitment to fostering a motivated and optimistic workforce.

Social Performance – Supply Chain

Leading and Transforming companies actively drive social responsibility culture and initiatives throughout their supply chain. They set high standards and work closely with suppliers to create open and trusted collaboration *and* incorporate this philosophy into their procurement practices. Below are the KSIs with selected examples.

Approach to Supply Chain Social Impacts (KSI 16.1)

To what extent is the company partnering with suppliers to drive down negative supply chain social impacts?
- **BlueScope Steel**, an Australian steel company, is training its second-level suppliers in Brazil to recognize and audit for indications of slave labor further down in its complex supply chain.
- **PepsiCo** collaborates with about 2,000 suppliers through the Sustainability Action Center and pep+ REnew to help them get renewable electricity.

Human Rights (KSI 16.2)

How has the company addressed sourcing from countries that exploit their people, including conducting and publishing the results of human rights impact assessments?
- **Eni** ranked third overall in the extractive and apparel sectors and second among energy companies in the 2023 Corporate Human Rights Benchmark.
- **Hitachi.** a member of the United Nations Global Compact since 2009, committed to ensuring no child labor or forced labor in their company or supply chain.
- **Rio Tinto** is consistently ranked as one of the top companies for human rights based on the United Nations Guiding Principles on Business and Human Rights.

Labor Relations (KSI 16.3)

To what extent has the company earned a reputation for demonstrated leadership in promoting labor relations throughout the supply chain?
- **Levi Strauss** launched its Worker Well-being initiative in 2011.In 2020 it covered 300,000 workers in 12 countries, with plans to cover 80 percent of the company's supply chain by 2025.
- **REI** works with tier 1 suppliers to ensure compliance with the REI Factory Code of Conduct, engaging them in corrective action plans when necessary.

Supply Chain Diversity (KSI 16.4)

To what extent has the company established and reported progress on supply chain diversity goals and publicly advocated for diversity across the supply chain?
- **Accenture**'s Diverse Supplier Development Program works with small, medium, diverse, and sustainable suppliers to drive resilience and innovation.

- **Bristol Myers Squibb's** supplier diversity program aims to spend $1 Bn globally with diverse-owned suppliers by 2025.
- **Gap**-owned athleisure brand Athleta continues its legacy of supporting women in sports via its impact fund, The Power of She collective.

Supply Chain Capacity Building (KSI 16.5)

How extensively has the company systematically partnered across the supply chain to eliminate negative impacts and improve overall supplier sustainability performance?
- **BASF**, **Bayer**, **Evonik**, **Henkel**, **Lanxess**, and **Solvay** founded Together for Sustainability in 2011 to promote sustainability in chemical supply chains.
- **Nike** exceeded its goal in 2023 of spending $1 Bn with businesses owned by underrepresented groups such as minorities, women, and veterans.
- **Target** developed Forward Founders, a collection of resources to help early-stage Black business owners and entrepreneurs scale their businesses for mass retail.

Social Performance: Community

Leading and transforming companies take philanthropy to a new level, fully aligned with a strategy of net-positive contribution to society. Below are the KSIs with selected examples.

Philosophy Regarding Community (KSI 17.1)

How is the company embedding itself in communities, driven by value to shareholders and to society – with a goal of creating positive **total societal impact**?
- **Intel** reaches underrepresented groups through Intel Scholars, Relaunch Your Career, and Talent Keepers, aiding people to upskill and work in **STEM** (Science, Technology, Engineering, and Math) fields.
- **OCBC Bank**, one of Southeast Asia's largest banks, expanded its Digital Silvers program to equip elderly customers with digital banking skills.

Engagement with Communities and NGOs (KSI 17.2)

How extensively is the company engaging with communities and NGOs on key societal challenges using a formal, structured process?

- **Natura** partners with families to help them farm sustainably. It provides up to 30 percent extra annual income for ~10,000 families in the Amazon.
- **Starbucks'** Coffee and Farmer Equity program, established with Conservation International, provides training, funding, and resources to help farmers implement sustainable practices and secure fair wages.
- **Warby Parker** aims to provide affordable eyewear. Through its "Buy a Pair, Give a Pair" program, for every pair of glasses sold, the company donates a pair to someone in need. It works with international partners to address vision care inequity globally.

Social Investment (KSI 17.3)

How extensively is the company investing in communities impacted by its full value chain impacts to earn high recognition and trust?

- **Albertsons** in 2023 launched with Uber a food rescue initiative to address food insecurity and food waste in major American cities.
- **IBM** Sustainability Accelerator is a pro bono program that helps nonprofits and governments scale projects for vulnerable populations globally.
- **Novo Nordisk** increased employee volunteer hours in 2023 by 130 percent year on year, the equivalent of five full-time employees for a year.
- **SC Johnson** since 1937 has donated 5 percent of pretax profits to charities.

Community and Stakeholder Partnerships (KSI 17.4)

To what extent is the CEO joining other leaders in high-impact partnerships with NGOs and supply chain partners to tackle a material value chain impact and major societal challenge?

- **Bayer** joined with Purdue University in 2024, launching the Coalition for Sustainable and Regenerative Agriculture to improve soil health while increasing crop outputs.
- **Cemex** partnered with nonprofit VeryNile to remove discarded plastic from the Nile River, converting it into biofuels for a cement processing plant.

- **IKEA,** partnering with the Forest Stewardship Council (FSC), commits to using only recycled or FSC-certified wood across all products by 2030, incorporating audits, certifications, and transparency protocols.
- **Levi Strauss** launched Time to Vote, a nonpartisan campaign that helps workers at more than 2,000 companies vote without losing paid hours.

Infrastructure Development (KSI 17.5)

How is the company partnering with others, such as in eco-parks and smart cities, to enhance societal value?
- **Holcim** has built the world's first plant to produce low-carbon cement (ECO-Pact). It can reduce the embodied carbon of buildings, infrastructure and homes by at least 30 percent without offsets.
- **IBM** partnered with a French NGO to analyze social media data to address deforestation and climate impacts where most of the world's palm oil is sourced.
- **Toyota** has raised $150 M for its climate fund, investing in companies and new tech-focused on combating climate change.

Community Job Creation (KSI 17.6)

To what extent does the company drive business development programs to enhance job creation nationally and in traditionally underserved communities?
- **Apple** launched its Racial Equity and Justice Initiative in 2023 to support minority businesses and funding access.
- **Enbridge**, a multinational pipeline and energy company, partnered with a consortium of six First Nations and Métis communities to develop a 200 MW wind energy project in Saskatchewan.
- **JPMorgan Chase**'s AdvancingCities initiative is a five-year, $500 M initiative that promotes inclusive economic growth across the country.

Part Three: **Chart Your Course**

Chapter 10
Preparing for Boardroom Discussions

It is difficult to get a man to understand something when his salary depends on his not understanding it.
Upton Sinclair

The most successful companies plan and execute over a five-to-seven-year horizon, according to McKinsey research.

The global climate that companies operate in five-to-seven-years from now will differ dramatically from today. Here is a peek at **The Climate Story** – for a sense of what's in store.

 The Climate Story: A simplified version[*]

1. **Population** explosion among the middle-class, alongside the demand for AI, are driving up electricity demand. Global energy demand is growing by the equivalent of Japan's annual use each year.
2. **CO_2** exceeded 420 parts per million in the atmosphere in 2024 and levels continue to rise. These levels were last seen 3 million years ago, with sea levels up to 60 feet higher.
3. **Air temperature** in 2024 exceeded the Paris Agreement target increase of 1.5°C (2.7°F) 26 years early. Temperatures will reach 2°C (3.6°F) above pre-industrial levels by 2040.
4. **Ocean temperatures** have surged sharply since 2000, and especially more recently, accelerating sea level rise.
5. **Sea level rise:** From 2005 to 2015, sea level increased at 2.5x the rate of the previous century, some areas more than others. Since then, the rate has increased. The coast of Savannah, Georgia, added 7 inches from 2010 to 2024.
6. **Adverse weather events** related to climate change directly affected one in five people from 2014 to 2023. The number of global events with over a billion dollars of damage has roughly doubled each of the past two decades.
7. **Insurance** plays an outsize role; pricing in the risk of storms and fires, raising premiums; cutting back coverage; leaving regions – after paying out more in claims than received in premiums in the US the past decade.
8. **Capital markets:** Banks are reducing exposure to climate risk, reducing carbon-intensive financing, and limiting lending to high-risk sectors.

[*]See Appendix A for full version of The Climate Story and visit https://the-climate-story.com/.

The climate story poses considerable financial impacts to companies over the next five years. **The trends are locked in. Impacts will accelerate**.

The consequences could be profound. *Without insurance, lenders won't offer a mortgage; without a mortgage, most Americans cannot buy a home.*

https://doi.org/10.1515/9783111548852-011

Strategic Plan Discussions

At the end of each fiscal year, the board typically reviews and approves the company's strategic and operational plans. At that point, it's likely too late to ask tough questions about the company's future direction.

The time for asking those provocative questions is months earlier, during the strategic planning working sessions. That's when to review these climate challenges in the context of the current sustainability goals and roadmap.

 Status of Company Climate Goals

Status:
- Over 90 percent of companies provide climate reporting.
- 88 percent of companies are committed to implementing TCFD or ISSB.
- 80 percent have a stated ambition to reach net zero by 2050 or sooner.

Challenges:
- Fewer than 40 percent of the Global 2000 companies have a net zero commitment covering Scopes 1, 2, and 3.
- Less than 10 percent publish a decarbonization pathway aligned with 1.5°C (2.7°F).
- Fewer than half of CEOs believe their firms will meet their net zero targets.
- Only 16 percent of these 2000 companies are on track to reach net-zero by 2050.
- Leading companies (Microsoft, Google, Walmart, etc.) are reneging on their climate commitments.

Questions:
- Is this situation acceptable?
- Are we satisfied with the current trajectory of our company's climate goals and progress?

Do we just carry on with our strategic planning and hope (in the US) that the second Trump administration will somehow reduce the urgency of climate action?

Every Corporate Leader has a Key Role

With CEOs and their teams focused on the one-to-three-year window, and climate risks and uncertainty escalating daily, there is only one conclusion:

Boards must, in collaboration with the CEO, own the climate and sustainability agenda as part of their fiduciary duty.

But that does not mean everyone else sits on the sidelines hoping for action. On the contrary, every leader has a key role.

- *Finance* owns the new sustainable growth metrics and systems; the impact of climate scenarios; assessment of life cycle product impacts; enterprise risk; and costing of carbon.
- *Human resources* partners with finance on sustainable growth metrics and systems and owns the system of incentives and goals. They can leverage the company's sustainability position to drive down recruitment costs, improve retention, and enhance productivity.
- *Supply chain,* in most companies, is accountable for around half of the company's full negative environmental and social impacts.
- *Operations* is directly responsible for climate change impacts caused by the production of products and services.
- *Marketing and sales* owns engagement with customers to help them decarbonize and dematerialize.
- *Public affairs* owns the calls for transparency.

Topics for Strategy and Boardroom Discussions

Table 10.1 lists 15 topics for discussion in the strategy development process and in the boardroom.

The topics are grouped in a simple planning framework ("Where do we want to go? Where are we today? How do we get there?").

In the balance of this chapter, each of the 15 topics is examined, with a key question followed by sub-questions, many gleaned during my recent research on enhancing board fluency in sustainability.

How to Position for Sustainable Growth

To define where the company wants to be five to ten years out to win in the marketplace, start with a clear picture of market signals, including how the climate story will likely unfold. I repeat a statement from the Introduction:

 Pause for Reflection

It's hard to make a good argument for being less smart than your competitors about the major trends impacting your businesses.

Table 10.1: Key Questions for Boardroom Discussion

15 Topics and Questions for Boardroom Discussion	Full Board & Executive Committee	Board Committees				
		Nominating & Governance	Audit/Finance	Human Resources; Compensation	Technology/ Operations	Corporate Responsibility*
How do we Position for Sustainable Growth?						
1. Grasp Market Signals and The Climate Story	✓					✓
2. Engage Tomorrow's Customers	✓				✓	
3. Examine Climate and Business Scenarios	✓		✓			✓
4. Review Purpose, Vision, Mission	✓					✓
5. Reimagine Product Offerings					✓	✓
6. Review Criteria for Key Business Decisions	✓					✓
How Good Are We Today – Really?						
7. Map Current Sustainable Growth Position	✓					✓
8. Assess Full Life-Cycle Impacts: Positive & Negative			✓			✓
9. Upgrade Disclosure and Transparency		✓				✓
10. Reassess Board Sustainability Oversight	✓	✓				
What's Our Roadmap and Action Plan?						
11. Set 10-Year Strategic Plan, Goals, and Roadmap	✓					
12. Build Sustainable Growth Metrics and Systems			✓	✓		✓
13. Create Inspiring Culture via Incentives and Goals	✓			✓		
14. Align Sustainability with Innovation Pipeline					✓	
15. Structure Sustainable Growth Leadership		✓		✓		✓

*Refers to the board committee having the greatest direct oversight of sustainability issues

To create a full understanding of how to position the company for sustainable growth, learn from customers and engage in robust scenario planning. Then, re-imagine the company's vision and purpose as well as the core customer offerings.

How do we Position for Sustainable Growth?

---

1. Grasp Market Signals and the Climate Story

Since many of the key business decisions we make this year will impact the company in the next decade, what do market signals and the climate story say about how to win in the marketplace in the next five to seven years?

- How is the organization building an understanding of key risks to our operations, business model, and offerings?
  - How will the EU, UK, CA, and other mandatory reporting standards likely play out over the next 2–3 years?
  - How are leading companies globally responding to CSRD, and other regulations? How do they see market signals unfolding in the next five years?
  - How will the growing impact of adverse weather events and the response by the insurance and banking sectors impact our company and industry?
- By 2030, Millennials and Gen Zers will comprise 70 percent of the workforce, customers, and investors. What impacts will they have on our business model and the long-term viability of our businesses?

---

2. Engage Tomorrow's Customers

How confident are we that the company is positioned to be the supplier of choice for customers embracing rapid decarbonization, dematerialization, and societal value?

- How does the current 'system' of engaging with customers – in terms of frequency, seniority, and impact of customer engagement – compare with best-in-class?
- Which customers are best aligned to grow as EU, UK, and CA standards come into effect over the next two-to-three years?
- Which potential new customers should management engage with?
- What specific actions can we take to help our customers accelerate reaching their net zero and other sustainability targets?

---

3. Examine Climate and Business Scenarios

Given climate impacts under both 1.5°C and 2.0°C scenarios, how is our company considering the potential business impacts of unforeseen events?

- How do the results of the climate scenarios the company has conducted compare with those of leading customers and competitors?
- How robustly have we summarized climate scenarios for the board, articulating risks to our operations and businesses the next five to seven-years?
- What is the best way for our board and management to engage in a robust *business* scenario process that builds on *climate* scenarios?
- How does the long-term viability of our core businesses look in the face of alternate climate and business scenarios?

(continued)

How do we Position for Sustainable Growth?

4. **Review Purpose, Vision, Mission**

How will our company fare in potential future rankings of "best global companies" where the core metrics *are truly sustainable growth* and *net-positive contribution to society*?

- What can we learn from successful sustainable growth companies that have been transforming their lines of business, offerings, and business models to achieve rapid decarbonization and dematerialization?
- What metrics should the company embrace to measure a net-positive contribution to society, looking ahead to 2030 and 2035?
- How clearly does the company's vision, mission, and purpose embrace decoupling growth from environmental impact, carbon and otherwise?
- How might we recast the company's vision, mission, and purpose considering a broader view of what constitutes sustainable growth going forward?

---

5. **Reimagine Product Offerings**

Over the next three to five years, what portion of the company's revenue can derive from products and services that deliver a measurable net-positive impact across the value chain?

- How robustly are we taking full ownership of the full life-cycle impacts of the products and services that we sell?
- To what extent are we measuring the full life-cycle GHG impacts of producing our products and services – along with measuring how much GHG emission reductions our products can help customers achieve?
- How well is the company capturing value from customer offerings that are traceable to raw material sources, durable, biodegradable, recyclable or reusable, highly water efficient, and/or highly carbon efficient?
- How thoroughly have we explored optimizing our portfolio of products and services to ensure long-term viability under different climate and business scenarios?

---

6. **Review Criteria for Key Business Decisions**

What criteria should the company have to ensure key business decisions made in the boardroom, and those down the organization, will ensure long-term, 'truly' sustainable growth?

- What criteria exist in our "key business decision checklist" for decisions made in the boardroom and by the C-suite?
- To what extent are management's business decision criteria grounded in decoupling growth from full life-cycle environmental and social impacts?
- How do we best incorporate an increasing cost of carbon, aligned with that of top-tier companies?
- How do we ensure decisions will enhance the long-term viability of our businesses and customer offerings in a future that prioritizes decarbonization and dematerialization?

Assessing Our Company Today

If we buy into the idea that sustainability is about decoupling growth from negative environmental and social impacts, we must be aligned on an honest, objective assessment of our company today.

How Good Are We Today – Really?

---

7. Map Current Sustainable Growth Position
How well is our company positioned today as the clean economy unfolds?
- How do our company's material environmental and social impacts – full life-cycle impacts including climate – break down across the value chain?
- As we benchmark peers, how good is the company, really:
  - On strategic positioning for future sustainable growth?
  - When compared with leaders decoupling growth from impacts?
- How extensively are we partnering with customers to drive increased recycling, reuse, and recovery at product end-of-life?
- How well positioned is the company to drive growth while systematically reducing full life-cycle impacts over the next five-to-seven years?

8. Assess Full life-Cycle Impacts: Positive and Negative
Stepping back from the hundreds of sustainability disclosure requirements regarding our operations and products, what is the overall full life-cycle impact of the company, positive and negative, on society?
- What is our total carbon footprint across the value chain? How does that compare with peers and leaders?
- How robustly are we:
  - Addressing the company's *resource inputs* (including raw materials and process components) to grow the portion that is renewable, recyclable, biodegradable, or otherwise sustainably sourced?
  - Growing the company's *resource outputs* (products and non-product outputs) that are biodegradable, recyclable, returnable, etc.?
- What is the social impact of our company throughout the value chain on core metrics including human health, human rights, **living wage**, etc.?

9. Upgrade Disclosure and Transparency
With growing pressure from regulators and investors on greenwashing, how closely aligned are the company's climate and sustainability positions with its marketing claims and public policy positions?
- What discrepancies would an outside analysis of the company's public policy positions via industry association membership, political contributions, and the like reveal, compared against the company's stated sustainability posture and goals?

(continued)

How Good Are We Today – Really?

- Which industry associations does the company belong to that are either neutral on global climate change impacts or question climate science – and what are the risks of continuing membership?
- What would a critical, science-based analysis of the product sustainability claims, such as green, biodegradable, recyclable and healthy, reveal?

---

10. Reassess Board Sustainability Oversight

How can we position the company to deliver 'truly' sustainable growth and profitability in a global marketplace, embracing rapid decarbonization and resource efficiency?

Structure

- What new skills, geographic insights, and life experience are needed to build and execute a five-to-ten-year 'truly' sustainable growth transformation path?
- How quickly can we build our 'ideal' board diversity, especially of gender, geography, and life experiences?
- What specific actions should we, as a full board, undertake? What material risks should each committee address? (See Table 11.1.)
- How robust are the climate and sustainability oversight duties as reflected in our board charters when compared with board charters of leaders across industry sectors?

Fluency

- How can we build our individual and collective knowledge about impacts and opportunities posed as climate and other material risks accelerate and the clean economy unfolds?
- How do we best enhance our climate and sustainability fluency:
  o   Learning from leaders of transformation companies?
  o   Outside advisors with expertise in our material issues and deep experience in board governance?
  o   Courses or other learning engagements to consider?
- How do we measure our individual and collective fluency in climate and other material sustainable issues?

Cadence

- How should we revise our board self-assessment process to address:
  o   The growing physical climate impacts and our company's need to transition in order to reduce risk and capture opportunities?
  o   The reporting and disclosure requirements from the EU, UK, CA, and other jurisdictions?
- How do we best integrate sustainability into next year's board scenario and strategy review sessions?
- How can we ensure the work of our individual board committees covers all the critical bases?
- How can we build a cadence of learning about climate and other material issues into a multi-year calendar of board meeting locations and agendas?

Roadmap and Action Plan

Driving successful sustainable growth, whether in the past or going forward, requires planning and executing on a five-to-seven-year horizon. For many companies, this requires a refreshed strategic planning process; considerable upgrading of financial, human resources, and innovation systems and processes; and truly exceptional organization structure.

What's Our Roadmap and Action Plan?

---

11. Set 10-Year Strategic Plan, Goals and Roadmap
Planning Process
How do we maximize the value of our annual strategy process to position the company for sustainable growth in the next five to seven years?
- McKinsey data strongly confirms that the most successful companies plan and execute over a five-to-seven-year horizon. As global climate risks escalate over that same horizon, how should we adjust our strategic planning timeframe and process to address that?
- How have we addressed the results of climate scenarios aligned with EU, UK, CA, and other standards?
- Have we translated those climate scenarios into business scenarios that help the company position core offerings to win in the marketplace in five to ten years?
- How different would our strategic plan be if we started with a ten-year net-positive impact, full value chain goal and built our strategy from that?

Goals and Roadmap
What few long-term goals help our company systematically decouple growth from negative environmental and social impacts?
- How does management's approach to addressing the company's material environmental and social impacts (full life-cycle impacts including climate) compare with best-in-class?
- How does our internal cost of carbon compare with that of industry leaders?
- What five-to-ten-year goal will help the company:
  - Track reduction of our impacts, including carbon and other material issues, while growing revenue?
  - Measure the portion of total revenue derived from sustainability-advantaged offerings?

12. Build Sustainable Growth Metrics and Systems
How fast can we build world-class systems that help the company efficiently track decoupling environmental impact from growth?
- How do our systems compare with best-in-class for measuring full life cycle:
  - Carbon reduction?
  - Nature of materials sourced?
  - Nature of product and non-product outputs, including waste?

(continued)

What's Our Roadmap and Action Plan?

- How completely do our internal systems align with the most aggressive global disclosure standards and what investors are increasingly looking for?
- How can we use our systems to drive competitive advantage?

---

13. Create Inspiring Culture via Incentives and Goals

How can we be sure our core incentives system, grounded in executive compensation and goals, supports growing pressure from investors and regulators?

- How does the portion of executive incentive compensation based on sustainability targets compare with best-in-class?
- How directly do the sustainability metrics in our executive incentive compensation program align with climate impacts and other material issues?
- How directly does our incentive system support decoupling revenue growth from negative environmental and social impacts across the value chain?
- How can we incentivize and align every employee to drive our company toward winning a future "most sustainable company" award?

---

14. Align Sustainability with Innovation Pipeline

How can we align our innovation and R&D investments to deliver rapid decarbonization and dematerialization solutions in the next five-to-seven years?

- How will the R&D investments made over the past five years impact our ability to decouple growth from negative environmental and social impact?
- What criteria should the company have today for screening innovation and research ideas to ensure they help drive decarbonization and dematerialization across the value chain?

---

15. Structure Sustainable Growth Leadership

How do we best organize for planning and executing 'truly' sustainable growth over the next five to seven years?

- Do we have the right sustainability leadership structure, including a:
  - Senior or executive vice president and CSO (reporting to the CEO) who is a strong advocate for and well-versed in sustainability; and whose portfolio requires a longer-term outlook (on innovation and technology, strategy, etc.)?
  - Vice president of sustainability with the resources and clout inside the company to impact key business decisions and business leader actions, such as providing key input to incentive compensation performance metrics?
- Do functional leaders each have explicit accountability for the relevant climate and sustainability roles – reporting to relevant the board committee?
- Is our executive sustainability council hardwired to the top operating committee (likely two-to-three individuals overlap)?
- How should we engage external advisor(s) or an advisory council to help calibrate with leadership actions of other companies?

Chapter 11
Conclusion – Making Companies *Fit*

Net zero 2050 is an absolute disaster for mankind, serving only one master: The fossil fuel sector.
Andrew Forrest, CEO, Fortescue (global mining company)

We stand at a pivotal moment in history. The entire global economic system is built on assumptions eroding in front of our eyes. Market forces, societal trends, and resource constraints are converging at a global scale for the first time in history.

Global, national, and local approaches to tackling climate change are not working. The business approach to addressing sustainability has failed.

ESG, as many have understood it, is dead for two reasons: the term never incorporated strategy and execution, the missing, critical components of sustainability and the recent politicization of the acronym.

It's simply more profitable in the short term to be unsustainable. Wall Street rewards short-term results. Companies can best deliver short-term growth and profits by milking current business models and staying under the radar.

After three decades of dancing around the edges of sustainability, it's time for companies to look in the mirror. **Sidestepping worked for a while, but the deadline now stares us in the face. Take off the blinders**. Climate is becoming a pocketbook issue for many Americans. We know fossil fuels are cooking the planet. The underlying trends are baked in. (See Appendix A: The Climate Story.)

The 2025 California fires are the most recent calling cards. As major insurers exited the state or cut back coverage, hundreds of thousands of homeowners shifted to California's state-run backstop, the FAIR Plan, whose exposure has tripled since 2020 to $458 billion. It had only $2.5 billion in reinsurance and $200 million in cash following the January 2025 fires.[1]

As extreme weather, ocean warming, and wildfires begin to impact capital values, the global outcry to decarbonize at pace will become impossible to ignore. High-emitting companies will become dinosaurs, unable to retain staff, leverage their balance sheet or win in new markets. **It is highly likely the tide will turn over the next five to seven years with a global outcry to decarbonize.** Companies will need to respond.

Regardless of industry sector, every company must rethink how it can generate 'truly' sustainable growth – not only growth of revenue and profits. Businesses must also *decouple growth and profitability from resource intensity*. Hitting pause on rapid decarbonization across the value chain is a fool's errand.

https://doi.org/10.1515/9783111548852-012

A handful of global companies – *Enel, Mars, Neste, Ørsted, Marks & Spencer, Schneider Electric, Trane Technologies,* and *Unilever* – have demonstrated this type of business transformation.

To guide boards, C-suite executives, and their teams to thrive in this new world, I've delivered three simple messages.

 Pause for Reflection

1. The **urgency of the global climate situation** presents huge risks to every company. It also offers the greatest business opportunities in over 100 years. But as Appendix A: The Climate Story conveys, hitting pause on rapid decarbonization across the value chain is a fool's errand.
2. Each company's **board of directors must own the climate agenda,** in collaboration with the CEO. Fiduciary responsibilities demand oversight of the company over the five-to-seven-year period. The one-to-three-year strategic planning horizon will not cut it.
3. **Citizens, students, educators, investors, and every business professional can influence how companies respond.** You can educate yourselves on The Climate Story and how to think about sustainable growth going forward. CEOs and corporate secretaries can use it to reframe board agendas. Boards can measure performance today and chart a course forward.

Barriers to Change

Twenty-five years ago, Shell asked me and my Arthur D. Little colleagues to define the business case for sustainability.

Yet, still today, far too often, **the business case rules for *not* being sustainable**.

A powerful inertia remains to maintain the status quo despite an imperative for reform. Only 12 percent of major change programs, such as those to drive operational efficiency, customer experience, and so forth, produce lasting results, according to McKinsey.[2] Often, the C-suite accepts partial outcomes and moves on.[3]

Three well-known paradoxes help explain why companies prolong the status quo.

– **The Tragedy of the Commons** arises when multiple people acting independently and rationally, with unfettered access to a finite, valuable resource such as a stable climate, pursue their own self-interest. They ultimately overuse the resource and may destroy its value.
– **The Prisoner's Dilemma** describes when two informed, rational agents either cooperate for mutual benefit or betray their partner for individual gain. The climate analogy goes like this: if companies collectively shift to cleaner

energy, a cooler climate benefits all over the medium and long term. But in the short term, each company has an individual incentive to cash in on fossil fuels.

- **Jevons Paradox:** Time and again, history shows that as technology advances, we often consume *more*, not less. The nineteenth-century English economist William Stanley Jevons noticed that as steam engines became more efficient, Britain's appetite for coal *increased*. This is playing out today with the demand for power from AI tools, such as ChatGPT. Efficiency improvements make them more accessible. More people adopt them, and existing users rely on them more frequently, increasing overall energy use.

The re-election of Donald Trump, who has called climate change a hoax, may seem like an open invitation for US corporate leaders to downplay sustainability. 'Drill, baby, drill' culture is back in power. CEOs continue to hit the pause button regarding climate – kicking the can down the road.

The temptation for many boards is to defer to their CEOs on climate and sustainability. However, **that is a big mistake**.

To help reimagine the company's future, it's useful to step outside the corporate world and consider *tomorrow's fit corporation*.

Tomorrow's *Fit* Corporation

Corporate leaders can gain insight from the attributes and habits of elite athletes competing in team events. **Picture what being *fit* looks and feels like.**

- **Eyes on the prize.** From a very young age, future Olympians hold close a clear, inspiring vision of what is possible. Whether they end up on the podium or not, once they compete, they remain Olympians for life. They have endured an arduous journey, buried in the daily grind. The end prize of permanent Olympian status steels them through the monotony.
- **A few simple metrics.** How does a junior athlete and aspiring Olympian measure progress? Answer: a few simple metrics and consistent improvement. Track what you did today. Focus on tomorrow. Win the next race. Learn new skills. Keep progressing. The initial focus is on individual metrics: what do I need to do to improve my scores; my times?
- **Ten year roadmap.** Athletes do not start with the perfect roadmap. They keep the vision close yet focus on the next day. They practice relentlessly and achieve short-term goals. They learn from mistakes. When pain or setback strikes, they keep a short memory, rebound, and hit hard. Even during failure, they succeed by keeping their eyes on the prize.

Elite athletes competing in team events understand what perfection looks like – when the team pulls in the same direction, in sync. Corporate leaders can do the same.

A CEO watching team events at Paris 2024 may have seen what a dream team looks and feels like. The women's rowing eight; the track and field mixed relay race; the men's football (soccer) final. What if your corporate team were as fit and in sync as those athletes?

 **Confession**

I have had the privilege of witnessing Olympic athletes up close. For ten years leading up to London 2012, I cheered our daughter, Kristin, as she pursued her dream of rowing in the Olympics.

The path was rough. Tracking daily workouts. Learning from mistakes. Perfecting skills to the tiniest detail. Enduring pain. What you hear about 10,000 hours to perfect a practice is true. In her case: three hours a day, seven days a week, fifty-two weeks a year, ten years, just to get in the arena. She kept her eyes on the prize and ultimately punched her ticket to London.

How fast can you say, "beep-beep?" In her case, qualifying for London 2012 Summer Olympics came down to winning a single race by 0.08 seconds.

While she was training, I spent that decade helping global companies begin to tackle ESG challenges. These were tough years for executives pushing the sustainability agenda during and following the Great Recession. Companies I worked with, including many industry leaders, made incremental progress. But they found it tough to operate outside their comfort zone.

Perhaps more than any other trait, **the need to operate outside of their comfort zone** is the immediate challenge for boards and company leaders. Every company that aims to reach the future prize, of competing in the marketplace in five or ten years, must:

- Set its eyes on becoming a true sustainable growth leader.
- Establish several simple metrics that will decouple growth from environmental and social impacts.
- Launch a ten-year transformation roadmap and ensure each key business decision drives toward the goal.

My advice for corporate leaders: **place yourself five to ten years from now and look back.**

Think about the time it takes to execute key business decisions made in the boardroom, such as making a major acquisition; launching a new product, service, or solution; closing a key plant; or building a new plant. Those decisions likely play out over many years.

The same is true for a major business transformation. What your company needs today is *not* a transformation *program*; it is transformation itself.
- *Transformation program:* often viewed as more work for all with questionable payoff.
- *Transformation path:* aligning with sustainability principles will inspire and energize your employees.

If the goal is to be a truly fit company, where are most companies today?

Today's *Unfit* Companies

Let's be blunt – most companies are not seriously engaging with sustainability.

They plod along, hitting snooze every time they hear about record heat or fires or floods or droughts. They carry on, profiting with business models crafted in the old economy. They design, make, and sell the same types of products as in the past. In their wake, they leave a trail of unintended consequences:
- Sourced materials with tons of embedded carbon pollution that leave mountains of waste in their wake.
- Dumpsters full of non-product output and waste discarded daily from the company's own operations, even by those claiming efficiency.
- Products that deliver to customers a burden of negative impacts – carbon pollution during use, plastic packaging that is not easily recycled.

Company leaders today find climate change and sustainability broadly important. CEOs assign a senior executive to look after it. They set goals and reduce their footprints. They report progress.

But, for all the time spent, they are almost all just ***dabbling*** in sustainability. Most companies are acting at the margins. ESG and sustainability have mostly been **bolted on, not woven in.**

Even companies widely regarded as sustainability leaders, like **Microsoft**, have backtracked on otherwise strong targets. Its overall GHG emissions were 30 percent higher in 2024 than in 2020 – as it doubles down on AI despite the carbon implications. **Google**'s GHG emissions rose 48 percent since 2019.

What about the "top half" companies across industries globally, the ones that have been investing significantly in sustainability over the past decade or more? The answer appears in Figure 11.1.

For 25 years, I have measured corporate progress on sustainability. ESG Navigator data from ~ 150 major global companies shows that they are only at an average Stage 2 on our four-stage maturity scale. They have been taking an incremen-

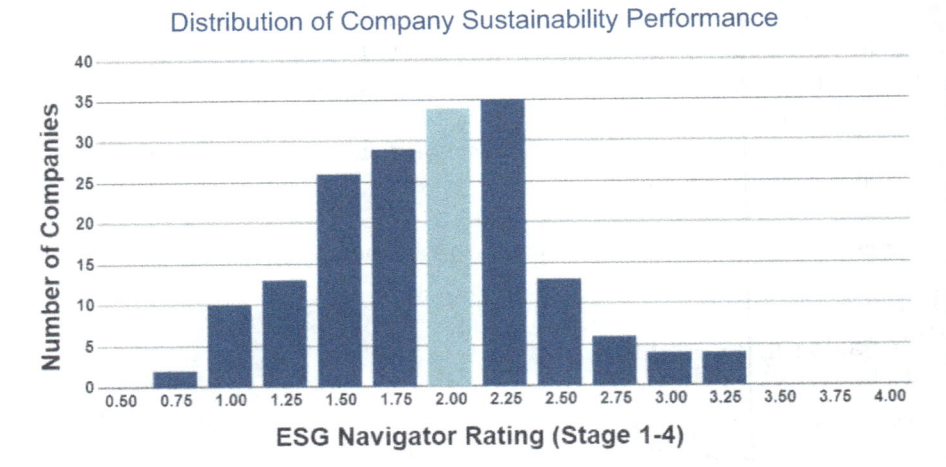

Figure 11.1: Overall Sustainability Performance of Major Companies
Source: ESG Navigator

tal approach. Yet many of these companies attract praise for being among the top half in their industry in sustainability reputation.

2035 is the New 2050

Andrew Forrest of Fortescue captured the challenge perfectly: the era of getting away with unintended consequences is over.

Net zero by 2050? Doesn't come close. 2050 was supposed to be the year society held global GHG emissions such that global temperatures remained no more than 1.5°C above preindustrial times. The problem: we reached that long-term target in 2024.

Climate risks are large, steadily growing, hardwired, and unswayed by political winds. The laws of nature do not allow businesses to carry on with current business models and gradually meet net zero in 2050.

Fossil fuels supply about 80 percent of global energy. The explosion of AI is driving up a ravenous hunger for energy, resulting in growing levels of CO_2 in the atmosphere.

Navigating Sustainable Growth

Sustainable growth of the past is evolving into **'truly' sustainable growth** of the future. As noted earlier, *more good; less bad.*

At its core, sustainability requires adopting an often uncomfortable set of assumptions about the world. It involves 'unlearning' the way industrial society has operated for 150 years. It demands learning a new route to deliver value for shareholders and society.

In any company, only a handful of individuals – the CEO supported by a few strong board members – can drive transformation.

If climate and sustainability are not key discussion topics for your board, they should be. Not just once or twice a year. Not just under the purview of a single board committee. Not as a bullet point in a board committee charter. Not limited to the board pack and pre-reads. Not just in reaction to external ESG ratings or internal company reports on progress and goals.

The board's role includes overseeing a set of five-to-seven-year indicators that drive the company transformation, decoupling growth from negative environmental and social impacts. Then, it must hold the CEO accountable for delivering.

The window of opportunity

The window of opportunity is closing, as shown in Figure 11.2. In five years, it may be too late to position your company ahead of competitors. You may be playing catch-up.

In 2030, 70 percent of the workforce will comprise Millennials and GenZers. They care about climate change. **Why would a young adult in 2030 want to work for a company making the climate situation worse?**

Established companies need to transform to win the war for talent, engage customers by helping them rapidly decarbonize and align with the circular economy, and earn the trust of stakeholders, including shareholders. **Enormous fortunes will be won and lost.**

Few companies recognize climate, sustainability, and ESG issues this way. But a growing number of leading companies do, and they are transparently reporting on it in the same way they account for and disclose their business performance.

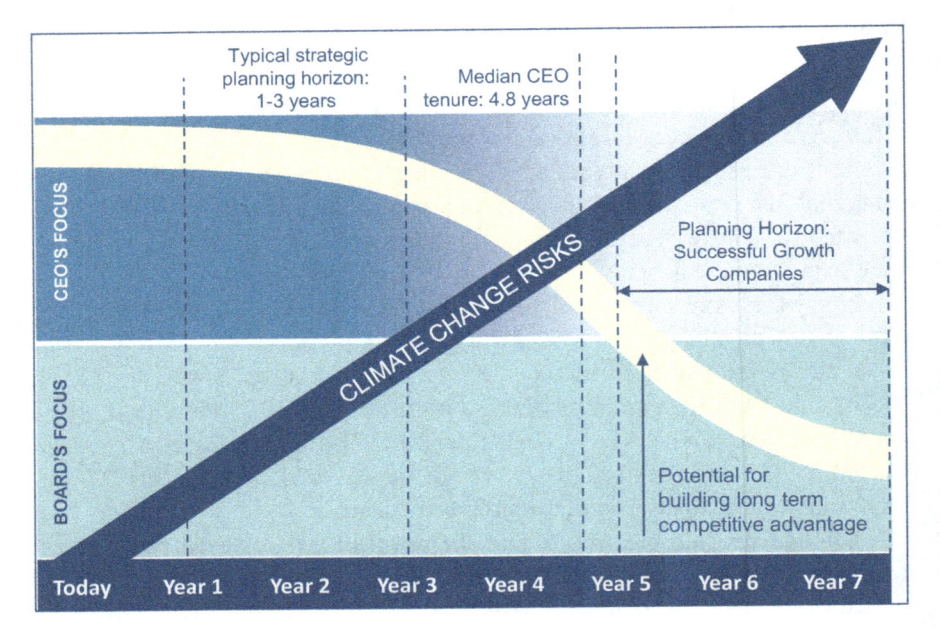

Figure 11.2: The Window of Opportunity is Closing

What's Next?

It's worth recalling a famous aphorism:

There are decades where nothing happens, and there are weeks when decades happen.

Sometimes, individuals and companies overcomplicate things. Yes, sustainability can be challenging, perplexing, and amorphous. Helping to solve climate change, tackle world hunger, protect human rights, and provide access to clean drinking water sounds daunting.

Since the first commercial oil well in 1859 heralded the modern petroleum industry, hydrocarbons have infused virtually every aspect of society. Within the next few years, however, humanity needs to make a 180-degree turn: continue enjoying the benefits of a modernizing society while rapidly decarbonizing the global economy.

At some point. . .

. . .the first light bulb goes on in the C-suite or boardroom. Board members reflect on the mess humans are making of the planet. They foresee the global impact of middle-class consumption doubling despite fixed planetary resources. They think about stranded assets, and they recognize that sustainability risks and opportunities are several orders of magnitude higher than in the past. They ask, *"If we were creating our company from scratch today, what would it look like?"*

. . .and then a second light bulb goes on. The executive team begins to see the climate situation not only as a source of risk, but also as a huge business opportunity. They imagine growing a profitable business without consuming nonrenewable resources.

To build tomorrow's fit company, follow this simple agenda –

- **Eyes on the prize:** A refreshed company vision anchored in truly sustainable growth will excite and inspire current and potential employees and business partners. Imagine building your company from the ground up, targeting zero carbon and zero waste throughout the value chain. Learn fast. Understand the magnitude, scale, and urgency of climate risks.
- **A few simple metrics.** Unilever's former CEO Paul Polman showed the simple metric: decouple growth from environmental impact. Since 2010, other companies have followed. Build powerful incentives and metrics driving a culture where all the executive team members pull in the same direction – with the rest of the staff rowing together.
- **Ten-year roadmap:** Take stock: measure your company's full value chain impacts. Build your net zero roadmap. Work with suppliers and customers to close the loop on waste. Engage with people who can influence your business.

Tomorrow's leading companies will systematically shed their old ways of thinking and working, the obsolete ways of doing business in the "take-make-waste" world. They will embrace, drive, and reap the benefits from the circular economy, reconsidering every business activity as a closed loop. They will change the way they talk about their company, shedding linear terminology such as supply chain and value chain. The refreshed vision, mission, and purpose, supported by aligned incentives, will inspire employees.

Business leaders have a choice: ***Will we "stay the course" and hope for the best? Or will we transform and position our company as fit for tomorrow?***

Game on!

Notes

1 https://www.wsj.com/economy/consumers/the-world-is-getting-riskier-americans-dont-want-to-pay-for-it-51901067

2 https://www.mckinsey.com/capabilities/implementation/our-insights/how-to-implement-transformations-for-long-term-impact

3 Michael Mankins and Patrick Litre, "Transformations That Work," Harvard Business Review, May-June 2024.

Epilogue: It's Your Legacy

Far and away the best prize that life has to offer is the chance to work hard at work worth doing.
Teddy Roosevelt

I have had the privilege of advising CEOs and boards of directors on dozens of occasions over the past few decades. I am not so naïve as to think a business leader should act on sustainability or ESG simply because "it's the right thing to do."

But I have a final plea for today's business leaders.

Step back. Learn about climate change. Ask how you would design your company from a blank slate today. The answer will provide inspiration.

Be proud to tell your kids what you do. It may also help cement your legacy.

> **Reflection:**
> I learned about legacy from my son, Matt, when he was five years old.
>
> As I tucked him into the upper bunk after the early days of pre-school, I was rubbing his back when he suddenly jerked up on his elbows, looked me in the eye, and said, "Galen's daddy is a firefighter!"
>
> "Wow," I said. "That's awesome," and resumed rubbing his back, knowing with trepidation what would come next.
>
> "Daddy, what do you do?"
>
> Ouch, I thought. How do I tell Matt I am a management consultant specializing in helping Fortune 500 companies manage their environmental obligations? I am a professional service provider, not a firefighter.
>
> I mumbled something about stopping big companies from littering.
>
> The next night, tucking Matt into bed, I asked what he told his class. "My daddy works for the world," he said.

https://doi.org/10.1515/9783111548852-013

Appendix A: The Climate Story in 8 Steps

Climate change features daily in our news. The most respected mainstream business press – the Financial Times, The Economist and Harvard Business Review – all acknowledge its complicity in escalating risks to businesses. Consensus is growing that significant negative climate impacts are already being felt, greater risks are imminent, and businesses must respond now. Failure to take bold action will affect long-term competitiveness.

Meanwhile, substantial opportunities exist to hasten the transition to a low-carbon economy while creating profitable, resilient and sustainable enterprises.

Despite widespread acknowledgment of urgent climate risks, however, companies mostly address climate and sustainability at the margins. They may take ad hoc action but mostly leave core business models and offerings unchanged. Three major factors influence the hesitancy to adapt:

- **Short-term Strategic Planning:** Most planning horizons are short-term, typically three years, leading to a mindset of compliance and cost-control.
- **Background Noise:** Non-scientific climate denial, often self-motivated, coupled with domestic and geopolitical uncertainties, allows companies to delay proactive, futureproofing—long-term action that would build climate resilience.
- **Lack of a Clear Storyline:** C-suite executives and boards lack a logical, clear, science-based storyline as background for sound, long-term decision-making.

As the frequency of climate-related disruptions increases, so do financial risks. Corporate leaders need to better understand how climate risk directly impacts their balance sheets and their ability to deliver sustainable growth.

Here is the climate story, at its most simple, for board members and corporate leaders.

We recognize the need for corporate leaders to articulate how these eight logical and sequential steps of the climate story make direct financial impacts on their company. (See Figure A.1.) The facts below are based on science and referenced in the remainder of this Appendix.

1. **Explosion in the Global Middle Class** – The global middle class is projected to more than double between 2010 and 2030, driving an unprecedented rise in consumption-driven carbon emissions, further driven by the growth of AI.

Note: The content of this Appendix is jointly researched and written by Gib Hedstrom and Lucy Carmody. The Climate Story was shared widely in advance of book publication.

https://doi.org/10.1515/9783111548852-014

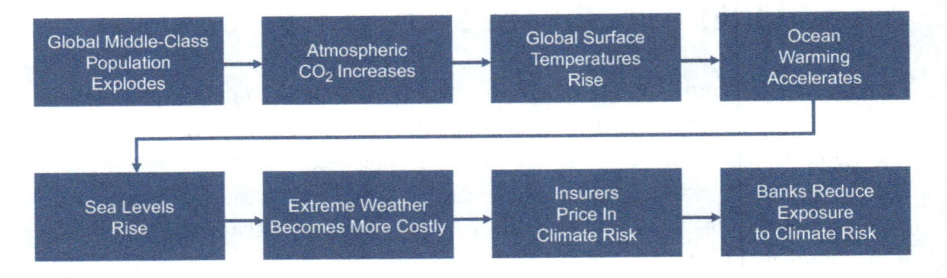

Figure A.1: The Climate Story
Source: Hedstrom Associates

2. **Atmospheric CO₂ Increases** – Concentrations of CO_2 and other GHGs have risen sharply since 1960, and this upward trend continues at a fast pace.
3. **Global Surface Temperatures Rise** – Average global temperatures have increased around 1.1°C (2°F) since 1900 due to the greenhouse gas effect. Recent increments have already surpassed the 2015 Paris Agreement 1.5°C threshold.
4. **Ocean Warming Accelerates** – Though oceans warm more slowly, due to their vast size, the warming trend has become easier to monitor since 2000, with temperatures rising rapidly, causing ice sheets to melt faster.
5. **Sea Levels Rise** – Global sea levels have risen by an average of 8 inches since 1900, with over 30 percent of that rise occurring since 2000. Many US coastal areas have experienced even faster rates.
6. **Extreme Weather Becomes More Costly** – Warmer air and oceans, along with increased atmospheric moisture, result in storms that develop faster, with greater negative impacts, especially when rising sea levels occur near highly populated areas.
7. **Insurers Price in Climate Risk** – Insurers increasingly model climate risk to ascertain premiums, including fire, hurricanes and tornadoes, passing costs onto customers. Some assets are becoming uninsurable due to successive extreme events.
8. **Capital Markets Reduce Exposure to Climate Risk** – With rising insurance costs and risks, the financial sector is cutting back on lending to high-risk sectors and is divesting from potentially stranded assets.

And, for context, below we present the long-term trends, recent trends (typically since 2000), and what to expect over the next five years.

Our hope is that this simple climate story connects the dots and compels action by executives wanting to thrive and deliver 'truly' sustainable growth beyond their existing planning horizons.

1) Explosion in the Global Middle Class

The global middle class is projected to more than double between 2010 and 2030, driving (alongside AI) rapid increase in energy demand.

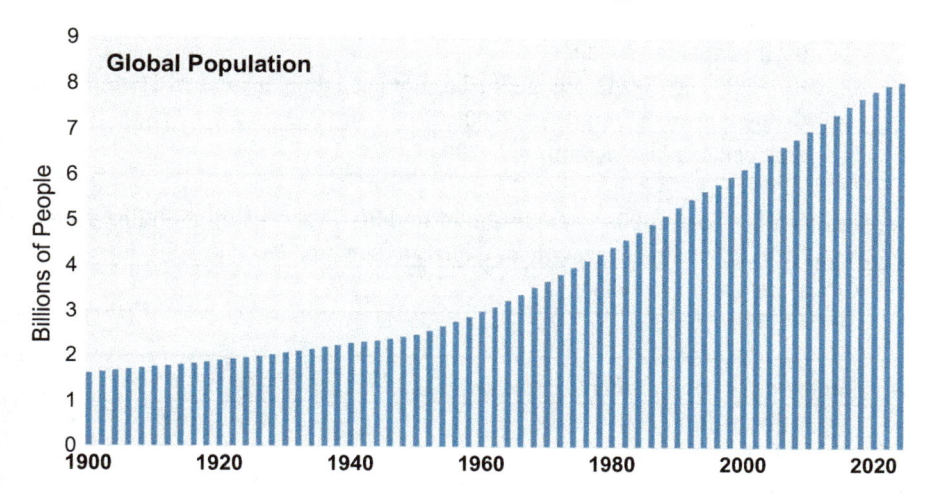

Source: HYDE (2023); Gapminder (2022); UN WPP (2024) from Our World in Data

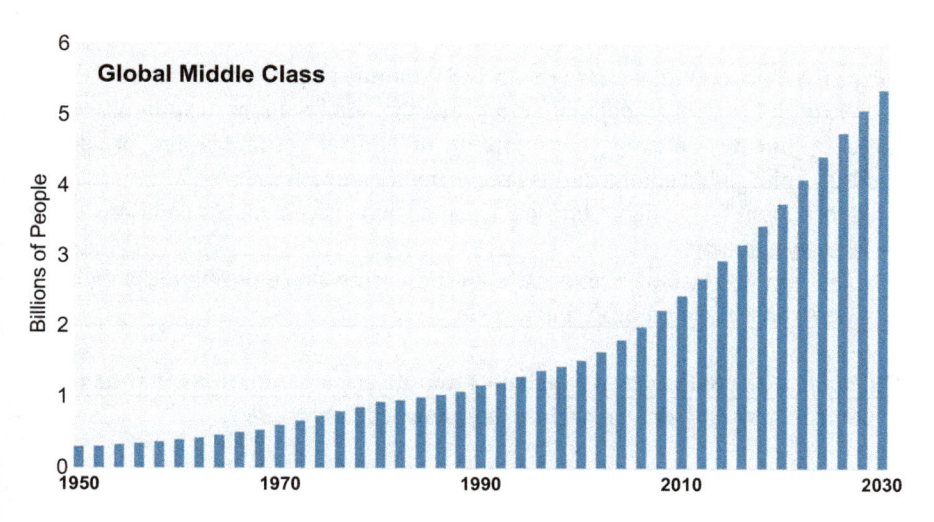

Source: Kharas, H. (2017), "The unprecedented expansion of the global middle class, an update"

Long-term trend: Global population growth has been accelerating since 1960. Middle-class growth has risen sharply since 2000:
- Global population:[1,2]
  - 4 Bn in 1974
  - 8 Bn in 2022
  - 9.7 Bn expected by 2050
- Global middle class (generally defined as having a daily income of $10 to $100):
  - Gradual growth from 1950–2000
  - Sharper increase beginning in 2000

Recent trends: Since 2000, an explosion of middle-class consumption has driven industrialization, economic growth, and energy demand.
- Global per capita income:[3]
  - $450 in 1960
  - $13,100 in 2023
- Middle-class population more than doubles:[4]
  - 2 Bn in 2010
  - 5 Bn by 2030 (est.-
- Global demand for energy per capita: 2023 up 65% from 1965.[5]
- The middle class was responsible for almost half of global CO_2 emissions, as of 2015.[6]

Next Five Years: Middle-class growth will continue globally, even as some countries experience overall population decline. CO_2 emissions per capita are set to increase, due to the rising consumption of natural resources and processed goods, despite global climate targets requiring the opposite.
- More fossil fuels will be burned, despite viable green energy solutions being widely available.
- The middle class will contribute an increasing share of overall global CO_2 emissions, based on projected growth trends.[7]

Outcome: **The continued expansion of middle-class populations that has propelled consumption-driven carbon emissions will continue.**[8]

2) Atmospheric CO₂ Increases

CO₂ concentrations in the atmosphere exceeded 420 parts per million (ppm) in 2024, a level last seen three million years ago, when sea levels were up to 60 feet higher.

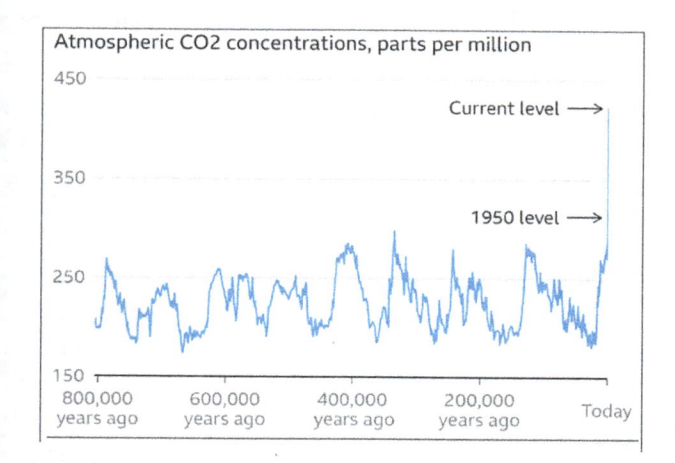

Source: NOAA, 2024

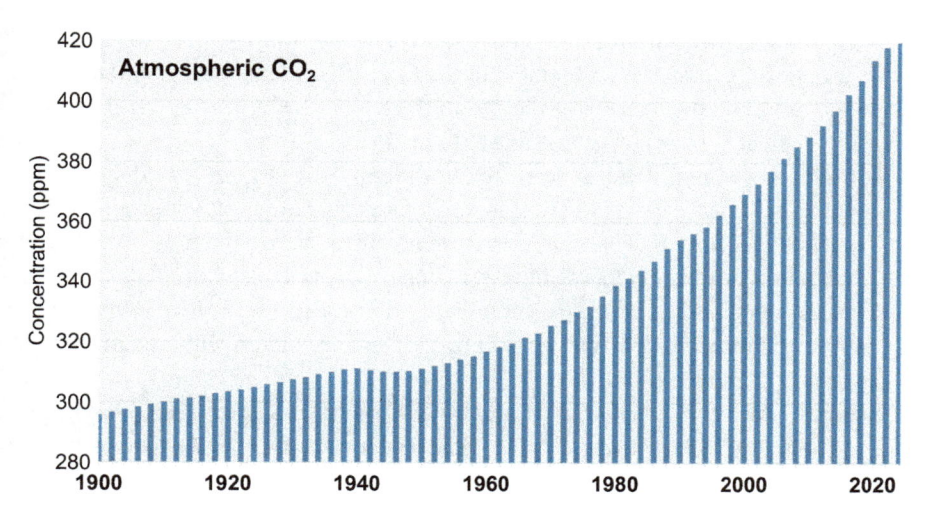

Source: GML/NOAA, 2024

Long-term trend: Atmospheric CO_2 has been increasing dramatically since 1960:[9]

- Pre-industrial (pre-1850s) CO_2 concentrations were ~280 ppm.
- CO_2 of 420 ppm last occurred in the Pliocene Epoch, 3 million years ago, before Homo sapiens. Sea levels were up to 60 feet higher than today.
- CO_2 concentrations remained steady for 800,000 years prior to 1850, rising to:[10,11]
  - 300 ppm in 1910
  - 400 ppm in 2015
  - a new high of 430 ppm in March 2025

Recent trends: Since 2000, CO_2 concentrations have accelerated sharply, along with other GHG emissions and water vapor in the atmosphere:
- 1960–2020: Annual increases of CO_2 ppm occurred at 100x rate of previous increases.[12]
- 2022–2024: Saw a record two-year increase in absolute CO_2 concentrations.[13]
- 2010–2020: CO_2 was released into the atmosphere at twice the speed that natural carbon sinks, such as oceans and forests, could absorb it.[14]
- Fossil fuel burning continues to rise;
- *Next Five Years:* Existing climate mitigation policies (we use the 'Stated Policies Scenario')[15] are insufficient to curb growing CO_2 and other emissions to allow us to meet Paris threshold targets:[16]
- Fossil fuels will continue to dominate global energy supply.
  - In 2023, fossil fuels accounted for 82% of global energy consumption.[17]
  - By 2030, the share is projected to drop to 73% but, to stay on track for global net zero targets, it must fall to 62%.[18]
- Under the Stated Policies Scenario, and before the Trump presidency, CO_2 emissions were expected to decline at an average annual rate of around 0.4% between 2025 and 2050, significantly short of the approximately 4% annual reduction needed to align with international targets.[19]
- Methane emissions have 80x the impact on warming of CO_2 (over 20 years)[20] yet are forecast to decline only 30% by 2050 against at least 50% required.

Outcome: **The rapid escalation of global GHG emissions since 1960 persists as fossil fuels continue to burn, driving increased air, surface, and ocean temperatures.**

3) Average Global Surface Temperatures Rise

Air temperatures have risen at an increasingly rapid rate since the 1970s,[21] with recent average temperatures breaching the Paris Agreement 1.5°C (2.7°F) threshold target.[22]

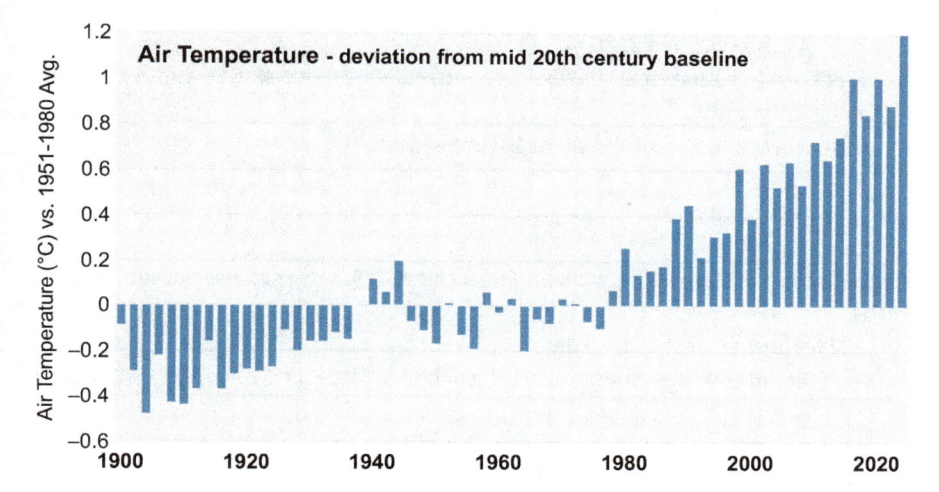

Source: NASA's Goddard Institute for Space Studies (GISS), 2024

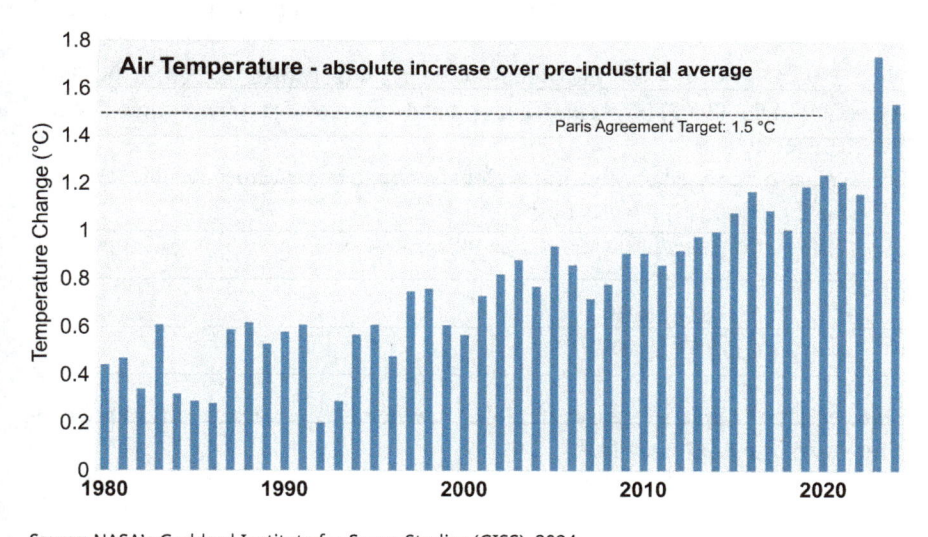

Source: NASA's Goddard Institute for Space Studies (GISS), 2024

Long-term trend: Rising global temperatures have caused longer, more frequent heat waves and droughts since the 1960s.[23]
- Average global air temperature is over 1°C (1.8°F) higher than 1900. Half of the increase happened since the mid-1970s.
- From 1970 to 2023:[24]
  - The US mainland warmed 1.4°C (2.5°F), faster than global averages.
  - Alaska warmed 2.3°C (4.2°F).
- Since 1980, global heat waves have moved 20% more slowly and occur 67% more frequently.[25]
- The average length of the US heatwave season:[26]
  - 1980s: 40 days
  - Today: 70 days

Recent trends: The rate of warming is accelerating; temperatures break new records.
- 2023: The warmest year to date[27]
  - Global average temperatures reached 1.74°C (3.1°F) over pre-industrial levels.
  - In Canada, the increase was even higher.
- 2024: Even warmer than 2023[28]
  - Antarctica temperatures soar 28°C (50°F) above normal.[29]
  - Australia experienced its highest-ever winter temperature: 41°C (107°F).[30]

Next Five Years: In 2024, the global average temperature exceeded the Paris Agreement 1.5°C (2.7°F) target above pre-industrial levels for the first time.[31] Without stronger action:
- We are on a trajectory towards a global average temperature rise of 3°C (5.4°F) above pre-industrial levels by 2100.[32]
- Temperatures are projected to rise to:
- 1.5°C (2.7°F) by 2030
- up to 2°C (3.6°F) by 2040
- up to 2.1°C (3.8°F) by 2050[33,34]

Outcome: **The rapid increases in global surface temperatures will likely continue over the next decade.[35]**

4) Ocean Warming Accelerates

The warming rate from 2000 to 2024 is approximately 3.5 times higher than that from 1920 to 2000, based on data tracked by NASA.[36]

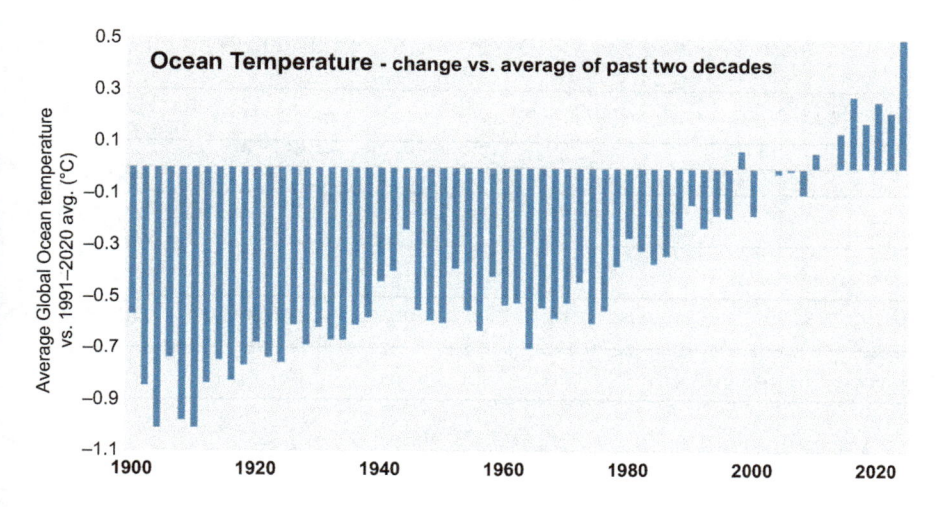

Source: C3S/ECMWF, 2024

Long-term trend: Ocean warming has resulted in the loss of sea ice and glaciers, even though oceans warm slowly due to their vast size.
–   Greenland and Antarctic ice mass:
    –   By the 2010s, the annual melt was 6x faster than the 1990s baseline of 81 Gt.[37]
    –   In 2019, Greenland alone lost a record 532 gigatons of ice (est.).[38]
–   Warming and ice melt have affected planetary heat circulation in air and oceans. Disruption of the global ocean circulatory systems is linked to extreme weather events,[39] impacting the jet stream, the polar vortex, and the El Niño and La Niña events.

Recent trends: Since 2000, ocean warming has been accelerating, driving record temperatures:
–   2013–2023: The warmest decade for the oceans since at least the 1800s[40]
–   2023: the warmest year on record[41]
–   2024: Greenland is losing around 30 million metric tons of ice mass hourly.[42]
–   Ocean warming rates have doubled in two decades, with 2023 seeing one of the largest annual increases since 1950.[43]
–   Elevated sea temperatures lead to more frequent, long-lasting tropical cyclones.[44]

Next five years: Increased average ocean surface temperatures will affect ocean ecosystems worldwide and cause storms to rapidly intensify.[45]

- Ocean warming:
    - As oceans warm, they become less effective at storing CO_2.
    - Higher CO_2 levels acidifies oceans, interfering with marine life cycles.
    - Mass coral bleaching will continue to negatively impact multiple marine species.
- Tropical cyclone impacts:[46]
    - The proportion of Category 4 and 5 storms will increase.
    - With a 2°C (3.6°F) rise in global temperatures, average rainfall rates within 100 km of storm centers are expected to increase by around 10–15%.[47,48,49,50]

Outcome: **The recent sharp increase in sea temperatures has caused ice sheets to melt faster, accelerating sea level rise and storm intensity, impacting marine life globally.**

5) Sea Levels Rise

Global sea levels have climbed by 8 inches since 1880. Since 2000, that rate grow by nearly 50%, and is even higher in many coastal areas.[51]

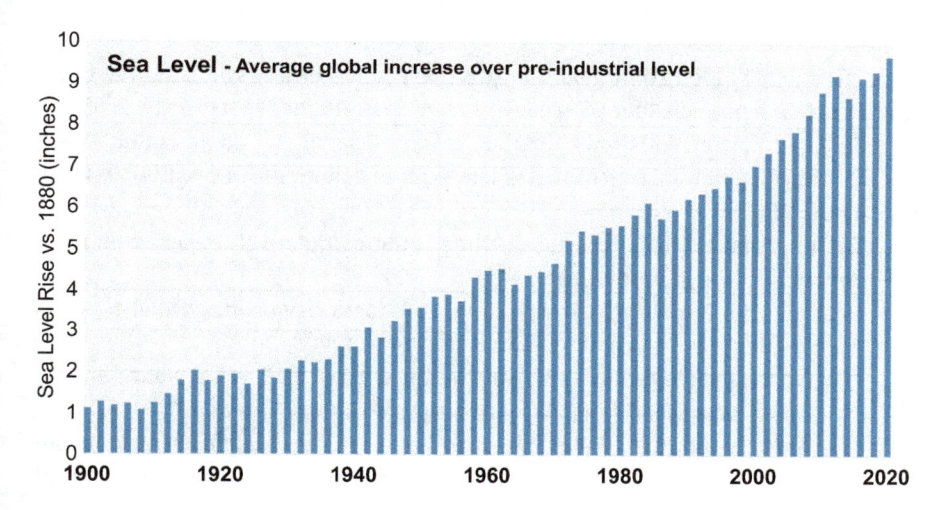

Source: EPA, 2024

Long-term trend: Global sea levels have steadily risen as oceans warm:
- The rate of sea level rise more than doubled from 1900 to 2020, half of it in the past 30 years alone (1993–2023)[52,53]
- Sea level rise in many US coastal locations has been higher than global averages due to coastal erosion, oil and groundwater pumping, and subsidence.[54]

Recent trends: Since 2000, sea level rise has been increasing:
- Global average sea level increases:
  - 1980–2000: 1.5 inches
  - 2000–2020: 2.6 inches
- 2006 to 2015: sea levels globally rose at 2.5x the rate of the previous century.[55]
- Sea levels in many US coastal locations continue to rise.
  - Since 2000, the coast of Maine saw a 2 inch rise per decade, over double the long-term average.[56]
  - The Gulf of Mexico is rising the fastest, half an inch annually since 2010, 3x the global average.[57]
  - The mid-Atlantic coast is rising the next fastest.[58]

- Higher sea levels and increased rainfall have significantly exacerbated flood risk.
  - In 2023 alone, extreme weather displaced 2.5 million Americans.[59]
  - Hurricane Helene in 2024 destroyed many homes beyond the 100-year floodplain, perhaps rendering the 100-year risk model obsolete.[60]

Next five years: Melt from mountain ice sheets and glaciers will continue to accelerate. NASA predicts that US sea levels could rise another 12 inches by 2050.[61]
- Failure to lower emissions, upgrade infrastructure, and adopt climate-resilient development practices will displace more communities from flood-prone areas.
- The financial toll from coastal flooding could cumulatively reach trillions of dollars by the end of this century.[62]
- Houston, the fourth largest city in the US, faces devastating flooding risks from higher sea levels and increased storm rainfall.[63]
  - Hurricane Harvey in 2017 was the third event in 3 years where annual rainfall exceeded 1 in 500-year levels in Houston.[64]
  - An over-saturated water table and poor structural engineering will continue to prevent stormwater from flowing safely back into natural waterways.

Outcome: **Climbing sea levels and expanding coastal populations globally leave one in ten people in low-lying coastal areas in danger from extreme weather events.[65]**

6) **Weather Events Become More Extreme and More Costly**

Warming air and oceans, with rising sea levels, have created conditions in which extreme weather events occur over 3x as frequently since 2000.

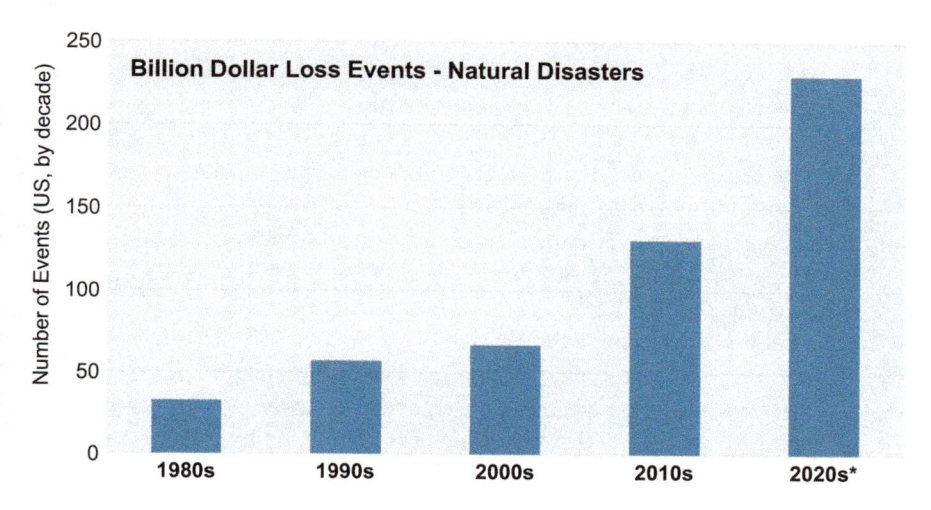

*Projected based on average from 2020–2024
Source: The State of the Reinsurance Property Catastrophe market, SwissRe Institute, 2023
Source: NOAA National Centers for Environmental Information (NCEI) U.S. Billion-Dollar Weather and Climate Disasters, 2025

Long-term trend: Extreme weather events have become more frequent and financially devastating.
- The average frequency of US extreme weather events with losses over $1Bn:[66]
  - 1980s: every 16 weeks
  - 2010s: every 4 weeks
  - 2023: almost every 2 weeks
- 2023 saw 66 global billion-dollar loss disasters, even higher than the 2020–2022 average of 52.[67]
- Extreme heat is now the leading cause of weather-related death in the US.[68]

Recent trends: The cost of extreme weather events is continuing to soar alongside increases in global temperature and population.
- The cost of extreme weather events in 2024 was $320 Bn, up from $268 Bn in 2023.[69]
- Nearly $600 Bn in debt in the US is reliant on repayments from communities at elevated risk of hurricanes, fire, or floods.[70]

- Rapid population growth in vulnerable coastal areas with already strained municipal infrastructure contributes to the increased cost of disasters.[71]

Next five years: Billion-dollar events will increase in cost and frequency and impact every sector. Economic harm from climate change is non-linear. Each additional degree of warming raises costs more than the previous degree.[72]
- Increased coastal flooding due to higher sea levels and rainfall rates will reduce the values of vulnerable coastal properties.
- Pricing of long-term municipal bonds backed by taxes from these vulnerable areas will be affected.[73] Bondholders will demand higher interest rates from higher-risk business and domestic communities.
- River, creek, and lake flooding is becoming more commonplace. Freshwater flooding, rather than coastal storm surges, caused over half of US hurricane deaths from 2012 to 2022.[74]
- Wildfires and hurricanes will:[75,76]
    - increase public expenditure, municipal borrowing, and healthcare needs;
    - decrease local tax revenues due to periods of lower productivity; and
    - increase annual wildfire suppression cost (40% more by 2050 to $3.9 Bn).[77]
- Economic losses from extreme heat will exceed $200 Bn annually by 2030 due to higher medical costs, productivity loss, and emergency response.[78]

Outcome: **Extreme weather events will amplify in frequency, intensifying economic impacts, public expenditures, municipal borrowing, and the healthcare burden.**

7) Insurers Price in Climate Risk

Insurers have 'priced-in' the risk of storms and fires, raised premiums, and cut coverage – leaving many vulnerable areas uninsured.

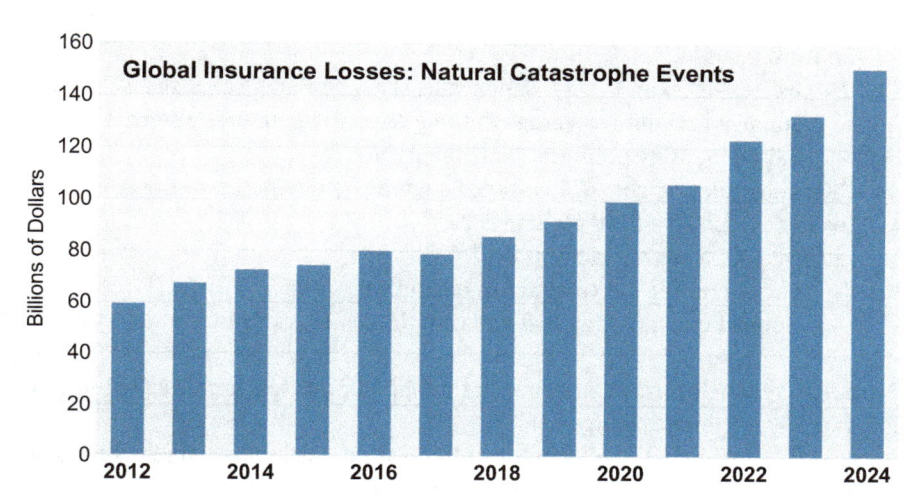

Source: Verisk 2024 Global Modeled Catastrophe Losses

Long-term trend: Insurance premiums have, in the past, tended to grow in line with inflation, enhanced property prices and other market conditions.
As climate risks accelerate:
– Uninsured losses have created a widening "global insurance gap."
– Over 60% of natural disaster losses are now uncovered.[79]
– Governments, businesses, and individuals increasingly bear the brunt when disasters happen, especially in emerging economies.

Recent trends: Since 2020, insurers have declined to cover high climate-risk locations and sectors. They are also reducing exposure to fossil fuels in their investment portfolios.
– 2012 to 2023: Annual insurance losses from global natural catastrophes doubled.[80]
– 2014 to 2023 – US property and casualty insurers:
    – Cut fossil fuel investments from 3.4% to 1.8% of their portfolios.[81]
    – Paid out more for claims than they earned in premiums,[82] largely due to climate-related disasters and higher rebuilding costs.
– 2023:
    – Insurers lost money covering homes in 18 of the 50 US states.[83]
    – Global recovery costs from extreme weather events rose to $108 Bn.[84]

- – Premiums rose by 18% for multifamily units, disproportionately affecting the poorest in society.[85]
  - – In some areas, insurers withdrew completely or raised premiums up as much as 50%.
- – 2024: Global natural disasters caused losses of $320 Bn, of which around $140 Bn were insured.[86]
- – US: Allstate, American Family, Nationwide, Erie, and Berkshire Hathaway have:
  - – Stopped providing coverage in some regions, including California.
  - – Raised monthly premiums and deductibles.[87]
- – UK: the escalating cost of insurance coverage contributed to the closure of the last British coal-fired plant in 2024;[88]
- – Europe: AXA, Zurich and Swiss Re:[89,90,91]
  - – Began phasing out coverage of oil and gas assets.
  - – stopped underwriting coal and coal-fired energy production.

Next five years: Insurance systems and public budgets are not designed to rapidly respond to climate change risk.[92]
- – Premiums will continue to rise, and state-run backstop insurers may become the only option for assets and homeowners in high-risk areas.
- – High-emitting companies will start to face higher penalties and will have to demonstrate mitigation activities to retain coverage.
- – Insurance costs could double by 2030 in states with high extreme weather risk.[93]
  - – Policies covered by state-sponsored insurance plans, the insurers of last resort, continue to grow as private insurers withdraw from risk-prone areas.[94]
  - – Costs to insure US commercial buildings will likely increase around 80% from 2023 to 2030.[95]

Outcome: **Uninsured losses will grow as the insurance sector passes costs on to customers. More assets are becoming effectively uninsurable within the private sector.**

8) Capital Markets Reduce Exposure to Climate Risk

Amid rising insurance costs and unpredictable risks, the financial sector is cutting lending to high climate-risk sectors and divesting from potentially stranded assets.

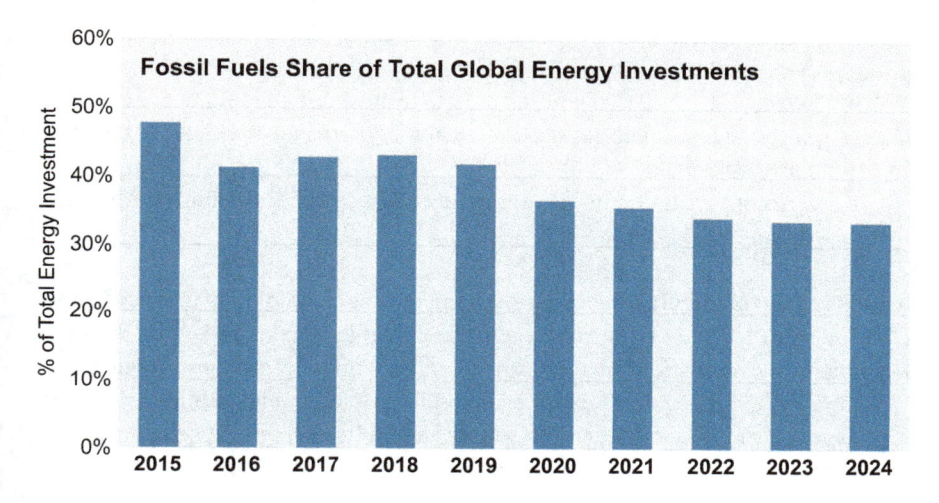

Source: IEA World Energy Investment, 2024

Long-term trend: Action has grown to mitigate climate risk since the Paris Agreement in 2015:
- Among the net-zero pledges from companies and governments:
  - 6,000 firms have committed to a science-based decarbonization target.[96]
  - 3,400 of these have a net zero commitment.[97]
  - As of 2024, 140 countries, covering 88% of GHG emissions, have made net-zero pledges, on behalf of around 85% of the global population and representing 88% of 2019 emissions.[98]
  - However, confidence in realizing corporate and national pledges remains low.[99]
- Bank climate stress tests:
  - An increasing number of global banks perform regular climate stress tests to assess physical and transition risk, a practice pioneered by Mark Carney at the **Bank of England** and by the **European Central Bank**.
- Global financial institutions have cut fossil fuels as a percentage of total energy investment, from 54% in 2015 to 35% in 2024.[100]

Recent trends:
- Older buildings generally face higher insurance rates and energy costs, yet are able to generate comparatively lower rents. Declining asset values encourage landlords to invest in energy efficiency.
- **HSBC**[101], **Barclays**[102], **Royal Bank of Canada**[103], and **Standard Chartered**[104] are among the leading banks reducing climate exposure[105] by:
    - declining to finance upstream oil, gas, and coal expansion or related infrastructure
    - setting science-based lending targets to cut CO_2 and methane emissions
    - boosting lending to support renewables and resource-efficient and circular business models
    - working with clients to rapidly accelerate the transition to a greener economy

Next five years: The link between asset prices and climate risks may lead to increasingly abrupt price adjustments over the coming years due to policy changes, technological shifts, infrastructural vulnerabilities, and increasing systemic risks.
- Lawsuits claiming damages against fossil fuel companies, utilities, industry trade associations, and their consultants and advisors, are expected to surge.
- Regulators will increasingly embed climate risks into financial models, systems, and policies.
- Institutional asset owners, such as endowments, foundations and pension funds, will pressure banks to:
    - reduce lending to high-risk sectors
    - improve disclosure on lending which is not aligned with net-zero targets
- Banks and investors will prioritize greater disclosure and focus on investments and lending that support the climate transition.
- Banks are starting to disclose their clean energy financing ratios[106] and sustainable investment commitments:
    - **HSBC** aims to provide up to $1 Tn in sustainable finance and investments by 2030 to support clients' transitions to net-zero emissions.[107]
    - **Citi** is committed to facilitating $1 Tn in sustainable finance by 2030, with $500 Bn allocated to environmental finance and $500 Bn to social finance.[108]
    - **Barclays** plans to invest over $400 M in global climate-tech startups between 2020 and 2027. It has committed to facilitating $1 Tn in green financing by 2030.[109]
    - **JP Morgan** intends to finance and facilitate more than $2.5 Tn over 10 years, from 2021 to the end of 2030. It focuses on sustainable development, including $1 Tn for green initiatives.[110]

Outcome: Banks will limit lending to certain high-risk sectors, and specific businesses and homeowners in high-risk regions. As a result, the economic impacts of stranded domestic, commercial, and municipal real estate assets will escalate.

Notes

1 https://ourworldindata.org/grapher/population?time=1890..latest&country=~OWID_WRL
2 https://www.un.org/en/global-issues/population#:~:text=The%20world%20in%202100,and%2010.4%20billion%20by%202100.
3 https://www.macrotrends.net/global-metrics/countries/WLD/world/gdp-per-capita
4 OECD https://doi.org/10.1787/888933888260
5 https://ourworldindata.org/grapher/per-capita-energy-use?tab=table
6 https://www.sei.org/wp-content/uploads/2020/09/research-report-carbon-inequality-era.pdf
7 https://www.sei.org/wp-content/uploads/2020/09/research-report-carbon-inequality-era.pdf
8 https://cepr.org/voxeu/columns/collapse-revisited-climate-change-and-development-middle-income-countries
9 https://www.climate.gov/news-features/understanding-climate/climate-change-atmospheric-carbon-dioxide
10 https://data.giss.nasa.gov/modelforce/ghgases/Fig1A.ext.txt#:~:text=Ice%2D%201850%20285.2%201900%20295.7%201950%20311.3,1905%20298.0%201955%20313.7%20ESRL/%202005%20379.46
11 https://gml.noaa.gov/ccgg/trends/weekly.html
12 https://www.climate.gov/news-features/understanding-climate/climate-change-atmospheric-carbon-dioxide
13 https://www.noaa.gov/news-release/during-year-of-extremes-carbon-dioxide-levels-surge-faster-than-ever#:~:text=That's%20an%20increase%20of%202.9,peak%20in%20the%20NOAA%20record.
14 https://www.ipcc.ch/report/ar6/wg1/downloads/faqs/IPCC_AR6_WGI_FAQ_Chapter_05.pdf
15 The Stated Policies Scenario (STEPS) is a model used by the International Energy Agency (IEA) to predict the future of the energy system based on current and announced policies
16 https://www.iea.org/reports/world-energy-outlook-2021/overview
17 www.energyinst.org/statistical-review
18 https://iea.blob.core.windows.net/assets/86ede39e-4436-42d7-ba2a-edf61467e070/WorldEnergyOutlook2023.pdf
19 https://www.iea.org/data-and-statistics/charts/global-energy-related-co2-emissions-by-scenario-1990-2050
20 https://www.unep.org/explore-topics/energy/facts-about-methane
21 https://earthobservatory.nasa.gov/world-of-change/global-temperatures
22 https://climate.copernicus.eu/surface-air-temperature-september-2024
23 https://www.science.org/doi/10.1126/sciadv.adl1598#T1
24 https://www.pbs.org/newshour/science/climate-change-harms-daily-life-across-the-united-states-new-federal-report-finds
25 https://subscriber.politicopro.com/article/eenews/2024/04/02/study-says-climate-change-makes-heat-waves-last-longer-00149995

26 https://www.epa.gov/climate-indicators/climate-change-indicators-heat-waves#:~:text=These%20maps%20show%20changes%20in,the%20trend%20was%20statistically%20significant.

27 https://climate.copernicus.eu/surface-air-temperature-september-2024

28 https://www.noaa.gov/news/2024-was-worlds-warmest-year-on-record#:~:text=Earth's%20average%20land%20and%20ocean,NOAA's%201850%2D2024%20climate%20record

29 https://www.sciencedaily.com/releases/2024/09/240904141509.htm

30 https://www.washingtonpost.com/weather/2024/08/26/australia-record-winter-heat/

31 https://climate.copernicus.eu/copernicus-2024-first-year-exceed-15degc-above-pre-industrial-level?utm_source=chatgpt.com

32 https://www.unep.org/resources/emissions-gap-report-2024

33 www.reuters.com/business/environment/climate-set-warm-by-31-c-without-greater-action-un-report-warns-2024-10-24

34 www.ipcc.ch/ar6-syr/

35 https://climatechange.chicago.gov/climate-change-science/future-climate-change

36 https://data.giss.nasa.gov/gistemp/

37 https://climate.nasa.gov/news/2958/greenland-antarctica-melting-six-times-faster-than-in-the-1990s/#:~:text=The%20team%20calculated%20that%20the%20two%20ice,trillion%20tons%20of%20ice%20since%20the%201990s.

38 https://science.nasa.gov/earth/climate-change/ice-glaciers/study-2019-sees-record-loss-of-greenland-ice/

39 https://science.nasa.gov/earth/earth-atmosphere/slowdown-of-the-motion-of-the-ocean/

40 https://climate.nasa.gov/vital-signs/ocean-warming/?intent=121#:~:text=The%20last%2010%20years%20were,the%20ocean's%20warmest%20recorded%20year.

41 https://climate.nasa.gov/vital-signs/ocean-warming/?intent=121#:~:text=The%20last%2010%20years%20were,the%20ocean's%20warmest%20recorded%20year

42 https://www.theguardian.com/environment/2024/jan/17/greenland-losing-30m-tonnes-of-ice-an-hour-study-reveals

43 https://www.unesco.org/en/articles/new-unesco-report-rate-ocean-warming-doubled-20-years-rate-sea-level-rise-doubled-30-years

44 https://www.climatecentral.org/climate-matters/hurricane-rapid-intensification

45 https://www.climatecentral.org/climate-matters/hurricane-rapid-intensification

46 https://www.gfdl.noaa.gov/global-warming-and%20%20hurricanes/

47 www.gfdl.noaa.gov/global-warming-and-hurricanes

48 www.ipcc.ch/ar6-wg1/

49 www.nature.com/articles/s41467-021-25685-2

50 www.public.wmo.int/en/our-mandate/focus-areas/natural-hazards-and-climate/tropical-cyclones

51 https://dev-04-drupal-climate.woc.noaa.gov/news-features/understanding-climate/climate-change-global-sea-level#:~:text=April%2019%2C%202022-,Highlights,–24%20centimeters)%20since%201880

52 https://www.climate.gov/news-features/understanding-climate/climate-change-global-sea-level

53 https://earthobservatory.nasa.gov/images/150192/tracking-30-years-of-sea-level-rise

54 https://dev-04-drupal-climate.woc.noaa.gov/news-features/understanding-climate/climate-change-global-sea-level#:~:text=April%2019%2C%202022-,Highlights,–24%20centimeters)%20since%201880

55 https://www.climate.gov/news-features/understanding-climate/climate-change-global-sea-level#:~:text=The%20global%20mean%20water%20level%20in%20the,year%20throughout%20most%20of%20the%20twentieth%20century

56 https://www.maine.gov/future/sites/maine.gov.future/files/2024-07/3-Slovinsky%20-%20SLR%20and%20Storms%20Infrastructure%20Rebuilding.pdf

57 ttps://www.sciencedaily.com/releases/2023/04/230410111643.htm

58 https://www.nature.com/articles/s41467-023-37649-9/figures/2

59 https://www.npr.org/2024/02/29/1234671424/the-human-cost-of-climate-related-disasters-is-acutely-undercounted-new-study-sa#:~:text=The%20U.S.%20Census%20Bureau%20recently,weather%20totaled%20over%20$90%20billion.

60 https://www.asce.org/publications-and-news/civil-engineering-source/article/2024/11/06/with-the-100-year-flood-model-seemingly-obsolete-what-now

61 https://climate.nasa.gov/news/3146/sea-level-to-rise-up-to-a-foot-by-2050-interagency-report-finds/

62 https://www.un.org/sg/en/content/sg/press-encounter/2024-08-27/secretary-generals-press-conference-sea-level-rise

63 https://www.washingtonpost.com/climate-environment/2024/07/10/houston-flooding-hurricane-beryl/

64 https://www.climatesignals.org/headlines/analysis-houston-experiencing-its-third-500-year-flood-3-years-how-possible

65 https://news.un.org/en/story/2023/02/1133492

66 https://www.climate.gov/news-features/blogs/beyond-data/2023-historic-year-us-billion-dollar-weather-and-climate-disasters#:~:text=Tropical%20cyclones%20have%20caused%20the,list%20of%20%20billion%2Ddollar%20events

67 https://assets.aon.com/-/media/files/aon/reports/2024/climate-and-catastrophe-insights-report.pdf

68 https://www.noaa.gov/news-release/biden-harris-administration-noaa-issue-national-heat-strategy-provide-200k-for-extreme-heat

69 https://www.munichre.com/en/company/media-relations/media-information-and-corporate-news/media-information/2025/natural-disaster-figures-2024.html#:~:text=Natural%20disasters%202024%20%E2%80%93%20a%20loss,in%20the%20pre%2Dindustrial%20era

70 https://www.bondbuyer.com/news/investors-bet-on-municipal-bonds-despite-accelerating-climate-concerns

71 Adjusting to the reality of sea level rise: reshaping coastal communities through resilience-informed adaptation | Climatic Change

72 https://nca2023.globalchange.gov/chapter/19/#:~:text=With%20every%20additional%20degree%20of,1%C2%B0F%20of%20warming.&text=As%20climate%20change%20advances%2C%20economic,projected%20to%20grow%20over%20time; and https://science.sciencemag.org/content/356/6345/1362

73 https://www.barrons.com/articles/municipal-bonds-climate-risk-c3353da7

74 https://blog.ametsoc.org/2023/08/08/recent-trends-in-tropical-cyclone-fatalities-in-the-united-states/

75 https://www.brookings.edu/articles/quantifying-climate-change-risks-to-the-cost-of-municipal-borrowing/

76 https://www.budget.senate.gov/chairman/newsroom/press/climate-change-is-destabilizing-the-municipal-bond-market-tune-in-as-dr-chris-hartshorn-explains-how-climate-change-is-threatening-funding-sources-that-enable-local-governments-to-invest-in-communities

77 https://www.fs.usda.gov/about-agency/features/economic-risks-forest-service-estimates-costs-fighting-wildfires-hotter

78 https://onebillionresilient.org/extreme-heat-the-economic-and-social-consequences-for-the-united-states/#:~:text=The%20economic%20costs%20of%20extreme%20heat%20are%20already%20huge.&text=The%20losses%20will%20increase%20as,and%20%24500%20billion%20by%202050

79 https://www.oecd.org/finance/insurance/climate-resilience.htm

80 https://www.verisk.com/4a9504/siteassets/extreme-event-solutions/2024-verisk-global-modeled-catastrophe-losses.pdf?__FormGuid=85eabd6c-286c-4f19-9b7d-cc70ab320339&__FormLanguage=en-US&__FormSubmissionId=5e9eab6f-a5d6-4df1-8b3c-bdd71b1d7239

81 https://www.wsj.com/us-news/climate-environment/the-two-big-insurers-still-betting-on-fossil-fuels-fa31bb15

82 https://cre.moodysanalytics.com/insights/cre-news/new-data-and-regulation-show-an-insurance-industry-in-flux/

83 https://www.nytimes.com/interactive/2024/05/13/climate/insurance-homes-climate-change-weather.html

84 https://www.swissre.com/dam/jcr:c9385357-6b86-486a-9ad8-78679037c10e/2024-03-sigma1-natural-catastrophes.pdf

85 https://cre.moodysanalytics.com/insights/cre-news/new-data-and-regulation-show-an-insurance-industry-in-flux/

86 https://www.munichre.com/en/company/media-relations/media-information-and-corporate-news/media-information/2025/natural-disaster-figures-2024.html

87 https://www.latimes.com/business/story/2024-07-11/allstate-seeking-34-rate-increase-for-california-homeowners-insurance

88 https://www.nytimes.com/2024/09/30/climate/britain-last-coal-power-plant.html

89 https://www.axa.com/en/press/press-releases/axa-extends-its-oil-and-gas-exclusions-to-support-the-energy-transition

90 https://www.insurancebusinessmag.com/us/news/environmental/zurich-insurance-stops-underwriting-new-fossil-fuel-projects-484241.aspx#:~:text=This%20initiative%20has%20been%20welcomed,to%20share%20your%20comments%20below

91 https://www.swissre.com/sustainability/stories/net-zero-underwriting-targets.html#:~:text=Since%202018%2C%20Swiss%20Re%20no,thermal%20coal%20utilities%20or%20mining.&text=Since%20July%202021%2C%20Swiss%20Re,carbon%2Dintense%20oil%20and%20gas

92 https://nca2023.globalchange.gov/

93 https://www2.deloitte.com/us/en/insights/industry/financial-services/financial-services-industry-predictions/2024/impact-of-climate-change-on-commercial-real-estate-insurance-costs.html

94 https://www.moodyscre.com/insights/cre-news/new-data-and-regulation-show-an-insurance-industry-in-flux/

95 https://www2.deloitte.com/us/en/insights/industry/financial-services/financial-services-industry-predictions/2024/impact-of-climate-change-on-commercial-real-estate-insurance-costs.html

96 https://sciencebasedtargets.org/blog/climate-action-milestone-6-000-companies-adopt-science-based-targets

97 https://www.ft.com/content/dc48634e-c9e8-40d6-88a4-87450907ef94

98 www.un.org/en/climatechange/net-zero-coalition

99 From Commitment to Implementation – An Analysis of Corporate Climate Actions

100 Global investment in clean energy and fossil fuels, 2015-2024 – Charts – Data & Statistics – IEA

101 Our climate strategy | HSBC Holdings plc

102 https://www.wsj.com/articles/shareholders-pressure-barclays-to-pull-back-on-financing-for-fracking-d2a889a7?utm_source=chatgpt.com

103 https://www.rbc.com/climate-action-institute/climate-action-24/index.html

104 Climate change | Standard Chartered

105 Top 50 Banks Tackling Climate Adaptation Download

106 https://about.bnef.com/blog/citi-jpmorgan-first-adopters-of-energy-finance-ratio/

107 https://www.hsbc.com/news-and-views/news/hsbc-news-archive/hsbc-sets-out-net-zero-ambition

108 https://www.citigroup.com/global/news/perspective/2021/citi-commits-1-trillion-to-sustainable-finance-by-2030

109 https://home.barclays/sustainability/esg-resource-hub/our-approach-to-sustainable-finance/

110 https://www.jpmorganchase.com/ir/news/2021/jpmorgan-chase-sustainable-development

Appendix B: Acronyms

CBAM (EU Carbon Border Adjustment Mechanism): A policy introduced by the EU that taxes imported goods based on their carbon emissions.

CDP (formerly the Carbon Disclosure Project): An international non-profit organization that helps organizations disclose their environmental impact, attempting to make environmental reporting and risk management the norm. CEP has separate programs for climate change, water, supply chain, forests, and cities.

CO_2 (Carbon Dioxide): The primary carbon source for life on Earth. In the air, CO_2 is transparent to visible light but absorbs infrared radiation, acting as a greenhouse gas.

CO2e (Carbon dioxide equivalent): Measures global warming potential and includes greenhouse gases besides CO_2. Often seen as a more accurate measurement (than CO_2) of global warming potential.

COP (Conference of the Parties): The United Nations Climate Change Conference or Conference of the Parties of the UNFCC has been held annually (except 2020 due to the COVID-19 pandemic) since the first UN Earth Summit in Rio in 1992, at which a major global climate agreement was agreed. The event is intended for governments to agree on policies to limit global temperature rises and adapt to impacts associated with climate change.

CSDDD (Corporate Sustainability Due Diligence Directive): A European Union law that requires companies to assess and mitigate their environmental and human rights impacts.

CSO (Chief Sustainability Officer): The most senior person in the company with responsibility for overseeing sustainability policy, positioning, and activities. Note: the person may or may not be officially designated as the CSO by the company.

CSR (Corporate Social Responsibility): Corporate practices designed to have a positive influence on the world. Often misused interchangeably with sustainability, CSR typically focuses mostly on the 'social' dimension of sustainability.

CSRD (Corporate Sustainability Reporting Directive): The EU requirement that came into force in 2023 that strengthens the rules concerning the environmental and social information that companies need to report.

https://doi.org/10.1515/9783111548852-015

DEI (Diversity, Equity, and Inclusion): Organizational frameworks that seek to promote the fair treatment and full participation of all people, especially groups that have historically been underrepresented or subject to discrimination.

EHS (Environment, Health, and Safety): The term commonly used in large corporations for this function.

ESG (Environment, Social, and Governance): The term often used by the investment community to refer to three central factors in measuring the sustainability of an investment. In this book (and ESG Navigator), we use the words sustainability and ESG interchangeably to include governance and leadership, strategy and execution, environmental stewardship, and social responsibility.

ESRS (European Sustainability Reporting Standards): Corporate sustainability reporting requirements for entities subject to the European Corporate Sustainability Reporting Directive (CSRD). Non-EU companies may be subject to the CSRD if their European turnover or operations exceed specified thresholds.

GHG (Greenhouse Gas): GHGs cause climate change by trapping heat in the atmosphere, and their cumulative total comprise a company's carbon footprint. The main GHGs are water vapor (H_2O), carbon dioxide (CO_2), methane (CH_4), nitrous oxide (N_2O), hydrofluorocarbons (HFCs), perfluorocarbons (PFCs), and sulfur hexafluoride (SF_6).

GRI (Global Reporting Initiative): An international independent standards organization that helps businesses, governments, and other organizations understand and communicate their impacts on issues such as climate change, human rights, and corruption.

IFRS (International Financial Reporting Standards): Refers to sustainability disclosure standards set by the IFRS Foundation – including general requirements (IFRS S1) and a climate-related disclosures standard (IFRS S2). IFRS focuses on sustainability-related risks and opportunities reasonably expected to affect a business's prospects over the short, medium, and long term.

IFRS Foundation (International Financial Reporting Standards Foundation): Mandates the creation and development of sustainability-related reporting standards to meet investors' needs.

IIRC (International Integrated Reporting Council): Launched in 2010 to aid businesses and investors as they adopt **integrated reporting**, typically a combination of a company's annual financial report with its sustainability report in a single document. The intent is to disclose how the company will create value over the short, medium, and long term.

ISSB (International Sustainability Standards Board): Established in 2021–2022 under the IFRS Foundation

KSI (Key Sustainability Indicator): The term used in ESG Navigator that refers to the (currently 100) corporate indicators of sustainability performance.

LCA (Life-Cycle Assessment): A technique to assess environmental impacts associated with all stages of a product's life (i.e., from raw material extraction through materials processing, manufacture, distribution, use, repair and maintenance, and disposal or recycling). Also known as life-cycle analysis.

LEED (Leadership in Energy and Environmental Design): One of the most popular green building certification programs worldwide, developed by the non-profit US Green Building Council.

NFRD (Non-Financial Reporting Directive): Adopted in 2014 by the EU, requires certain companies with more than 500 employees to provide non-financial and diversity information, driving greater business transparency and accountability on environmental and social issues.

NGO (Non-Governmental Organization): An organization that is neither a part of a government nor a conventional for-profit business, seen to represent "civil society."

REC (Renewable Energy Certificate): An energy procurement option that certify the bearer owns one megawatt-hour (MWh) of zero-carbon electricity that has been generated by renewable energy sources and delivered to the power grid.

SASB (Sustainability Accounting Standards Board): A non-profit organization founded in 2011 to develop sustainability accounting standards. In 2021, the SASB and International Integrated Reporting Council (IIRC) combined to form the Value Reporting Foundation (VRF). Subsequently, the VRF and the Climate Disclosure Standards Board (CDSB) combined to form the new ISSB in 2022.

SBTi (Science-Based Targets Initiative): A global organization that helps companies set science-based targets to reduce greenhouse gas emissions.

SDGs (Sustainable Development Goals): A set of 17 "Global Goals" with 169 targets, adopted by 193 United Nations member countries, to galvanize and guide the world's efforts to eradicate poverty, end hunger, and address climate change by 2030.

STEM (Science, Technology, Engineering, and Math): An umbrella term used to group together technical disciplines. Typically used in the context of education, workforce development, or national security.

TCFD (Task Force on Climate-related Financial Disclosures): Established by the Financial Stability Board (an international body that monitors and makes recommendations about the global financial system), issued its final report in June 2017. Offered recommendations to the industry for disclosure to investors, following a simple structure: Governance; Strategy; Risk; Metrics. (Almost identical in structure, ESG Navigator separates risk into E and S; puts Metrics in Governance).

TNFD (Task Force on Nature-Related Financial Disclosures): A market-led, science-based, and government-supported global initiative to provide tools to organizations to act on nature-related issues.

VRF (Value Reporting Foundation): A global nonprofit organization that offers resources to help businesses and investors develop a shared understanding of how enterprise value is created, preserved, or eroded over time. In 2021, VRF combined with CDSB to form the IFRS Foundation.

Appendix C: Definitions

Biodegradable (also biodegradability): The capacity for biological degradation of organic materials by living organisms down to the base substances such as water, carbon dioxide, basic elements, and biomass.

Biodiversity: The enormous variety of life on Earth including every living thing – plants, bacteria, animals, and humans. It can be used more specifically to refer to all species in one region or ecosystem.

Board: Refers to the external Board of Directors (as with all US-based public corporations); the governing body with oversight fiduciary responsibility for the corporation – or equivalent for privately-held companies. [Note: the 'Supervisory Board' referred to often in Europe, consisting of the CEO and his/her direct reports, is not part of this section. That is covered under CEO Leadership and Culture and Organization.]

CapEx (Capital Expenditure): Funds used by a company to acquire, upgrade, and maintain physical assets such as property, plants, buildings, technology, or equipment. CapEx is often used to undertake new projects or investments by a company.

Carbon Neutral: Refers to having a net-zero carbon dioxide (CO2) footprint by balancing a measured amount of carbon released to the atmosphere with an equal amount removed through carbon sinks or other offsets – or buying enough carbon credits to make up the difference.

Carbon Price: an instrument that captures the external costs of greenhouse gas (GHG) emissions, tied to their sources through a price, usually in the form of a price on carbon dioxide emitted; pricing can be set internally or through regulations.

Chatham House Rule: whereby information disclosed during a meeting may be reported by those present, but the source of that information may not be explicitly or implicitly identified.

Circularity: Organizational practices that optimize resource use and minimize waste throughout the full value chain.

Circular Economy: An alternative to the traditional linear economy (of "take, make, waste"), in which resources remain in use for as long as possible, extracting the maximum value from them while in use, then recover and regenerate products and materials at the end of each product or service life.

https://doi.org/10.1515/9783111548852-016

Climate Change: Significant changes in global temperature, precipitation, wind patterns and other measures of climate that occur over several decades or longer.

Climate Positive means that an entity absorbs more emissions than it emits, or that it removes more greenhouse gases from the atmosphere than it creates.

Climate Risk: Includes both **physical risks** and **transition risks**.

Closed Loop: Also referred to as the **circular economy**, where materials, at the end of their useful life, are consistently repurposed, recycled, reused, reclaimed, restored, or otherwise converted to some use rather than discharged as waste.

Cradle-to-Cradle: A framework typically used for product design where materials are viewed as nutrients circulating in a healthy, waste-free environment.

Ecosystem Services: Humankind benefits in a multitude of ways from ecosystems (e.g., cleaning drinking water, removing/storing carbon, decomposing wastes, etc.). Collectively, these benefits are known as ecosystem services.

ESG Raters: Independent sustainability frameworks, ratings, and rankings that major companies view as particularly influential or worthy. Common frameworks are *CDP, GRI, SASB, and TCFD*. ESG ratings targeting investors include, for example: *Bloomberg; CDP; Dow Jones Sustainability Index (DJSI); FTSE4Good; MSCI; Morningstar/Sustainalytics*. Other highly regarded ratings include *EcoVadis* and *Global 100 Most Sustainable Companies*.

Externalities: The cost or benefit that affects a party who did not choose to incur that cost or benefit. For example, manufacturing activities that cause air pollution or carbon emissions may impose health and cleanup costs, or other impacts on society.

Footprint: A measure of an organization's (or human's) demand on the Earth's ecosystems. Used as a measure of the full impact across the **supply chain** of an organization's operations, including consumption, use and emissions of energy, materials, resources, water, etc.

Green Bonds: Sometimes referred to as Green, Social, and Sustainability (or GSS) Bonds – provide investors with the ability to finance environmental and socially impactful projects while securing about the same risk/return profile to conventional bonds.

Green Chemistry: The design of chemical products and processes that reduce or eliminate the use or generation of hazardous substances across the full life cycle of chemical production, from design and manufacture to product use and disposal.

Green Financing: Financial flows from banking, micro-credit, insurance, and investment that are directed towards companies, investments, or projects aligned with sustainable development priorities.

GRI Reporting Principles: The Global Reporting Initiative (GRI) lists principles that help ensure high-quality sustainability reporting. Includes: accuracy, balance, clarity, comparability, completeness, sustainability context, timeliness, and verifiability.

Key Business Decisions: The handful of major decisions the CEO and Board make each year – typically involving merger, acquisition, or divestiture; large capital expenditure; new product launch; major research and development expenditure, etc.

Living Wage: An independent review to assess the percentage of a company's workforce (full-time employees, contractors, etc.) earns a living wage or better.

Material: Information is material if its omission or misstatement could influence the economic decision of users based on the financial statements. (See **Materiality**.)

Materiality: A concept or convention within the financial community relating to the importance/significance of something relevant to the corporation. Materiality in relation to information in an integrated financial and sustainability report refers to matters that could substantively affect the organization's ability to create value over the short, medium and long term.

Materiality Assessment: A process to identify, refine, and assess important S/ESG issues that should inform corporate strategy and reporting. GRI uses "materiality" in this context in a very broad way – any ESG issue that is important to stakeholders – whether or not it might have a (financially) material impact.

Natural Capital: The world's stock of natural assets, providing critical services and resilience. Examples include supporting water cycles and soil formation; protecting communities from major storms, floods, fires, and desertification; absorbing CO_2 to limit the pace of climate change.

Net Positive (Environmental Impact): A situation where the sum of the full environmental impacts of an organization – across the full **supply chain** – is less than the net reduction in environmental impact caused by use of the company's products and services.

Net Zero: The state where emissions of greenhouse gases due to human activities and removals of these gases are in balance over a given period. To reach net zero requires actions to reduce CO_2 or all greenhouse gases (e.g., by shifting from fossil fuel energy to sustainable energy sources). [See also **Carbon Neutral**.]

Physical Risk: Risk to assets from the impact of climate change. Can be acute risks that are event-driven (e.g., increased severity of extreme weather events, such as fire, drought, flooding, water scarcity, etc.) or chronic risk associated with longer-term shifts in climate patterns (e.g., sustained higher temperatures, sea level rise, changing precipitation patterns, etc.).

Root Cause Analysis: A term that describes a range of approaches, tools, and techniques to uncover the causes of problems.

Scenario Analysis: A structured way for organizations to develop strategic plans that are flexible and robust, given a range of plausible future states under conditions of uncertainty. Scenario analysis can be qualitative, relying on descriptive, written narratives, or quantitative, relying on numerical data and models, or some combination of both. Executives develop a small number of **scenarios**—how the future might unfold and affect an issue that confronts them.

Scenario (climate-related): a future anticipated mean temperature rise based on an assumption of action or inaction by society on limiting greenhouse gas emissions. Organizations that are significantly affected by transition risk (e.g., fossil-fuel-based industries, energy-intensive manufacturers, and transportation activities) and/or physical risk (e.g., agriculture, transportation and building infrastructure, insurance, and tourism) typically need to undertake in-depth and robust scenario analysis. A key type of transition risk scenario is a so-called 2°C scenario, which lays out a pathway and an emissions trajectory consistent with holding the increase in the global average temperature to 2°C above pre-industrial levels.

Science-Based Targets: Refers to science-based emission reduction targets that are independently verified against a set of criteria developed by SBTi. These typically refer to energy and greenhouse gas reduction goals aligned with the 1.5°C or well-below 2°C criteria.

Scope 1 GHG Emissions: Direct emissions from owned or controlled sources.

Scope 2 GHG Emissions: Indirect emissions from the generation of purchased energy.

Scope 3 GHG Emissions: All indirect emissions (not included in Scope 2) that occur in the **value chain** of the reporting company, including both upstream and downstream emissions.

Stage Gate Process: A technique used in product development to manage the work from one phase to the next. Each phase, or "stage" of the project is separated by a "gate" that prevents progressing onto the next stage without certain milestones, check, and decisions.

Stakeholder: Individuals or groups who can be significantly affected by an organization's business activities or whose actions can reasonably be expected to significantly affect the ability of the organization to create value over time. *Internal stakeholders* include the board (or equivalent), management, employees, and owners. *External stakeholders* include communities, government, NGOs, suppliers, customers, and consumers.

Supply Chain: The system of organizations, people, activities, information, and resources involved in moving a product or service from point of origin to point of consumption. Supply chains underlie **value chains**; environmental impact lies in the value chain – either upstream (supply chain) or downstream (product use) phase.

Sustainability: The pursuit of a business growth strategy that creates long-term shareholder value by seizing opportunities and managing risks related to the company's environmental and social impacts. Sustainability includes conventional environment, health, and safety (EHS) management; community involvement and philanthropy; labor and workplace conditions; as well as elements of corporate citizenship, corporate governance, **supply chain,** and procurement.

Sustainability Principles: Various ways of characterizing the concept of sustainability, including meaningfully progress on the Sustainable Development Goals (**SDGs**). Examples include using regenerative energy sources; continuously recycling non-regenerative resources; affecting a closed-loop flow of materials and energy; minimizing waste throughout the value chain. Can also include advancing a service; conserving and enhancing biodiversity; accounting for externalities; and enhancing social equity.

Total Societal Impact: The full economic, social, and environmental impact (both positive and negative, across the **value chain**) of a company's products and services; operations; core capabilities; and activities.

Total Societal Value: The value to society, measured by an analysis of the full economic, social, and environmental cost, impacts, and benefits – across the full **value chain**. (Connected to **Total Societal Impact**)

Traceable (also **Traceability):** The ability to identify and trace (e.g., from raw material extraction to product end-of-life) the history, distribution, location and use of products, parts, and materials, to ensure the reliability of sustainability claims, in the areas of environment, human rights, anti-corruption, etc.

Transition Risk: Risks from the transition of the economy/society to a clean, low-carbon economy. Risks typically include legislative, reputational, and market risks.

Value Chain: Includes all the individual steps taken to create a marketable product. The process by which a company transforms an idea to a finished product or service, adding value at each step: production, transportation, marketing, and after-sales service. Includes both the physical components and the value-adding activities such as design, marketing, etc. Environmental impact lies in the value chain – either upstream (supply chain) or downstream (product use) phase.

Water Positive: Refers to the quantity (vs. quality) of water. Includes replenishing more water than used, and (especially) putting back more water in stressed water basins.

Water Neutral: A situation where an organization returns to surface water or groundwater the volume of water it uses – across the full **supply chain** – at a level of purity that equal to or higher than the quality of the receiving body or aquifer.

Appendix D: ESG Navigator
An Industry-led Conversation on Sustainable Growth

It's a simple tool using clear language that helps us understand what good, better, best look like—and what's expected of our company as we progress.
Scott Tew, VP, Sustainability – Trane Technologies

ESG Navigator is a solution to the question busy CEOs and boards ask: "How do we use sustainability or ESG to reduce risk and grow our business?"

The benchmarking and strategic planning platform has been a work in progress for decades, continually shaped and refined by industry leaders, for industry leaders. More than a hundred senior corporate sustainability executives from global companies across most industry sectors have used the platform and contributed to its development.

Why Companies Use ESG Navigator

ESG Navigator is equally helpful to companies early or advanced in their sustainability journey. Businesses use the platform for different reasons, such as:
- Plotting sustainability performance on a simple maturity scale
- Assessing materiality of KSIs
- Generating internal engagement and alignment on sustainability measurement and objectives from stakeholders
- Agreeing on strategic priorities
- Benchmarking a company against industry sector and sub-sector peers as well as against all companies in the ESG Navigator database and the top ten performers overall
- Mapping coverage of external raters and regulators
- Tracking customer expectations
- Using the library of best sustainability practices globally and reviewing the ambitions of leading companies.
- Using the ESG Navigator summary PowerPoint presentation to share with the C-suite and board.

https://doi.org/10.1515/9783111548852-017

The Early Years

In 1997, Gib Hedstrom returned from a stint in Brussels, where he ran Arthur D. Little's environmental strategy practice. He had previously advised boards of over 20 Fortune 500 companies, but, this time, he noticed the boardroom conversation had changed.

Hearing of his time in Europe, and the strengthening sustainability agenda there, board directors asked how they should think about sustainability. They wanted to learn of the best practices in Europe, and how they performed against their industry broadly and their sectoral or sub-sectoral peers. Mostly, **CEOs and boards of leading companies wanted to simply understand how they could capture value from sustainability.**

Following several highly energetic board meetings, Gib began framing his explanations of sustainability as a jigsaw puzzle.

At the time, sustainability was commonly known as 'people, planet, profits.' Since the logical first step with a jigsaw puzzle is to create the border, Gib visually referred to the sustainability puzzle with people and planet as the two sides, profit at the top, and governance as the base. These four sections have framed ESG Navigator ever since.

With input from consulting colleagues and clients, Gib cast a net to capture global best practices that would constitute the individual pieces of the puzzle. As an early member of the World Business Council for Sustainable Development (WBCSD), Gib and his Arthur D. Little colleagues had access to many examples of global best practices. By 1999, a rough draft of the first corporate sustainability scorecard emerged. Two decades later, the scorecard was expanded and repositioned as ESG Navigator.

In 1999, the CEO of **Anheuser Busch** commissioned a review of its risks and opportunities from sustainability issues. Gib led a cross-functional team, using an early version of ESG Navigator that contained nearly 50 indicators in a simple rating scheme. This team assessed how Anheuser Busch stacked up and, in the process, helped to refine the scorecard. They later reported to the CEO, who accepted the recommended goals for climate change, water stewardship, energy use, and packaging.

After that initial engagement, Gib and his colleagues continued to capture global best practices and expanded and refined the benchmarking criteria, making them general enough to apply across industry sectors.

The Conference Board Conferences and Councils

In the early 2000s, The Conference Board (TCB) asked Gib to run its conferences and councils for sustainability executives.

At early annual global sustainability conferences the leaders of NGOs such as WBCSD, World Resources Institute and The Conservation Fund listened to CEOs of leading companies (including **Dow, DuPont** and **Nestlé Waters**) share their journeys. These events were always illuminating and provided provocative insights into the best practices that Gib folded into the growing ESG Navigator benchmarking tool.

Peter Senge, a social systems modeler from MIT, inspired and challenged the audience to instill a learning organization culture. Hannah Jones, then **Nike** CSO, explained how its approach to board oversight of sustainability strengthened after the US Supreme Court settled Kasky v. Nike, Inc., a case highlighting sweatshop labor.

In 2008, Gib started running TCB's Chief Environment, Health, and Safety Officers' Council. In 2012, he was asked to develop and launch two sustainability councils, one focused on strategy and implementation and the other on innovation and growth.

Each of these focus groups of corporate sustainability executives met three times a year for several days. Collectively, over 100 executives from 75 major companies participated. They shared challenges, lessons learned, and best practices. Meetings provided a valuable forum to dive deep into topics of interest to CEOs and led to dozens of measurable 'indicators' that would later become the organizing structure of ESG Navigator.

These discussions, combined with years of experience working with hundreds of companies, helped to fine-tune the benchmarking tool. A common theme at every meeting: but how do we stack up vis-à-vis our peers?

Agreeing on a Rating Scale

Thirty company leaders volunteered to participate in a 2015 pilot. ESG Navigator was already organized as it is today: four sections (governance, strategy, environment, social). More than 100 indicators, distilling hundreds of hours of conversations rolled up into 17 subcategories, or elements.

The next challenge was to agree to the rating scale. TCB member companies were eager to develop a model where the apex score would be awarded to the model sustainable corporation of tomorrow, not simply best quartile practices today.

In 2015, the pilot participants recommended a four-stage rating model:
- Stage 1 – **Engaging**: Basic compliance and conformance with industry practices.
- Stage 2 – **Accelerating**: Beyond compliance – still thinking about environmental stewardship and social responsibility in a traditional manner

- Stage 3 – **Leading:** Beginning to change business and business model, creating new products and shedding more environmentally and socially impactful ones.
- Stage 4 – **Transforming:** The model sustainable corporation of the twenty-first century with sustainable objectives and sustainable growth at its core.

The same year, TCB introduced this model of increasing maturity in an article by Gib called "Navigating the Sustainability Transformation." It laid out the basic structure of what was then called the Corporate Sustainability Scorecard™ and reflected insights from years of council meetings.

In 2018, Gib invited 60 corporate members of the TCB Councils to try the first version of the benchmarking tool. They eagerly embraced the strategic benchmarking approach.

As one Director, Corporate Responsibility, of a healthcare leader with a market cap of around $250 Bn summarized:

ESG Navigator is a roadmap. It shows us what best practice looks like (with hundreds of examples) – and helps us understand where we should be headed.

The ESG Navigator Collaborative

In In 2018, Gib moved on from managing TCB councils but further developed ESG Navigator by continuing to engage with sustainability leaders. Using the peer council concept, the "ESG Navigator Collaborative" grew as a series of monthly webinars, held under the **Chatham House Rule.**

The number of KSIs had reached an unwieldy 150, based on a growing set of global best practices. Leading sustainability executives and outside experts advised how to streamline the maturity model. The number of KSIs was eventually trimmed to 100.

The Collaborative webinars have grown in popularity since 2018. ESG Navigator access is freely available although NGOs, consultants and ESG service providers are not eligible to join. Employees of any for-profit company with over 100 employees, or revenues of at least $100 M can attend for free, after they request and are granted access via login credentials.

Each month up to 45 corporate sustainability leaders share their learnings. Since 2019, over 200 individual corporate leaders have participated.

One Chief Sustainability Officer of a $14 Bn revenue food producer summed up what many expressed of these webinars:

ESG Navigator is much more than a tool. Gib brings together a diverse group of leading companies to discuss and address the latest sustainability topics companies are wrestling with.

Quantifying the Unquantifiable

A core distinguishing feature of ESG Navigator is its measurement of both sides of the sustainability coin: those actions, programs and activities which are subject to external disclosure, and those that are not.

Some indicators are easy to measure across four stages of maturity. These are ones that companies disclose and include most of the environmental topics and more than half of the social ones.

However, *many indicators essentially quantify the unquantifiable*, soft topics. For example,
– Board oversight: agendas, time spent on sustainability in board meetings, etc.
– Customer engagement: CEO/C-suite interaction with customers; exploring the market strategy for new products and services, etc.
– Innovation pipeline: research and development of new products, services and solutions that can win in the marketplace.
– Workplace culture: how the internal incentive system defines the 'unwritten rules of the game' and how employees engage with sustainability.
– Strategic planning: the process and extent to which it incorporates robust scenarios and comprehensive board deliberation.

ESG Navigator measures both the quantifiable and the unquantifiable. The outcomes are summarized in 'Snake Charts' and other visuals and analytics that become a backdrop for discussions. The overriding theme of the webinars is to discuss how companies can create sustainable growth and value.

As the Deputy Chief Sustainability Officer of an international integrated chemicals company based in Europe said:

ESG Navigator provides benchmarking insights that other frameworks simply cannot give.

ESG Ratings Cover Only Half of Activity: Of Course They Fail

In 2019, when Pacific Gas & Electric (PG&E) filed for Chapter 11 bankruptcy protection due to liabilities for catastrophic California wildfires, The Wall Street Journal declared it "The first major corporate casualty of climate change."

What was most striking was that external ESG ratings providers had given PG&E gold stars:
- Sustainalytics had named PG&E an "outperformer," ranked in the 82nd percentile on governance and the 88th on environment.
- Corporate Responsibility magazine rated PG&E the #1 utility.
- Newsweek Green Rankings placed PG&E as the #1 utility and listed the company #4 overall.

How did the ESG ratings agencies miss that PG&E's lack of governance oversight would deliver such existential risk to its shareholders and lenders?

The answer is simple: **ratings only access data and information that companies disclose publicly**. It turns out that the items disclosed, prior to the EU, UK, and CA reporting standards, make up around 50 percent of the actions companies take. Ratings do not access the other half because:
- The information is confidential
- The information is qualitative and not easily measured
- The information was not requested by ESG ratings organizations.

Shortly after the news PG&E news broke, TCB published an article by Gib "Beware the 80/20 Governance Trap: Focus on the "G" in ESG."

At the time of the PG&E bankruptcy, eight major US utilities had self-assessed their performance on ESG risk management and governance using ESG Navigator. Collectively, these utilities had objectively rated themselves an average of Stage 1.7 on the four-stage maturity model. The ESG risk gap related to the lack of governance oversight.

Those eight utilities were basically saying, "we are at early stages of *accelerating* our work on sustainability. We are clearly neither *leading* nor *transforming* (on the four-stage ESG Navigator rating scale).

The article noted that, while relatively straightforward for a corporation to score highly on most external ESG rating criteria, even those integrated into investment decision-making, **those raters had very little idea of what was going on internally** – how key business decisions were being made and what behaviors the culture was promoting.

ESG Ratings Maps

The PG&E situation caused considerable discussion among the ESG Navigator Collaborative members. During webinars, company leaders discussed how much pressure they were under to achieve strong ratings, (for, amongst other things, reducing the company's cost of capital), while knowing that they were methodologically flawed. They asked Gib and his team to help.

The 80 companies participating in the monthly ESG Navigator webinars in 2019 needed a new dimension. They wanted to understand how well positioned their company was to perform against the criteria used by 15 major ESG reporting frameworks and ratings, including CDP, GRI, Sustainalytics and MSCI.

In response, in 2020 ESG Navigator developed a new analytical tool, **ESG Ratings Maps,** to assess the extent to which these reporting frameworks and ratings *cover* the 100 KSIs, the library of actions that companies take independently and ESG Navigator assesses. Many companies shared the 'stoplight' (red, yellow, green) maps with their C-suite and board.

Data from ESG Navigator confirms that roughly **half of corporate sustainability activities are *not disclosed* to the raters.** They are treated as competitive intelligence.

The Sustainability Group Chair at a multinational engineering and construction firm valued at over $9 Bn noted that the ESG Ratings Maps are valuable so they and their peers can be more confident and open in their company assessments. She said:

> *The data we provide is confidential; no other company can see our ratings. We can candidly assess where we are in our sustainability journey – and where we should focus to improve.*

Identifying Leading Sustainability Indicators

By 2022, the ESG Navigator database contained input from about 150 companies who, for the previous four years, had used the platform to assess performance across a tough maturity scale and to identify *which KSIs they should be focusing on to creating value.*

Patterns had emerged. Members expressed a desire to understand which of the 100 sustainability KSIs were widely viewed as the most important.

Gib launched a study in partnership with a key client to understand which KSIs should be viewed as the leading sustainability indicators. The team surveyed leading sustainability VPs to supplement the ESG Navigator data and the results were presented at a joint meeting of TCB's two sustainability councils in early 2023 and later shared in various webinars.

Along Comes CSRD, IFRS, CA and More

In early 2024, as the onslaught of new disclosure and reporting standards emerged from the EU, UK and California, companies actively engaging with the monthly ESG Navigator webinars clearly needed a new feature covering regulations.

A new analytical tool was born on the ESG Navigator platform – one analogous to the ESG Ratings Maps but this time comparing company performance on the 100 KSIs with the coverage of the major emerging disclosure standards.

The ESG Regulations Maps were launched in mid-2024 and are consistently growing in complexity and usefulness.

The ESG Navigator research team annually updates the analysis comparing against each of the KSIs the methodology of key regulations (EU, UK, California, etc.), and of external reporting frameworks and ratings. The team evaluates the coverage of these standards, compared with the detailed Stage 1, 2, 3, and 4 descriptors of each KSI.

Summary: By Industry – For Industry

ESG Navigator has been **developed, used, shaped, tested, and *refined by industry leaders for industry leaders* for over 20 years**. Today, over 150 major global companies use it and an additional 80 companies periodically join the ESG Navigator webinars. All data entered by companies is confidential. Some pay a membership fee for extra features and personalization; others use the free version.

Companies say it provides a top-down view of sustainability for the C-suite and board. They appreciate that the ESG Navigator rating scale is tough; no company is fully Stage 4 today. The average overall rating of ~150 major companies using ESG Navigator is slightly below Stage 2.

Each year the research team, with input from users old and new, review and update the ESG Navigator Maturity Model. External developments and new regulations are assessed and KSIs are refined, with descriptors checked for integrity and relevance.

Each sustainability leader extracts different aspects of value from ESG Navigator. As noted in Chapter 5, a long-time sustainability leader and vice president of Sustainability at IBM shared this perspective:

"**ESG Navigator is my library.** It organizes current and emerging ESG topics in one place; helps us assess the relevance of these topics to our business; shows our organization's maturity; and identifies improvement opportunities."

To become a member, use the basic tools, and join the free monthly webinars, please contact *admin@esgnavigator.com.*

Appendix E: ESG Navigator KSIs

The high-level structure of ESG Navigator is depicted in Figure E.1. This is virtually identical to the structure we started with two decades ago, but with more emphasis to impacts across the full value chain.

Governance & Leadership
- Company Purpose
- CEO and C-Suite Leadership
- Board Leadership
- Goals and Metrics
- Culture and Organization
- Disclosure and Reporting

Strategy & Execution
- Customers and Markets
- Strategic Planning
- Innovation, R&D
- Product Offerings
- Supply Chain Management

Environmental Stewardship
- Environment: Operations
- Environment: Supply Chain
- Environment: Product

Social Responsibility
- Social: Workplace
- Social: Supply Chain
- Social: Community

Figure E.1: ESG Navigator Structure
Source: ESG Navigator

As companies pursue sustainable growth, they will ultimately save time and money by weaving climate and sustainability into the fabric of how they manage the company – not bolting it on.

Each of the 17 elements in Figure E.1 relates to a core corporate activity or function. These are not sustainability terms. For example, Environmental Stewardship is not about climate, water, and waste. Instead, it is organized by the way a CEO runs the company, including operations, supply chain, and products.

The following pages depict the individual KSIs that comprise each of these 17 elements. For reasons of space, we include only the Stage 1 and Stage 4 descriptors. (For more information, visit www.esgnavigator.com.)

https://doi.org/10.1515/9783111548852-018

1. Governance: Company Purpose

Stage 1 *"Engaging"*	Stage 4 *"Transforming"*
Purpose, Vision, Mission	KSI 1.1
Sustainability (**S**) is viewed as **CSR**** and/or an extension of **EHS** and philanthropy. Company purpose, vision, and mission can enable **S** but the extent of **S** ambition is not explicit.	Sustainability (**S**) is the North Star *at the core* of the company's distinctive role in society. Every strategic and key operational decision is guided by purpose, with **S** driving goal of **net-positive** impact.
Operationalizing Sustainability	KSI 1.2
The C-suite broadly communicates traditional **S** positions (e.g., ethics, EHS, corporate responsibility, etc.). Business systems and controls are in place to adhere to those policies.	The C-suite is driving deep integration of **S** into core business processes, cascading (via individual performance goals) throughout the company's regions, businesses, and organization.
Public Commitments	KSI 1.3
Company conforms to common industry practices and standards (e.g., **GRI**). Commitments are general, not calling out **material** issues.	Company's CEO and board of directors publicly commit bold **S** action (e.g., rapid decarbonization, investment in natural capital, etc.)
Long-Term Viability of Core Businesses	KSI 1.4
Core businesses do not align particularly well with **sustainability principles** (e.g., using renewable energy, fully recycling, minimizing waste throughout the value chain, enhancing social equity).	Core businesses engage with customers and **value chain** partners to measure and drive toward decarbonization, social equity, and net-positive impact.
Key Business Decisions	KSI 1.5
S elements are typically not major factors in **key business decisions** (e.g., major investment, new product launch, acquisition, divestiture, etc.).	Material **S** issues guide strategic planning and capital allocation. Company demonstrates a track record of factoring material **S** risks into key business decisions.

*****S** is used as shorthand for sustainability in Appendix E
******Acronyms (defined in Appendix B) and potentially unfamiliar words (defined in Appendix C) are bold the first time used

2. Governance: CEO and C-suite Leadership

Stage 1 *"Engaging"*	Stage 4 *"Transforming"*
Public Positioning	KSI 2.1
CEO/C-suite rarely speaks publicly about **S*** issues or the material environmental or social impacts of the company or overall industry.	CEO often speaks publicly about material **S** risks and opportunities, highlighting the company's purpose, role, and responsibility in addressing global **S** challenges.
Financial Strategy	KSI 2.2
S does not drive financial strategy or decision-making. Transparency regarding material **S** issues is limited.	Cost of borrowing is directly related to achieving **S** goals. Invest in sustainability-linked products, e.g., green bonds, carbon credits, and climate insurance. Partner to drive sector-wide transformation.
Engagement with Investors/Owners	KSI 2.3
CEO/C-suite responds to **S** questions from investors (or owners if a private company) but shares relatively little insight regarding **S** risks or opportunities.	CEO/C-suite actively engages with key investors regarding societal impact topics. Leads on addressing climate change and connecting climate-related issues to long-term resilience.
Collaboration with Key Customers	KSI 2.4
CEO/C-suite responds to customer requests regarding **S**.	CEO/C-suite collaborates with key customers to create **S**-advantaged products and services core to the company's growth strategy.
Messaging to Employees	KSI 2.5
CEO/C-suite encourages compliance and efforts on selected **S** topics beyond EHS, CSR, and philanthropy.	CEO/C-suite actively ties **S** to company strategy. Messages cascade down and encourage deep integration of **S** with daily operations and business processes.
Engagement with NGOs	KSI 2.6
CEO/C-suite discusses relevant global **S** issues mostly among colleagues with similar worldview (e.g., other members of the same industry associations).	CEO/C-suite frequently engages with a wide pool of stakeholders on sector-relevant topics. CEO/C-suite provides industry leadership and spends considerable time (e.g., >20 hours/year) engaging directly with NGOs and educating others.

***S** *means sustainability*

3. Governance: Board of Directors Leadership

Stage 1 **"Engaging"**	Stage 4 **"Transforming"**
Full Board Oversight	KSI 3.1
Full **board** oversight of *S* is neither explicit nor extensive. Board self-assessment process does not focus on *S* fluency.	Full board is actively and frequently involved (during and between meetings) in discussing *S* issues, risks, and opportunities. Board self-assessment process builds robust cadence of *S* learning.
Committees, Charters, and Roles	KSI 3.2
Board roles and committee charters focus on conventional EHS and public policy issues, with only summary reference to *S*. No designated *S* leader.	Each board committee incorporates relevant *S* topics, explicit and detailed in charters (which are updated frequently).
Sustainability Fluency	KSI 3.3
Board *S* fluency (especially environment and social) is little to moderate. The board relies mostly on internal experts and external industry associations.	Board fluency is robust on material *S* risks and opportunities across the value chain. Board members engage in systematic cadence of learning between board meetings.
Meeting Agendas	KSI 3.4
Board meetings cover EHS, philanthropy, *S* benchmarking, trends, and emerging issues. CSO reports goals and metrics related to own operations. Pre-reads: limited, with few *S* thought leadership articles.	Board meetings involve *S* learning (e.g., scenario planning), with business leaders discussing full value chain *S* risks and opportunities. Board calendar drives *S* learning cadence. Pre-reads: periodic deep dive requiring considerable preparation.
Time Commitment in Meetings	KSI 3.5
Time spent on *S* (full board or committee) is 2–4 hours a year, with *S* a key agenda item at least one meeting per year. No special *S* strategy sessions.	Time on *S* at every meeting is significant (>12 hours per year, full board or board committee). A half-day special (e.g., scenarios) session, in addition, deliberates long-term implications.
Board Diversity	KSI 3.6
Board diversity representation (gender, ethnicity, religion, etc.) is cumulatively less than 20%. May or may not have a board diversity policy.	Board reflects diversity of workforce and market, with at least 50% women. In addition, board reflects highly diverse life experiences and key geographic areas of strategic importance.

4. Governance: Sustainability Goals and Metrics

Stage 1 *"Engaging"*	Stage 4 *"Transforming"*
Goals and Roadmap: Near Term	KSI 4.1
Near-term (e.g., 2–5 year) *S* goals focus on own operations and are likely achievable (if a stretch). Mindset stays within comfort zone, with interim steps to achieve goals.	Near-term goals are highly rigorous (e.g., **net zero** or net-positive impact, with third-party validation such as **science-based targets**). A detailed roadmap links to longer-term targets.
Goals and Roadmap: Long Term	KSI 4.2
Company lacks long-term (e.g., 5+ year) *S* goals. Company *S* goals align with typical industry practices.	Company keeps goals and metrics driving toward net positive across its value chain. Also addresses opportunities for **circularity**.
Materiality Assessment	KSI 4.3
Materiality assessment mostly covers impacts from own operations.	Materiality assessment drives significant **footprint** reductions, with C-suite executives personally owning material *S* issues.
Tracking Footprint Reduction	KSI 4.4
Assess *S* impacts informally. Report footprint of own operations vs. baseline year (or when footprint reduction efforts began).	Measure cuts in footprint, aligning with circular economy principles. Carbon reductions are on track to align with 1.5°C or well-below 2°C goals.
Tracking Revenue	KSI 4.5
Informally assess *S* attributes of products and services.	Derive 80%+ of revenue from products and services that create a net-positive impact on the planet and society.
Accounting for Material Risks, Externalities	KSI 4.6
View (financial) accounting for material *S* risks and **externalities** as a compliance requirement.	Incorporate externalities across value chain into financial accounting, aligned with leading global impact accounting principles, consistent with financial controls.
Ratings and Rankings	KSI 4.7
Engage with external **ESG raters** to gain recognition, if applicable, and enhance credibility of external reporting.	Earn recognition as a model *S* performer by key ESG raters, peers, and NGOs, who value company's track record of investing in best-in-class *S* governance and strategy.

5. Governance: Culture and Organization

Stage 1 *"Engaging"*	Stage 4 *"Transforming"*
Compensation and Goals	KSI 5.1
CEO and C-suite KPIs (tied to compensation) may include a few traditional *S* topics (e.g., compliance, safety, EHS). Annual employee *S* goals are largely limited to these *S* topics.	CEO and C-suite compensation (20%+ or more if defined by a regulator) is based on performance against material *S* issues (full value chain). Cascade down to all staff and relevant contractors, reinforcing sustainability as a core value and core purpose (North Star).
Organization	KSI 5.2
A C-suite member has *S* oversight and addresses sustainability risks during crises and risk reviews. One or more cross-functional *S* teams may have a C-suite sponsor.	The CEO and C-suite drive *S* during CEO meetings and as a core part of strategic plans and performance reviews. *S* council has several C-suite members and meets at least quarterly.
Accountability and Leadership	KSI 5.3
The most senior, full-time corporate *S* leader reports below the CEO and runs cross-functional *S* team(s).	A C-suite member leads *S*. Every C-suite member and senior leader has explicit *S* responsibilities.
Reward and Recognition	KSI 5.4
Company executives recognize *S* excellence, though limited to traditional sustainability topics only (e.g., compliance, safety, EHS).	CEO and C-suite recognize *S* excellence (tied to bold company *S* goals) in a high-profile way, perhaps awarded annually by CEO and/or board member(s).

6. Governance: Disclosure and Reporting

Stage 1 *"Engaging"*	Stage 4 *"Transforming"*
Annual Reporting and Financial Disclosures	KSI 6.1
Mention material *S* issues briefly (if at all) in CEO letter. Financial disclosures are mostly conventional. May issue a sustainability report. Discuss *S* as corporate responsibility or CSR.	Publish and integrate *S* information with annual report. *S* issues are not easily distinguished from core business issues (100% core business language). Strategic messaging is aligned with net-positive impact.
Disclosure of Material Impacts and Strategy	KSI 6.2
Disclose required information. Follow *S* disclosure and reporting frameworks and tools generally accepted among industry peers.	Reporting includes comprehensive qualitative information on positive and negative impacts across the value chain, with efforts to quantify impacts where possible.
Assurance and Verification	KSI 6.3
Company does not solicit formal verification of *S* business processes or data.	Company's third-party review is consistent with the company's review of financial controls (e.g., "reasonable' assurance" of data) and addresses alignment with leading *S* reporting frameworks.
Transparency and Marketing	KSI 6.4
Adopt a cautious approach, remaining consistent with industry sector average. Commit to protecting consumer data and privacy. Address customer concerns (though perhaps not addressing material *S* risks). Communicate *S* impacts when necessary.	Earn recognition as a leader in transparency – addressing each of the **GRI reporting principles** or equivalent. Engage with ethical advertising standards bodies to ensure alignment with best practices and earn ethical marketing credentials.
Public Policy (e.g., Lobbying) Alignment	KSI 6.5
Company's public policy positions on *S* issues and risks (e.g., lobbying, political contributions, etc.) are aligned with industry association positions.	Company's lobbying and *S* policy positions and actions are robust (e.g., net zero or net-positive impact), transparent, and consistent with *S* goals.

7. Strategy: Customers and Markets

Stage 1 *"Engaging"*	Stage 4 *"Transforming"*
Customer Engagement	KSI 7.1
Engage with customers to instruct on safe product use. Respond to customer *S* requests. Solicit feedback about *S* features and impacts of existing products and services.	Engage with customers to jointly create or expand the market for sustainable products and services that meet rigorous criteria for *S* attributes. Pioneer innovative business models (e.g., **closed loop**).
Market Strategy: Existing Products and Services	KSI 7.2
Sell existing portfolio of products and services into traditional markets and market segments. Expand into new markets motivated by traditional business factors (e.g., regulations, economics).	Launch industry product and service breakthroughs with new *S* features. Differentiate from competitors based (in part) on *S* features.
Market Strategy: New Products and Services	KSI 7.3
Expand product offerings motivated by traditional business factors (e.g., regulations, economics, etc.).	Reimagine the market to advance *S* agenda. Map *S* investments to most material issues across the value chain.
Product Portfolio Transformation	KSI 7.4
Consider sustainable attributes occasionally, when extending existing product lines.	Transform company's products and services to fully embrace *S* attributes. Lead as the market grows, while rapidly exiting less sustainable offerings.
Impacts on Brand	KSI 7.5
Company brand does not focus predominantly on *S*. Company publicizes activities in favorable *S* light.	Company brand is tied directly to driving **total societal value.**

8. Strategy: Strategic Planning

Stage 1 "Engaging"	Stage 4 "Transforming"
Strategic Planning Process	KSI 8.1
Strategic planning incorporates conventional social responsibility and EHS topics. *S* is not a key driver of business strategy.	*S* issues drive strategic plans (at least 5-year horizon), resulting in a bold roadmap for decarbonizing, reducing footprint, and enhancing total societal value.
Use of Scenario Analysis	KSI 8.2
Use informal processes to identify potential future *S* impacts on the business.	Use **scenario analysis** to identify key determinants of resilience and integrate actions and monitoring into strategic planning and risk management. Engage with board to explore business scenarios, building on climate scenarios.
Cost Reduction	KSI 8.3
Employ traditional costing. Focus on reducing footprint (emissions, packaging, waste, etc.).	Calculate and report on mitigation of value chain externalities in cost management. Incorporate a moving cost/t/**CO2e** for future GHG emissions in investment decisions.
Enterprise Risk Management	KSI 8.4
Material *S* risks are not fully integrated into the company's (formal or informal) risk management process(es).	Material *S* issues are considered as drivers of risk and integrated into **enterprise risk management** as stand-alone risks. C-suite member(s) are accountable for material *S* risks.
Revenue Pipeline from Sustainable Products and Services	KSI 8.5
Sustainability attributes of products and services are not widely viewed as a revenue driver (unless a customer asks).	Sustainability drivers dominate growth options. Company is on track to generate majority of revenue from offerings linked to sustainability.
Capital Allocation	KSI 8.6
CapEx (e.g., about 25% for many sectors) is driven by *S* risks, using traditional metrics.	CapEx (often >75% for certain sectors) aligns with company rapidly transforming to achieve net-positive *S* impact. Invest considerably in **natural capital** where relevant to sector and company.

9. Strategy: Innovation, Research & Development

Stage 1 *"Engaging"*	Stage 4 *"Transforming"*
Linkage: Sustainability and Innovation	KSI 9.1
No formal linkage between *S* and the company's innovation processes.	*S* drives long-term growth. Goal is to decouple sales growth from full value chain footprint.
Materials and Labor Inputs	KSI 9.2
Regulations are the main *S* driver in evaluating materials and labor inputs into new products and services.	Processes are in place to eliminate high-hazard materials and labor inputs and to maximize use of natural and highly recycled or recyclable materials.
Product Design and Development	KSI 9.3
Use basic **stage gate process** for product development with *S* issues considered, if indirectly. Limited or no use of eco-design tools.	Determine "go/no-go" decision early in the process, fully incorporating product *S* risk assessment and related metrics. Use innovative eco-design tools, aimed at closed-loop processes.
R&D Partnerships	KSI 9.4
Engage in some *S*-related R&D partnerships (e.g., with universities, incubator start-ups, etc.) to collaborate on *S* issues.	Aggressively seek *S*-related R&D partnerships that could have a significant business and societal impact. Work with *S* thought leaders.
R&D Investment	KSI 9.5
Rarely invest in R&D or new technologies targeted at sustainable products and services. Work with customers to refine and upgrade offerings with incrementally better *S* benefits.	Make major investments in disruptive technologies, aligned with corporate purpose, to reduce full value chain footprint – driving to net zero. Partner with customers to systematically reduce material *S* impacts across the value chain.

10. Strategy: Product Offerings

Stage 1 *"Engaging"*	Stage 4 *"Transforming"*
Product* Value Proposition	KSI 10.1
Focus is selling products and providing value (e.g., price and quality) to customers and shareholders, while ensuring products and services do not harm health or environment.	Focus moves increasingly to products supporting net zero, as well as services and solutions. Societal value of offerings and driving toward a closed-loop value chain are core.
Product Stewardship	KSI 10.2
Working to reduce or phase out hazardous substances. Build/enhance positive *S* features. Do not conduct formal product audits.	Quantify *S* and financial benefits for existing and new products and services. Purposefully invest in green and/or healthy offerings. Demonstrate track record of positive *S* performance.
Product Risk Assessment	KSI 10.3
Use product *S* risk assessment selectively, for products that are high risk and/or high business impact. Do not use formal **LCA** or equivalent.	Use **cradle-to-cradle** metrics (or equivalent) for existing and all new products and services.
Product Labeling and Rating	KSI 10.4
Use standard industry codes, certifications, and labels. Disclose hazardous substances.	Use industry-leading product labeling and ratings supporting portfolio changes across businesses.
Product Quality and Safety	KSI 10.5
Product quality and safety standards are driven predominantly by laws and regulations.	Product quality and safety standards across portfolio are fully aligned with sustainability and **circularity**.
Product Marketing and Advertising	KSI 10.6
Encourage safe and responsible use. Company is "selectively quiet" about potential product *S* risks.	Communicate (often LCA-based) cradle-to-cradle impacts. Actively promote responsible consumption, 100% recycling, etc.

*The word 'product' incorporates the full range of products, services, and solutions

11. Strategy: Supply Chain Management

Stage 1 *"Engaging"*	Stage 4 *"Transforming"*
Responsible Sourcing Approach	KSI 11.1
Sourcing and supplier vetting process includes *S* criteria limited to basic compliance with regulations and common industry practices.	Embed responsible sourcing policies, standards, and processes throughout the company (regions, businesses, functions) – setting a high standard for industry peers.
Engaging on Material Issues	KSI 11.2
Assess *S* issues in own operations to gain baseline awareness. Engage in dialog across **supply chain** about *S* issues.	Engage in ongoing dialog on all material *S* issue(s) across full supply chain, with a focus on growth and opportunity. Foster peer learning on addressing material *S* issues.
Standards for Supply Chain Impacts	KSI 11.3
Impose conventional contract requirements, focusing primarily on compliance. Share industry-wide standards with key suppliers.	Impose non-negotiable *S* requirements for demonstrated impact reduction. Apply **root cause analysis** to actively reduce *S* footprint in the entire supply chain.
Measuring Supply Chain Impacts	KSI 11.4
Measure supply chain *S* impacts by relying primarily on suppliers' reports. Protect privacy through secure information storage and privacy policies.	Measure, track, and report material *S* impacts throughout the supply chain with a goal of net-positive impacts. Investigations analyze root causes and implement revisions to procurement processes.
Verifying Supply Chain Impacts	KSI 11.5
Conduct basic due diligence and rely on suppliers to conduct compliance assurance (self-audits).	Conduct third-party audits of suppliers in higher-risk countries (as defined by Human Rights Watch or similar list). Publish audit results.

12. Environmental Footprint: Operations

Stage 1 *"Engaging"*	Stage 4 *"Transforming"*
GHG Emissions: Owned/Controlled Sources (Scope 1)	KSI 12.1
Company is on target for about 10–20% reduction in **Scope 1 GHG emissions** from baseline year.	Company is on target for being **carbon neutral** or better (use of unbundled **REC**s or low-integrity offsets is not permitted).
GHG Emissions: Energy Purchased (Scope 2)	KSI 12.2
Source most energy (e.g., fuel, electricity, transport, etc.) from conventional sources (oil, gas, coal) with <10% renewables.	Source 100% renewable energy. Company is on target for being carbon neutral or better (use of unbundled RECs or low-quality offsets is not permitted).
Non-Carbon Emissions	KSI 12.3
Manage emissions (e.g., SOx, NOx, particulates, VOCs, TRI compounds, etc.), spills, and releases for compliance.	Achieve zero discharge of hazardous substances and 100% fully benign emissions.
Buildings and Equipment	KSI 12.4
Launch targeted efforts to reduce energy use in owned buildings and equipment.	Drive all owned or leased buildings to net-zero energy within five years. Working towards **LEED** certification for all buildings.
Water Management	KSI 12.5
Achieve incremental reduction of water consumed. Focus on compliance in own operations.	Achieve **water neutrality** in all operations. Manage for net **water positive** impact on stressed aquifer supply.
Biodiversity and Land Management	KSI 12.6
Focus on compliance and protection. Remediate (clean up) or restore land as required.	Reduce nature-related impacts as much as possible. Restore and protect habitat aggressively. Invest in (and promote the value of) natural capital as part of an integrated approach to addressing habitat loss and climate change.
Waste Management	KSI 12.7
Implement goals to reduce hazardous waste and report progress on waste reduction (e.g., per unit of production).	Achieve **zero waste to landfill** from own operations, 100% recycling, and zero hazardous waste to the extent economically feasible.

13. Environmental Footprint: Supply Chain

Stage 1 *"Engaging"*	Stage 4 *"Transforming"*
Approach to Supply Chain Environmental Impacts	KSI 13.1
Comply with industry standards regarding environmental footprint. Focus on quality, cost, and dependability (more than environmental impacts).	Partner with suppliers to drive supply chain environmental footprint toward zero. Monitor performance vs. joint customer-supplier goals. Collaborate around growth opportunities.
Materials Sourced: Human-Made *(e.g., chemicals, metals, plastics, etc.)*	KSI 13.2
Adopt some resource efficiency efforts with a focus on compliance. Source about 10–20% recycled content.	Approach closed loop with 75–100% recycled content. Align with **green chemistry** principles or leading sector-specific guidelines.
Materials Sourced: Biological Based *(e.g., forest products, etc.)*	KSI 13.3
Source in conventional ways, with a compliance focus, incremental reductions, and aligned with industry codes.	Source 100% from responsible and/or certified *S* sources: 100% bio-based materials if proven (e.g., through LCA) to be better.
Scope 3 GHG Emissions	KSI 13.4
Engage across supply chain on major *S* issues/risks – but with limited or no focus on supply chain GHG emissions.	Engage actively with suppliers, customers, and others, successfully meeting a science-based target to cut **Scope 3** GHG emissions.
Supply Chain Impact: Biodiversity	KSI 13.5
Manage biodiversity to maintain compliance and minimize risks. Focus on the company's own operations.	Source 100% sustainably to restore, preserve, and enhance **biodiversity** in value chain, independently verified. Lead protection and restoration beyond areas of direct impact.
Supply Chain Impact: Water	KSI 13.6
Manage supply chain water issues to maintain compliance.	Achieve water neutral status across supply chain with no upstream negative social impacts from usage. Lead on water quality preservation.
Supply Chain Impact: Waste	KSI 13.7
Manage supply chain waste issues to maintain compliance.	Collaborate with suppliers to report "zero-waste to landfill" (or equivalent).

14. Environmental Footprint: Products

Stage 1 *"Engaging"*	Stage 4 *"Transforming"*
Responsibility for Product* Use and End-of-Life	KSI 14.1
Focus on compliance, with typically informal systems for product take back, recycling or reuse of products and services sold.	Implement robust systems ensuring end-of-life responsibility that approaches closed loop and preserves or restores **ecosystem services.**
Product Traceability	KSI 14.2
Focus on compliance when monitoring inputs through life-cycle stages, with little or no focus on traceability of source materials.	Ensure that all high-risk **S** source materials inputs are **traceable** (e.g., from raw material extraction to product end-of-life).
Product Carbon Impact	KSI 14.3
Focus on low cost. Carbon impact associated with customer/consumer use is not a major priority.	Design all products and services for minimum carbon (GHG) impact and maximum energy efficiency.
Product Durability	KSI 14.4
Focus portfolio on traditional elements (product quality and low cost), with most products being single use and disposable.	Build a robust product life-extension business. Sell highly durable products; sell products as a service where possible.
Product Biodegradability	KSI 14.5
Pursue **biodegradability** associated with products and services as beneficial, though not a major consideration.	All product offerings are biodegradable (as applicable), with calculations externally validated by respected rating agencies.
Product Recyclability and Reusability	KSI 14.6
Achieve product recyclability, reusability when economically beneficial.	Achieve product recyclability and reusability for entire product portfolio (as applicable).
Product Water-Use Efficiency	KSI 14.7
Increase water-use efficiency when driven by customer requests and goals, or when required by regulatory standards.	Improve product water-use efficiency (e.g., >50%) during customer use (as applicable). Design offerings for minimum water use.
Product Packaging	KSI 14.8
Reduce product packaging when economical. Use some renewable, recyclable, or reusable packaging.	Provide renewable, recyclable, and/or reusable options approaching 100% of total packaging.

*The word 'product' incorporates the full range of products, services, and solutions

15. Social Performance: Workplace

Stage 1 "Engaging"	Stage 4 "Transforming"
Workplace Environment	KSI 15.1
The company meets basic needs, honors individual privacy, and fosters pay equity – including a **living wage**. Focus is mostly "inside the fence line" of company operations.	The company highly values human capital and *"walks the talk."* Employees are truly living the company purpose – driving achievement of robust *S* goals.
Diversity, Equity, and Inclusion	KSI 15.2
Provide a workplace with equal opportunity without discrimination. Make public commitments (e.g., equal opportunity). Outline DEI-focused programs and training.	Push the boundaries of industry sector with a highly diverse C-suite and staff. DEI policies extend to business partners, vendors, and suppliers (e.g., 30%+ spending with minority businesses).
Recruitment and Retention	KSI 15.3
Emphasize traditional benefits in hiring and managing workforce (e.g., childcare, telecommuting, etc.).	The company's bold purpose and vision, reinforced by CEO's distinctive sustainability leadership, attract the best and brightest.
Safety Programs and Performance	KSI 15.4
Company promotes safety performance generally consistent with industry peers.	CEO/C-suite drive safety culture that is pervasive across the company and constantly reinforced. A leader across all industry.
Health and Wellness	KSI 15.5
Provide a comfortable work environment with insurance coverage, exercise benefits, voluntary programs, etc.	Provide formal health and wellness programs to all employees and business partners. Provide robust mental health programs.
Training and Staff Development	KSI 15.6
Provide basic safety, ethics, diversity etc. training for all employees. Provide *S* skills training and career development.	Invest in robust *S* training tools and infrastructure so that all staff are aligned with company ambitions. Provide *S* leadership training and *S* learning for high-potential employees.
Employee Engagement	KSI 15.7
Provide opportunities for employee *S* engagement – largely based on individual initiative.	Monitor, track, and support employees actively working on high-impact projects with major *S* value contribution.

16. Social Performance: Supply Chain

Stage 1 *"Engaging"*	Stage 4 *"Transforming"*
Approach to Supply Chain Social Impacts	KSI 16.1
Comply with social responsibility standards and requirements. Focus on quality, cost, and dependability (over social impacts).	Partner with most suppliers to drive down negative social impacts across supply chain. Actively monitor performance vs. joint customer-supplier goals.
Human Rights	KSI 16.2
No formal human rights policy (other than perhaps protecting human rights of direct employees). Comply with laws, regulations, and global conventions. Conduct basic risk assessments to identify issues related to forced labor, child labor, abusive treatment, etc.	Publish results of human rights impact assessments across supply chain. Ensure extra levels of diligence when sourcing from countries with a higher risk of modern slavery, child labor, or forced labor, with a strong drive to eradicate child/forced labor.
Labor Relations	KSI 16.3
Ensure that suppliers support minimum standards of worker health and safety, work hours, and wages. Support basic, structured relations with trade unions by key suppliers.	Demonstrate leadership as a strong promoter of labor relations throughout supply chain. Eliminate abuse of temporary contracts. Commit to independent whistleblower protections.
Supply Chain Diversity	KSI 16.4
Define supply chain diversity baseline (e.g., based on current spend data). Include diverse businesses in supply chain where required by law or industry expectation. Engage in dialog with local or regional diversity organizations.	Publish progress against supply chain diversity goals. Publicly advocate for diversity across supply chain. Achieve external recognition for program and results.
Supply Chain Capacity Building	KSI 16.5
Work with key supply chain partners to ensure quality, dependability, and compliance.	Systematically partner with supply chain partners at multiple levels to eliminate negative impacts and improve supplier *S* performance overall.

17. Social Performance: Community

Stage 1 "Engaging"	Stage 4 "Transforming"
Philosophy Regarding Community	KSI 17.1
Focus on community initiatives (often locally or regionally) where it fits business goals and doesn't significantly affect bottom line.	Embed company in communities, driven by shared value (value to shareholders and to society). Actively measure and track **total societal impact.**
Engagement with Communities and NGOs	KSI 17.2
Approach communities and NGOs with the intent to win approval. Defend company positions. Respond to concerns to protect brand and reputation.	Engage deeply with communities and NGOs, focusing on key societal challenges. Use a formal, structured process (from C-suite to site managers) to engage stakeholders.
Social Investment	KSI 17.3
Invest resources (money and time) devoted to social action (often philanthropy in USA) consistent with industry peers in the same markets.	Earn high recognition and trust from communities globally that are impacted by the company's (full value chain) activities.
Community and Stakeholder Partnerships	KSI 17.4
Partner with local industry groups and selected **NGOs** to address community priorities.	CEO joins other leaders in high-impact partnerships with NGOs, value chain partners, and a range of stakeholders to tackle a major relevant social challenge with material value chain impacts.
Infrastructure Development	KSI 17.5
Invest in physical structures or systems that enhance societal value at a local level near company operations or offices (e.g., parks; schools).	Invest at scale globally. Partner with others to drive the circular economy and enhance societal value (e.g., eco-parks, smart cities, etc.) in all relevant locations.
Community Job Creation	KSI 17.6
Company emphasizes local talent in purchasing and hiring decisions.	Company drives business development programs to enhance job creation nationally and in underprivileged communities.

List of Figures

https://doi.org/10.1515/9783111548852-019

List of Tables

https://doi.org/10.1515/9783111548852-020

Index

https://doi.org/10.1515/9783111548852-021

www.ingramcontent.com/pod-product-compliance
Lightning Source LLC
Jackson TN
JSHW061115250625
86703JS00004B/51